THE TORONTO

1979/1980

Stan Obodiac

MAPLE LEAFS

Edited by John Gault

McClelland and Stewart

McClelland and Stewart Limited
The Canadian Publishers
25 Hollinger Road
Toronto, Ontario
M4B 3G2

Canadian Cataloguing in Publication Data

Obodiac, Stan, 1922-
  The Toronto Maple Leafs, 1979-80

ISBN 0-7710-6840-9

1. Toronto Maple Leafs (Hockey club)
I. Title.

GV848.T602   796.96'2'06   C79-094809-5

Printed and bound in Canada by
T. H. Best Printing Company Limited

Contents

Acknowledgements

To the nearly 400 Leafs, past and present, who have worn the sweater.

Thanks to the contributors and photographers who have been caught up in the enthusiasm of what the Toronto Maple Leafs mean to Canada.

My thanks to Jack McClelland for believing in my work, *The Leafs The First 50 Years,* and who made it into the most successful book in world hockey history, and who continues to believe in the Leafs with the publication of this book.

My thanks also to Harold Ballard for the encouragement and help in the production of this book.

Stan Obodiac
Toronto,
October 10, 1979
(the opening day of the Leaf 1979-80 schedule)

Book design:
James McLachlan

Colour Photo Credits:
Robert Shaver: 9, 12, 14 top left and right, 16 all photos, 17 all photos, 20 bottom right, 22 right, 23 left, 24
Dennis Miles: 13, 15, 20 bottom left, 21, 22 left, 23 right
Jerry Hobbs: 10-11, 14 bottom, 18-19, 20 top

Additional Photo Credits
Jerry Hobbs: 2-3, and 5
John Maiola: 4
Robert Shaver: 8, 176

Blue and White in Colour

The Sittler-McDonald-Maloney line (that's Lanny betwixt two defenders) making life miserable for Tony Esposito and the Chicago Black Hawks

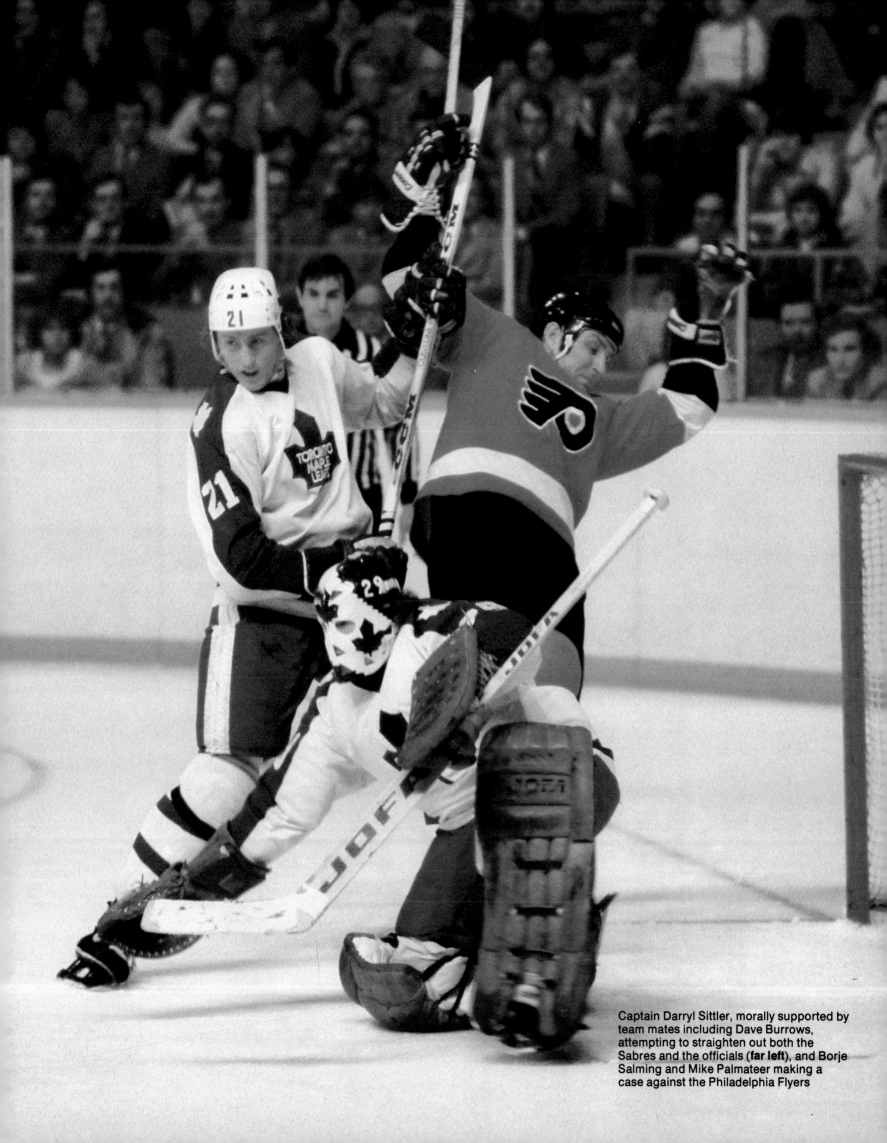

Captain Darryl Sittler, morally supported by team mates including Dave Burrows, attempting to straighten out both the Sabres and the officials (**far left**), and Borje Salming and Mike Palmateer making a case against the Philadelphia Flyers

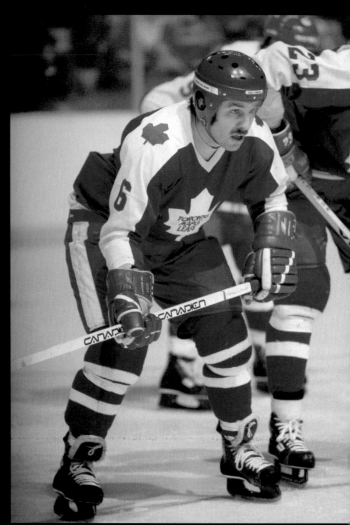

Darryl Sittler pondering the situation, Ron Ellis patiently waiting for the puck to be dropped and (**bottom**) Lanny McDonald blazing one – unsuccessfully this time – against the New York Rangers

Even Borje Salming can't do it all with grace every time, but he did manage to keep the Kings' Charlie Simmer and the puck out of the Maple Leaf nets, nonetheless

Clockwise from right: Darryl Sittler making one of his patented moves; Ian Turnbull taking the puck out of harm's way; Dan Maloney showing his well-documented hustle; young Joel Quenneville thinking out his move when the puck is finally dropped in a faceoff; and Walt McKechnie, looking a bit impatient for the game to get underway once again

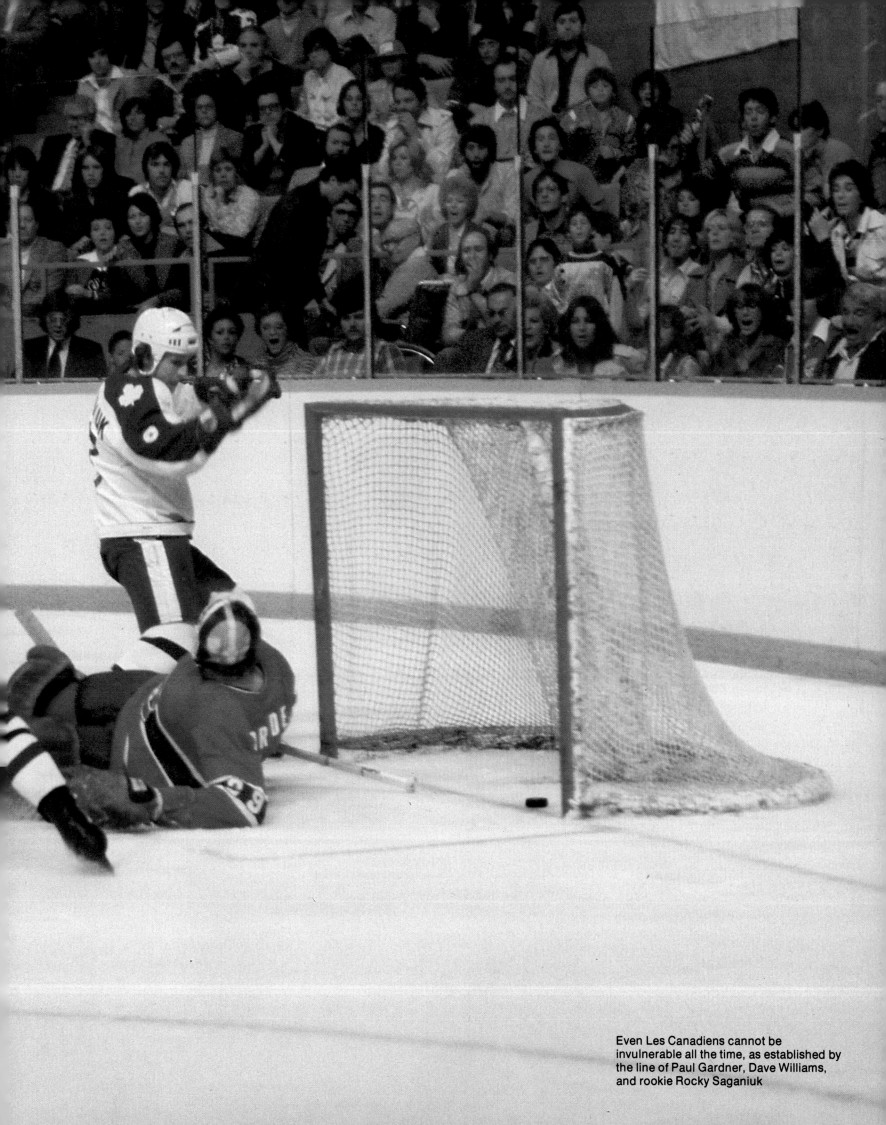

Even Les Canadiens cannot be invulnerable all the time, as established by the line of Paul Gardner, Dave Williams, and rookie Rocky Saganiuk

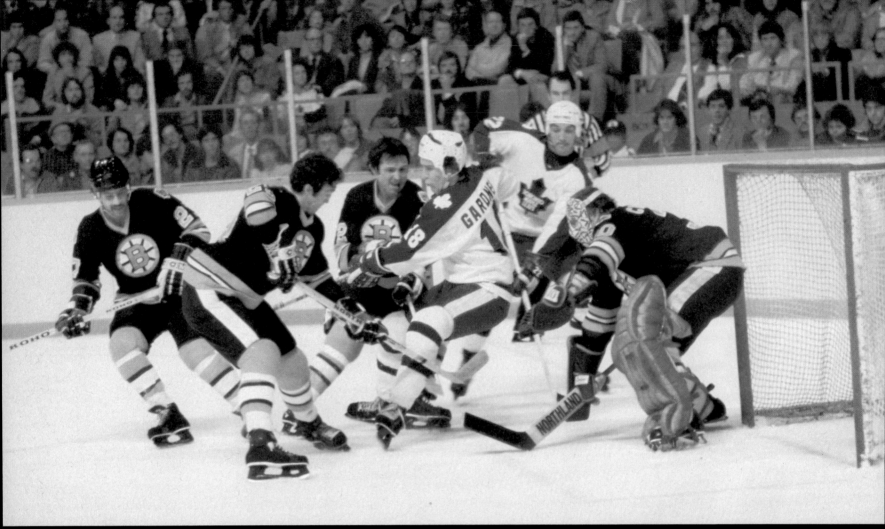

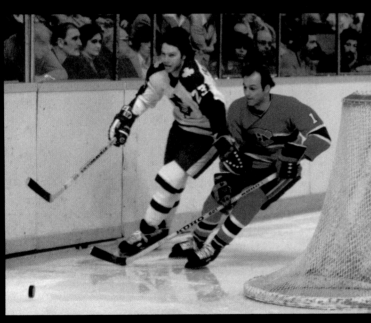

The fact that they're battling two-to-one odds seems to bother Paul Gardner and Dave Williams a little bit (**top**); Dave Hutchison tries to keep Guy Lafleur at bay (**above**); Rocky Saganiuk follows the play; and (**on opposite page**) John Anderson moves Yvon Lambert out the the way – or tries to – as they jockey for position on a faceoff

Ron Wilson in a good old-fashioned foot race for the puck against the Canucks

Mike Palmateer and Jerry Butler don't seem to notice Gil Perreault coming up from behind

Pat Boutette appears to have more
important things to worry about than a
fallen Sabre

It may not be legal, but Dave Burrows does
keep Phil Esposito off the scoreboard

The Word From on High

John Gault

Hal's pals John McLellan, Floyd Smith, Gerry McNamara (standing), John Bower, King Clancy, Punch Imlach, and Dick Duff (*Jerry Hobbs*)

The Master's Voice

It is a rare thing in sports for a team owner to be at least as well-known – or more so – than the people who play for him. Charlie Finley of the Oakland As comes immediately to mind, as does George Steinbrenner of the Yankees, and Big John Bassett when he owned the Argos. But of all the owners of all the teams in all the world, there is none more notorious (in every sense of that word) than Harold E. Ballard, president and general manager and chief executive and 85 per cent shareholder of Maple Leaf Gardens. He is King Lear by way of Norman Lear, the last of the buccaneers, a fiery or funny quote in search of an author.

He is easy to like and, apparently, just as easy to hate. Eight years ago, when I was profiling him for *Toronto Life* magazine, a respected fellow journalist urged me to ''nail the son-of-a-bitch to the wall.'' I guess I didn't, because even today that article brings me vituperative responses or, in the case of the friends I didn't lose over it, a rapid change of subject. But whatever anybody thinks about Harold Ballard, who took control of the Gardens and the Leafs in a series of manoeuvres that would have made Howard Hughes' head spin, it must be conceded that the world would be a much duller place without him. As you will see in the interview which follows, there is no subject that he will not touch, be it that attempt, last season, by the then-coach Roger Neilson to unload star defenceman Ian Turnbull, or the use of illicit drugs by athletes.

And lest anyone wonders why there is no mention of the fraud and theft convictions that sent him to prison in the early 1970s, it is because I edited them out, partly because of the complexity, and mostly because Ballard's candor would have undoubtedly dumped both of us into a cauldron of steaming libel suits. Our conversation – it was more that than a structured interview – was pretty free-wheeling, and I also found it necessary to clean up both his language and my own. Other than that what follows is pure Harold Ballard, a not-so-venerable 76-year-old who is still pickin' them up and layin' them down the way he's done all of his life.

Gault: The obvious question is, What made you bring back Punch Imlach?
Ballard: As you know, Punch and I have been friends for years. As a matter of fact he played for me when I coached and managed the Marlboros. He played hard and he was a good hockey player, a good junior and a good senior. And as far as I was concerned, a fellow who was a good player and who is as interested in the game as he is – and has proven he is – well, when he became available from Buffalo, it prompted me to go after him. Although I had talked to Punch, I couldn't do it before; I couldn't interfere because it was a $10,000 fine. But he knew what I had in the back of my mind for two or three years. I never thought the [Buffalo owners] Knoxes would be so stupid as to fire a guy like

Punch. I didn't think there was ever any chance of me being able to rehire him here in Toronto. Another thing: with a guy like Punch, there's never been any prize for second.

Gault: Then why was he let go in the first place 10 years ago? He'd won four Stanley Cups for you, and admittedly the team was on the wane, but every team wanes.
Ballard: It was a tough situation. As a matter of fact there was a little bit of . . . I don't know whether you'd call it jealousy . . . there was some conflict between Imlach and [the late Leaf president, Stafford] Smythe that went deeper than I could understand.

Gault: And you weren't in a position to intervene?
Ballard: Well, I was and I did because Stafford often said to me that he was considering releasing Punch from his contract, and I said: 'I don't want that, and I don't see eye-to-eye with you.' And I think Stafford did pay a lot of attention to what I said and what I did . . . But he and Punch didn't get along and I knew that and it was a little bit strained for me because I liked Punch and I liked Stafford and I couldn't understand why the two of them couldn't pull together. [Ballard was not at the Gardens the spring night of 1969, when Imlach was fired. He was driving into his garage with his late wife, Dorothy, who had taken sick at the game, and heard the news on the car radio.] There was a news flash, and it was that

Harold Ballard, managing once more to turn the hot seat – in front of a battery of mikes – into the catbird seat *(Jerry Hobbs)*

Stafford had gone into the coach's room and fired Punch. Well, that disturbed me terribly but it was done and I couldn't do anything about it. But I tell you, I wasn't any too pleased because I knew what Punch could do and what he had done. And yes, the team had backed up a bit, but that's natural. Every team is bound to have a relapse or go into a slumper.

Gault: But he did trade away the future, didn't he? At least that's the mythology of it. He did win four Stanley Cups in seven years, but he did it with great old pros who only had two or three years left.
Ballard: Let's say this: he played the game for today, and when he traded away some of the younger fellows such as Garry Unger and Frank Mahovlich, he brought in guys that were a little bit mature – Allan Stanley, Marcel Pronovost, Red Kelly, and guys like that. They weren't speedballs or anything, but they played with their heads and naturally they were more up to winning than the younger generation. The younger kids could beat them in legs but they couldn't beat them in the knowledge of the game and the way it should be handled.

Gault: Okay, but let's talk about the Leafs of today. What do you expect Imlach to do with this team? What kind of hockey can we expect? Do you have the people now who can play the kind of hockey he wants?
Ballard: We have a nucleus of that, and I think Punch can get it out of them.

Gault: Why?
Ballard: I think he has the ability, and I think he'll gain the respect of the players and that they'll give out a little harder for Punch than they will for anybody else.

Gault: But the consensus among the sportswriters seems to be that this is a sixth- or seventh-place team, that it doesn't have enough guns to win the Stanley Cup or get into the Stanley Cup finals. But there have been Leaf teams that have played over their heads, because of motivation, and I think that's one of the things that attracts you to Imlach, isn't it? He had teams here that shouldn't have won, but did.
Ballard: That's right. We had no right to beat Montreal in 1967 [the year the

Leafs squeaked into fourth place and knocked off the Hull-led Chicago Black Hawks, perhaps the best team in hockey, in the semi-finals before facing the Canadiens]. That was the Expo year and they had everything set up down there at the fairgrounds for the celebration, skyrockets and everything else. And we blew their lid for them. So you see, you never know what's going to happen to a team, and a guy like Imlach can inspire these fellows.

Gault: But what is it about him, how does he operate?
Ballard: That question can be easily answered: by success. And anybody who has success is on my side of the fence.

Gault: But how does a guy like Imlach, as opposed to a guy like [former Leaf general manager] Jim Gregory, say, inspire people to play that much better?
Ballard: He's had the experience. He's been on championship teams himself. He knows what makes things tick, and he knows how to handle different personalities. Now with Imlach and Mahovlich, they never got along . . .

Gault: I was going to bring that up.
Ballard: And the reason they never got along is that when Mahovlich would come back to the bench, Punch would say: 'You son-of-a-bitch, what the hell are you doing out there, you goddamn crazy Croatian,' or whatever he is. And if Punch had gone in his pocket and thrown him a fish like they do with a seal, or handed him a sucker, well, Christ, he could have put the guy back out there the next minute and he'd probably have scored a couple of goals for us. But Punch always aggravated him, and that's why he couldn't get . . . see, in the playoffs [in 1967] against Chicago, I don't think Mahovlich was on the ice more than once or twice. On the other hand a guy like Brian Conacher played a hell of a game and he never did play for us the next year. But Punch seems to have a method of getting those [kind of] fellows aroused to where they give to the best of their ability.

Gault: Do you have the idea that he may be able to do that with some of your journeymen right now?
Ballard: I don't think there's any doubt about it. I think Punch can get more out of fellows – I don't think out of McDonald; McDonald gives you 100 per

cent every game; you don't need to inspire McDonald, he inspires himself. Sittler inspires himself to a point, but he didn't play the kind of hockey last year he was capable of playing.

Gault: But how hurt was he? It's pretty hard to determine that. I mean, if you have a bad leg . . .
Ballard: You don't have a bad leg all year. And if you do, you know about it.

Gault: And you really think that Imlach is going to inspire these guys?
Ballard: Do you think I would have hired him if I didn't think he could?

Gault: No, I don't. But there are patterns, aren't there?
Ballard: There aren't two characters the same. You can't treat one hockey player differently than the other, and yet there's not two the same on a hockey club.

Gault: But don't you have to treat them differently? We talked about Mahovlich . . .
Ballard: You do. To a point.

Gault: What is that point?
Ballard: That you're not going to let them walk all over you. Now hockey players are just boys and they're like kids in a school: you'll always find there're two or three bastards in your class who are always trying to get the teacher's goat.

Gault: But Imlach doesn't treat people differently, does he? Or he didn't. That was the great knock against him, wasn't it?
Ballard: Well, you know, there're lots of guys who hated Imlach when they played for him, but they think he's a hell of a guy.

Gault: Why did they hate him?
Ballard: Imlach's something like I am. A needler. For instance, when Bob Pulford was playing with us Punch used to take dead aim at Pulford; he used to call him Mortimer Snerd, 'cause he looks like Mortimer Snerd lots of times and he acts like him. And Imlach, he's like I am, needling people. He takes great enjoyment out of it.

Gault: Doesn't he worry about his health, about his heart? Don't you? This isn't going to be easy, is it?
Ballard: I don't worry about his health. I think if he wasn't doing anything he'd

Ballard and Imlach, together again for the second time and, obviously, enjoying every minute of it *(Jerry Hobbs)*

be more subject to heart conditions than he's going to be now. I mean he knows me well enough to know that I'm not going to do anything that would hurt him. He knows I'm in his corner and always have been. Big!

Gault: Okay, but what about Floyd Smith? Is Floyd Smith's career distinguished enough to bring him in here as coach at this time in history?
Ballard: There are very, very few fellows who ever played pro hockey that have been good coaches, so you can't use that as a criterion. Is Floyd Smith a good coach? He's not dynamic, but he's well-read, generally; he speaks well and I think he can demand the respect of the players. That is one of the big things in coaching a club – to demand the respect of the players.

Gault: Which is what Scotty Bowman has. You went after him. You wanted him pretty badly.
Ballard: I wanted him. But first of all I wanted Don Cherry, because I thought Cherry would be a great guy for the news people and . . .

Gault: Well, you are in the entertainment business.
Ballard: That's right, that's what I'm selling. Sure I'm trying to win the Stanley Cup, but I've got to get people into the rink, and be it good, bad or indifferent, I've got to get stuff going in the ink and on the idiot box and the radio. And if you employ people like Cherry, you've got it made. I mean a guy picks up the paper in the morning and reads it going down on the streetcar or the subway, and he turns to the guy next to him and says: 'Did you hear what that goddamned Cherry said today?'

Gault: But, further to the 'entertainment business,' the Leafs in the last couple of years have played very dull hockey. Is this going to change?
Ballard: Without a doubt. Imlach plays a different type of game than Roger Neilson.

Gault: But you're still a great admirer of Neilson.
Ballard: Oh yes, I am. I'll tell you why: if he wanted to write a book or lay down game plans, I think he would be a perfectionist at it. But to execute what he knows, he can't do.

Gault: But isn't it tougher in the pros,

when you're dealing with all that high-priced help, to get people to play the kind of disciplined game that Neilson was obviously striving for, the kind of game the Russians play, say, or the Czechs?
Ballard: I would say yes. It's a little different today in view of the fact that juniors are pampered and they're not disciplined the way they used to be years ago.

Gault: It's too easy to get into the league now, isn't it?
Ballard: Absolutely. There are many openings for hockey players today and you don't have to be that good. But back to Roger Neilson: I take full responsibility for employing him because there weren't too many people here who wanted him as coach.

Gault: Why? Because he was academic? Because he studied the game?
Ballard: When we hired him to take over the team in Tulsa, he did a great job with guys like Dave Williams and some of the vets down there. They were only mediocre hockey players when we sent them down to the minors, to the Central League, and they were only there a short time before they became pretty good hockey players. As a matter of fact, Randy Carlyle came back here and he was one of our better defencemen. Then, when it came time [in 1977] to hire a coach I thought: 'Well, goddarnit, here's a guy who's done such a great job in the minors . . .' And I did it against my own thinking, because he'd never won a championship and I always like to hire somebody that has tasted championship blood. So I brought him back – and I honestly thought with his knowledge, being a schoolteacher and having the requirements to handle kids, especially in high school because they're a bunch of bastards as you know, I honestly thought he would be able to speak their language, whether it was to go out with them or whatever . . . I thought he would be able to weld them together.

Gault: But aside from owning the team, you are the number one hockey fan in the city. Were you unhappy at the way the Leafs were playing the game in the last couple of years? Were you being bored by it?
Ballard: Well, he didn't do badly the first year, but as time went on, in the

second year, it was disastrous. I didn't like the way he was coaching the club. You see, we didn't have any body contact in practice. Now how in hell are you going to play the game to win if you practise one way and play another? If you're a pianist you're going to have to perfect the number you're playing at the recital. Well it's the same with this: he skated them around pylons and they skipped down the ice and jumped up and down – all the kind of crap that the Russians do. But the Russians have such control over their players that they can say, 'Here, skate on your hands . . .'

Gault: Nevertheless, you did let the team get into playing boring hockey.
Ballard: Well, that was on account of I had people here who were satisfied with that. And strange as it may seem, changing things around here has been in the back of my mind for the last year. But I've got people I talk to, hockey people, right here in the building, and they were always saying: 'Give it another chance, give it another chance.' But it went on so long I couldn't stand it any more so I just took the bull by the horns and said: 'To hell with you, I'm going to do this myself right now!' And that's what happened.

Gault: Was it hard to replace Jim Gregory, who's been a loyal employee of yours over a hell of a lot of years?
Ballard: Well, he understands the situation, and . . .

Gault: I know he understands the situation, but was it hard, nonetheless?
Ballard: Sure it was. He'd been with me a long time

Gault: I suspect, knowing you, that you held off a couple of years longer than you should have because of those personal considerations. That's something of your pattern, isn't it?
Ballard: That's right. And besides, you don't like to let a guy down. But I kept telling him: 'Lookit, we can't go on here. How long are we going to take people's money with these kinds of performances?' And I said: 'Jimmy, we can't make deals like we've been making them.' We've traded away some pretty good hockey players.

Gault: Who has been traded away, in the past five years, say, that you wish you had back?

Ballard: Well, Rick Kehoe, for instance, who went to Pittsburgh. Carlyle should have been kept here. And I think that probably Jack Valiquette should have stayed. I think that if Punch had been here and he'd had Valiquette, he'd have had him playing hockey. He's not a good skater, but he's a son-of-a-bitch in front of the net and he can score goals for you, and that's the name of the game.

Gault: The return on players you've sent to other teams hasn't been that great in the past while, has it?

Ballard: No. We've traded away some pretty good hockey players.

Gault: Yes, and it could be argued that you didn't exactly get return on your dollars . . .

Ballard: You don't have to argue about it, it's a fact.

Gault: Why?

Ballard: I don't think our scouting system was that good, or they wouldn't have agreed to make those trades. Now you've said that I try to run everything. I don't. When they were going to make a deal I'd say to Gregory – a hell of a nice guy and everything but he just doesn't know the score – I'd say to Gregory: 'Are you sure you're going to do it?' You see, they would have gotten rid of Turnbull if I hadn't asserted myself last year and stopped it. Roger and Gregory wanted to get rid of Turnbull and I wouldn't allow it. He couldn't get along with the coach, so the coach wanted to get rid of him. As a matter of fact, Roger was quite adamant about it. And I said: 'Lookit. If he's going to go, you're going to go.' It was that bad.

Gault: I doubt that Neilson would have argued that Turnbull wasn't a good hockey player, surely?

Ballard: Well he did. He had these 'points.' He was a great guy with those replays, those little pictures, you know. And he used to pick out all the bad things Turnbull did, but he didn't pick out many of the good things.

Gault: But in fairness, you have been known to interfere at other times with the coaching function. You've often been accused of that.

Ballard: That's entirely wrong. If you talk to the players, any of the players, you will find that I've never interfered

with anything on the club.

Gault: But you went on the record about Inge Hammarstrom. I can't remember the precise quote, but I think you said he could go into the corner with a dozen eggs in his pockets and not break a single one.

Ballard: That's right. That was my observation on the way he played. I didn't go and say: 'Hey, lookit, take the eggs out of your pockets!'

Gault: But it's like *Murder In The Cathedral*, isn't it? Henry II said, 'Will someone rid me of this meddlesome priest,' and the four knights took him up on it. I mean, when Harold Ballard talks, presumably the people who work for him listen.

Ballard: Look, what I said about Hammarstrom was only a comment. I was asked what I thought, and that's what I thought. They asked, 'What about Hammarstrom?' and I said he's a great guy if he'd only take the eggs out his pocket when he went into the corners. And the newspapers made a big show out of it.

Gault: But of course they made a big show out of it. You own the team and you put down one of your players; it's the equivalent of saying the guy's got no guts.

Ballard: I could have said that. It wouldn't have been so drastic, I suppose, or cutting. On the other hand I told him: 'You score some goals and I'll kiss your ass on the City Hall steps.'

Gault: But then he was gone.

Ballard: No, he lasted two years after that – but he didn't play any different on the seven hundredth day than he did on the day I said it. What happened to him proves the fact. He's still running around with eggs in his pocket.

Gault: But I'm afraid you probably reinforced that old 'Chicken Swede' thing that certainly doesn't apply to some of the other Swedes in the league.

Ballard: Oh no . . . Well, listen, there's none of them too brave.

Gault: Salming wouldn't be pleased to hear that, would he?

Ballard: Well, I wouldn't . . . No, he's not scared, but he doesn't . . . Let's put it this way: they don't play as rugged and robust as the average Canadian.

Gault: So who is your kind of hockey player? If you could get a hockey player, any hockey player in the league, who would you go for? Lafleur? Gillies?

Ballard: You'd have to say Lafleur. And Gillies is certainly one of the choice. And Robinson. The kind of guys who can go both ways, and you don't push them around. Now I don't believe that a fellow should do something stupid enough to get himself a punch in the mouth without defending himself, and there isn't any room in hockey for stick-swinging or kicking or spearing or anything like that: those things are absolutely out in my book. But if a fellow did that to me, I would think nothing of punching him in the mouth.

Gault: Do you think it's still possible, with the guys making the kind of money they're making, and with 20 other teams in the league, to get more out of the players than you've been getting? What if they don't like the way they're being handled and just say, 'To hell with it?'

Ballard: If they say to hell with it, they shouldn't be playing for me.

Gault: But there may be some pretty skilled hockey players who will say to hell with it.

Ballard: If there are, they're not going to play here, and they're not going to play for anybody else if they play with the attitude you're talking about.

Gault: But even recent history shows that players have gone from one team where they weren't happy to do well on another.

Ballard: Yeh, but now wait a minute. The average player has a little bit of pride, you know. If he hasn't got pride I don't want him and I wouldn't be bothered with him. And I admire the players for sticking up for their rights – as long as they don't get stupid about it.

Gault: Speaking of that, when the players stuck up for Neilson last year, you rescinded your firing order. Then you made the whole thing out to be just a big hoax or a joke or whatever. It wasn't though, was it?

Ballard: No. What actually happened was that we were going so goddamned badly it looked as though we weren't even going to make the playoffs. At one time we were only 8 points ahead of Minnesota and they were breathing down our necks. So I said: 'Lookit (I was talking to myself at the time) if we don't do something on the night we play Montreal (I forget what date it was) I'm going to have to make a change.' So I arranged with Johnny McLellan that he was going to take over the team and run it for the rest of the year . . . But when I told Roger he was through the players didn't actually make the big fuss that they tried to claim they did. However, I let it rest for a day. I said I wanted to have a meeting with the players and I told the trainer to have them there by 11.00 o'clock because I was going to talk to them. So I went in and said: 'Lookit, you guys, I didn't fire Roger Neilson, you did, everybody in here. The reason I fired him is because you're not playing hockey the way you can play, you don't resemble the team you were last year in any shape or form. There's only one way you'll get Roger back to run this club and that's if you make up your minds you want to play. Any of you guys don't want to play on this team, you just hang your goddamned uniform up because I can get players to play this game for half the price of what I'm paying you.' After it was all over Sittler came right out and said the team took the blame for the way they were playing, that they had let Roger down. They went out and won five games. Then they went into a slumper again. That was the only time I went into the dressing room last year.

Gault: You just mentioned the Canadiens. It seems to me that you play good hockey against the Canadiens, almost always.
Ballard: We play better against the Canadiens than we do against anybody else. But as soon as we play the Canadiens, then we fall back into the category of a mediocre hockey team.

Gault: And that's how you see the team as it stands right now, as a mediocre hockey team?
Ballard: Yeh.

Gault: But what, if anything, can you expect Punch Imlach to do about that?
Ballard: I think he'll correct that. He'll get them skating. I think our practices will be a lot better to watch, and I think our games will be a tremendous amount better to watch. You'll see interesting hockey – we have the personnel to do that. And talking to the

players, as of today, I know they're looking forward to it.

Gault: But the situation with the Leafs as it stands is that you have a core of five stars, five fine hockey players who could star with any team in the league. But to go along with that, you have mostly only those young legs we talked about earlier. Couldn't this season be just a repetition of last?
Ballard: No. I think what we have is the nucleus of a darn good hockey club.

Gault: But it's only a nucleus.
Ballard: That's all . . . No, the quality's there too. I mean to say we've got three of the best hockey players in the league. No, four: Sittler, Lanny McDonald, Salming, and, I think, Turnbull.

Gault: I was thinking of Palmateer as the fifth.
Ballard: Yes, you'd have to consider Palmateer, so that gives you five. We have some fringe players down from there, down to players that would be tradable. And that's what we're going to do now. We're going to work at making deals whether we have to pay two for one or whatever. Whatever deals we can make, we're going to make them.

Gault: You've been urged by various columnists to open the strongbox and buy yourself a winning team the way George Steinbrenner did with the Yankees in New York . . .
Ballard: Which I've done. There's never been any time when I've objected to paying for players, or not tried to buy players when I could. I made a bid for the Swedes [Anders Hedberg and Ulf Nilsson, late of the then-WHA Winnipeg Jets] but the $200,000 I bid was a lot different from the $3 million they got from the Rangers.

Gault: But I'm sure there are a lot of people in Toronto who think you ought to have bid that $3 million.
Ballard: Probably so. But when the tax guy comes around and you haven't got the money, there wouldn't be any hockey here because they'd goddamned soon close you up.

Gault: But we both know that there's no possible way the Gardens will close up, whether you're here or not. There would be a minor – no, major – insurrection if that happened.

Ballard: But after all, there's only so much you can do. In Madison Square Garden, for instance, their take in the playoffs was $300,000 a game, which is a little different from mine at $145,000 or $150,000; they advanced their ticket prices $25 and $30. You've got to be sensible about the thing: how in the hell could I go to the bank and say, 'Lookit, I want to increase my payroll from $3 million to $7 million.'

Gault: But as you told me once before, you've always been able to go to the bank and get what you've asked for.
Ballard: Well, I have – but you don't want to press your luck. And remember, I have to pay that money back. None of the bankers is going to say, 'Hey, you're a great guy, don't worry about your loan.'

Gault: At the risk of sounding cynical, the Gardens is sold out for every game anyway, isn't it? Doesn't that create a problem, doesn't that make you just a little bit complacent about building up a team? If you're going to fill the place for every game – at least theoretically – with a sixth or seventh place team, then why bother . . .
Ballard: If you're not going to try to better your position, you might as well get the hell out of the business. As I've told you before, there's no prize for second as far as I'm concerned, and I'm just as eager to win the Stanley Cup today as I was 10 years ago.

Gault: It's been 12 years since the Leafs won. In the vast scheme of things perhaps that isn't necessarily so bad, but in a town like Toronto and with a team that has the tradition of the Leafs, it must be galling for you.
Ballard: That's right. It burns my ass. You think I get any pleasure walking out of that box at the Gardens and having everybody say: 'Ya son-of-a-bitch, you should give me my money back,' and things like that?

Gault: What else do they say?
Ballard: Oh, 'What the hell are you doing, stealing my money again?' and 'Why don't you give me my money back?' and 'You should write this one off and give me a free ticket to come in.' I don't blame them. That's the way they feel. But they don't say, when they've enjoyed themselves, 'Gee, we're going to pay you double tonight!' That's their privilege. If they want to

Floyd Smith speaks, Ballard seems to be checking the press's reaction, and Imlach weighs the words *(Kent Jones)*

say I'm a son-of-a-bitch, that's up to them. If they want to say I'm a good guy, that's up to them too. I'll tell you something else: with all of the crap they throw at me, all the nasty things they say, I don't think they really mean it; I think a lot of it's endearment.

Gault: But the fact is you are such a public figure. You put yourself out there so people will take pot-shots at you.
Ballard: That's right. I'm not scared to walk right into tiger dens. That doesn't bother me; I love it.

Gault: And the fans here are pretty knowledgeable, aren't they?
Ballard: Oh, Jesus! And the ones that are the best are up there in the Greys and the Greens where people come religiously every week and they know every move those players make – privately, professionally, and every other way. They have a book on them; they know exactly how many breaths-per-minute they take.

Gault: That puts a hell of a lot of pressure on you and the manager and the coaches and the team. It's something that wouldn't occur in places like Atlanta and Denver, would it?
Ballard: Are you kidding? The Rangers walk out of the rink in New York and do you think anybody bothers those players? Here, Christ, they can't move. They follow the players all the way up into the parking lot; they won't let them get into their cars, looking for autographs and all kinds of crap. Every day of practice the whole goddamned street's full of kids, taking their pictures and giving them presents and stuff like that.

Gault: But isn't hockey today nothing more than a business and an entertainment medium?
Ballard: People don't look at hockey as a show. They look at it as something different, though it's not. You and I know it's not any different from showbusiness, but the people don't: they look at it as something that's so close to them, you don't make fun of it.

Gault: It is sacred, isn't it? More than one writer has called it our national religion. But is it still that, or is it going the way of other traditional religions?
Ballard: No. No. You and I might criticize the Maple Leaf Hockey Club, but

you go out on the street and talk that way about the team or individuals on it and you could end up wearing your teeth for a necklace.

Gault: You have, in fact, a pretty strong responsibility to that paying public, don't you?
Ballard: That's right.

Gault: And after a particularly bad string of games, do you get a lot of angry letters from those fans?
Ballard: Everybody gets them. I get them by the dozens. And I answer every one of them as long as I have a return address.

Gault: Are the criticisms generally valid?
Ballard: They're like the newsmen. They all want to be coaches and managers.

Gault: They also want to win, though. They figure they own the team as much as you do.
Ballard: Everybody figures they own the team. They talk about 'My Team.' The team belongs to them. 'To hell with you, Ballard, I've got something to say about this!'

Gault: And they do, don't they?
Ballard: Oh, sure they do. And I listen to them – how do you like that? I get some very intelligent letters, very intelligent. I've had five- and six-page letters on what to do and how to do it and when to do it with the hockey club. Now, for a guy to sit down and write that and worry his goddamned brain out, he deserves some consideration.

Gault: So it's safe to say that the Leafs are still as important to Toronto and to English-speaking Canada as they ever were?
Ballard: I think they're more so. There's more controversy, and not just because of me . . . though I'm very controversial.

Gault: You are that, yes.
Ballard: I'll walk into places – like a year ago [1978] when the draft was on in Montreal and I walked into the press room and they must have had 150 or 200 typewriters in there, and the guys are sitting there, dead – and I'll start things going. I'll start all kinds of crap flying one way and another.

Gault: Do you do these things on purpose?
Ballard: Sure, I do! Sure.

Gault: Well, I get the feeling that by and large you can't help yourself, that it's just who you are.
Ballard: That's right. I walked into that press room and they said: 'Thank Christ you're here. We've been sitting here with our fingers up our noses.' So I started in and I gave everybody a shot. Everything they asked me, I gave them a shot, and it's usually controversial, what I say. I get something going and arouse people's anger and get their fur up, and naturally it goes across the country and people say: 'What kind of a son-of-a-bitch is that?'

Gault: On the other hand, you do get a certain amount of what most people would consider bad press.
Ballard Oh yeh. But I don't worry. That doesn't worry me.

Gault: You don't think you get a bum rap, then?
Ballard: Oh no, I don't get a bum rap. I'm friendly with a lot of those guys.

Gault: And, after all, you start it.
Ballard: Sure I start it, and if they're gullible enough to grab it, let them grab it . . . Then they say all I'm looking for is ink: they're the guys who give me the ink; they don't have to write it. If it's never been written, what the hell . . .

Gault: I suppose nobody's made fun of you more or criticized you more than Dick Beddoes of the *Globe and Mail*, but you still like Beddoes.
Ballard: Beddoes and I are great friends. When Beddoes and I are serious, we talk seriously. But naturally, when we're out for the kill, we go at one another. And don't think that doesn't create a lot of interest and a lot of talk.

Gault: So you think being as public as you are helps the team?
Ballard: I think so. I think people say, 'Let's go down and see what the crazy bastards are doing,' and they talk about it. When they don't talk about you, you're in trouble; you know that.

Gault: One of the things that got you a lot of ink, as you call it, was your opposition to merger with the World Hockey Association. While that hasn't really

happened, four new teams from the old WHA are in the National Hockey League this year. You effectively scuttled a number of merger talks in the past . . .
Ballard: Well, I did. And I'm sorry that I didn't sink them to the depths of the sea, because there's not one of them that's going to add anything to the National Hockey League. I told them that right in the boardroom; when this thing was passed I said it was the worst day that the National Hockey League had ever experienced. You mark my word, there'll be more goddamned trouble . . . I don't think a city like Winnipeg will be able to last in the league. I don't think that Denver [an always-NHL team] will last. Hartford might have a tough time . . .

Gault: Of course you lost a few good hockey players to the WHA . . .
Ballard: I lost 18 players.

Gault: Including guys like Jim Harrison, and Paul Henderson when he was

strong.
Ballard: And Ricky Ley, who was picked as an all-star of the WHA.

Gault: Do you think the league is going to shrink again?
Ballard: Yeh.

Gault: How many teams do you think are reasonable?
Ballard: Well, it's hard to say. What actually should have happened, I think, is that they should have left the WHA intact and [eventually] it would have been like the American League and the National League in baseball. And another thing I'd like to see is a Canadian League.

Gault: But weren't you one of the people who opposed having a Canadian league? Didn't you effectively keep Quebec City and Edmonton and Winnipeg – and Calgary, when it existed – out of the NHL?
Ballard: Oh, not necessarily. No, not any more than anybody else. I thought

we expanded too fast, and that's why I didn't want to take four or five teams in at a time. You can't afford to do it, you water down your league too much. It's all right for the people who don't know the difference, but a long time elapses between today and tomorrow for these teams. With the 21 teams we have today, people will look at us and say: 'Jesus, this is great.' But you bring a team over from Russia, where they probably have five or six good teams in the whole country, and they're bound to kick the crap out of us.

Gault: And not only on a team-to-team basis, either. They also kick the crap out of us on an all-star basis.
Ballard: That's right, and they do it in any sport that you want to go into, because that's really a business with them there. That's the hockey player's job; and if they don't excel at it, they're going to be grinding salt for the rest of the world.

Gault: I guess some of us would see

that more as dedication than fear. But let's talk about dedication; some of us older fellows suspect sometimes that it's becoming a lost character trait in hockey. But that's not really true, is it?

Ballard: I don't think so. I think fellows like McDonald and Sittler may say all they play for is the money, but that just isn't true. They have a lot of pride and they think just as much about the Stanley Cup as Sweeney Schriner did, or Turk Broda or any of those guys. Naturally the monetary end is a big thing, and it should be. That's the way they make their living.

Gault: But everybody's not Sittler or McDonald. What does a player have to do to get on your wrong side? What does he have to do to get you to the point where you'd be just as happy if your general manager sent him elsewhere?

Ballard: The main thing is the I-don't-care attitude.

Gault: And there are players on this team who have that attitude?

Ballard: Well, you know, you can tell by the way they act. They pull their skates on and they go out and play and they come back in and they can't get the skates off fast enough, and that's it.

Gault: I don't know how any coach or manager could live with that. Is it because they have to?

Ballard: What are you going to do?

Gault: Do you personally have trouble dealing with the kids on this team, or with any kids, for that matter, or with the things that they find important?

Ballard: I used to, but I've gotten over that now. It took me a long time to realize that they don't think the same way as I do.

Gault: But suppose, for example, that you found out one of your better hockey players was smoking dope occasionally?

Ballard: I do. I know it now.

Gault: What would you do about it? Or maybe it's better to ask what you are doing about it?

Ballard: First of all, I'd get after the coach to find out if it was true, and how bad the guy was . . . Mind you, I don't condone smoking marijuana, but – and I think you've heard this so often it's old hat – guys that drink whisky are

a lot worse off than guys who smoke marijuana.

Gault: Well, I certainly know that to be true. This sort of brings up the Don Murdoch case. Murdoch [of the New York Rangers] was convicted of possessing cocaine and he was fined in the courts, but then the league suspended him for a year.

Ballard: I was sympathetic to Murdoch and I think you probably read it in the papers at the time. I thought they had a lot to do to publicize it and I thought that [NHL president John] Ziegler was a little bastard for the way he handled it. He's no judge. We have the courts to handle the situation, and whether we agree with the courts or not, we hire those people to hand out punishment and they did what they saw fit.

Gault: Do you think the fans today care one way or another whether or not an athlete does drugs?

Ballard: I think the real dyed-in-the-wool fans, the Murdoch fans or the Sittler fans or the McDonald fans, take it seriously, because they feel these guys are a part of them.

* * *

Gault: How old are you now?

Ballard: I was born in 1903. I'm 76 years old.

Gault: And since you've taken over control of the Gardens and the team, you haven't won a Stanley Cup. You were associated closely with winners in the past, but you've never won one. What would you do with it if you got it, walk up and down Yonge Street with it?

Ballard: I'd have to. I'd have to take it to bed with me.

Gault: But as healthy as you may be, you are 76 years old and your time is running out. Is that one of the reasons behind the push right now, behind revamping everything and . . .

Ballard: Oh yeh. I would have done this before if I hadn't been so soft. I would have done it long ago.

Gault: But you want a Cup before you die.

Ballard: Oh yeh.

Gault: And are you going to get one?

Ballard: Yes sir . . . And I'm going to live to be 100.

Once and Future Punch

George (Punch) Imlach did not spend much time in his customary and long-held seat in Maple Leaf Gardens last season, and it wasn't just because the team's wagons-in-a-circle style of play was making him crazy. The real reason, he insists, was the endless stream of fans asking him the same question, game-in and game-out: "When are you coming back to Toronto?"

On July 3, 1979, a decade plus a couple of months after he'd been fired by the Leafs as coach and general manager, the question was answered. Dropped by the Buffalo Sabres, a team he once built into respectability and contention, and with no Stafford Smythe around to say him nay, Imlach returned to the scene of his greatest hockey triumphs – four Stanley Cups in the 1960s. The last one, in 1967, turned out to be the last one, period, for the Leafs. He won those championships by getting older players, guys like Andy Bathgate and Terry Sawchuk and Allan Stanley and Marcel Pronovost, and then getting the very best that was left in them. The critics, when the team began to go into eclipse, accused Imlach of trading away the future. His response is that he was never given the chance to finish the rebuilding program that he started. Now he has the chance, as director of hockey operations, to prove that what he did in Toronto, and again in Buffalo, was no accident.

Today's Imlach contemplating a photo of yesterday's Imlach – a reminder of the first of his eras *(John Maiola)*

This Leaf team, he observed before the 1979-80 season was even at the training camp stage, ''is not the best in the league and not the worst in the · league; it's somewhere in between, they've proved that.

''But what everybody was worried about was that the team was going down, rather than up, and I'm hoping to reverse that trend.''

The obvious question is, of course, how? And the obvious answer is to either a) get better players, or b) get a lot more out of the players you've got, or c) all of the above. In the short run – again, this was pre-season – Imlach was a great deal more intent on seeing precisely what he already had to work with, and how much better he could make it work. He knows, as well as or

better than anybody in sports, what a change in approach and a little inspired leadership can do.

''In theory, everybody can be better. It doesn't matter who the hell he is. Sittler can be better. Palmateer can be a better goalie. Even the worst hockey player can improve. And if you can get even 10 per cent more out of five or six different players, that's going to make a hell of a lot of difference overall.'' He is also looking to his coach, Floyd Smith, to win four games or so with strategy and leadership, and he's counting on assistant coach Dick Duff for a similar contribution. That's 14 or 16 or 18 points and in the tough Adams Division, despite the presence of Boston and the still-dangerous Sabres, that could well mean first place.

Imlach's approach to leadership is relatively uncomplicated. ''I tell the players: my job is to get a better hockey team here. In black and white terms, that means I'm supposed to get better hockey players than you are, and your job is to see that I can't get better hockey players than you are. You do that and everybody will be happy. It's no easy job for me, and it's no easy job for you.''

The one thing he promises to do, which is the very same thing he was hired to do and which the team, fans, and media expect him to do, is to send the team on the attack. "We're going to take the leash off them, and if they've got the talent, then it'll show.

"I think you can teach anybody to play defensive hockey," he said, referring to the Leafs of 1978-79 as much as anything else. "But the result is they tend to stand around when they get the puck, and are very slow in moving it." And while he believes that offensive hockey can be taught to some extent, he is much more willing to rely on the basic ingenuity and instincts of the players. "The Canadian kid learns to think for himself in hockey; he's not disciplined into a narrow range of thinking. You can lay down certain plays, but the good hockey players, when they see that they're blocked, that those plays aren't going to work, will change course instinctively."

His rule is simple: you go all out when you've got the puck, and when they've got it, you'd better get it back. It may lack profundity, but on careful examination it's as good a definition of hockey as anybody's likely to come up with, and it's served Imlach pretty well over his 45 years in the game. He practises something else that he preaches too, which will be a welcome relief to Leaf fans: his teams do not play dull hockey. Succinctly: "You can win with spirit, and you can lose with spirit. You can lose with Dullsville too, but the chances of winning with Dullsville aren't too goddamned good."

Given what Imlach has said about the relative chances of this Leaf team, it might seem a little ludicrous and more than a little self-contradictory for him to be talking about winning Stanley Cups earlier rather than later, but he doesn't seem to have too much trouble with that notion.

"The best team doesn't always win the Stanley Cup," he says. "I've proven that in the past. What I say is: 'Let's get out there and we'll see what we can do.' And I'm sure of one thing, that this club is going to get there."

Punch Imlach, barring a recurrence of his heart problems, or some other unforeseen illness or emergency, won't miss many games in the Gardens this season; but instead of having to answer questions about when he's coming back, he may find himself pinned to the wall by fans who want to know what he's going to do for his next miracle. Or, if the worst happens, when he's leaving again.

A Good Old-Fashioned Guy

It could be argued that Bernie Geoffrion occupies the hottest seat in hockey; he is being asked, after all, to take a weakened legend in Montreal and add to the Canadiens' seemingly endless string of Stanley Cups. On the other hand, Al Arbour has to do something with a New York Islander team that seems capable of winning everything except when it counts. But not to be forgotten in the pressure-to-perform world of NHL coaching is Toronto's Floyd Smith.

He must take a team that the local sports media, by consensus, think isn't good enough, and make it good enough. He must take a team that has developed a reputation for plodding hockey and give the tough, knowledgeable, and increasingly impatient fans something to get excited about. He must prove to the Roger Neilson partisans that his old-fashioned, two-way approach to the game is better than Neilson's scientific, defense-minded system. And to add to the temperature of the seat he's now occupying, Smith realizes he wasn't the Leafs' first choice as new coach, or even the second.

Smith, however, entered this 1979-80 season with far more excitement than trepidation. As a journeyman player who kicked around the NHL in the sixties and early seventies, and as a major league coach at Buffalo (his 1975 Sabres were the last team to beat the Canadiens in a playoff series; they lost in the finals to the Philadelphia Flyers) and the WHA's Cincinnati franchise which folded under him last year, he knows the boulder-strewn terrain pretty well.

So . . .

"There's no question it's not going to be easy – on the other hand, this is the Toronto Maple Leafs, and how many people get the opportunity to coach in one of the great places in hockey?"

And . . .

"Roger did what he thought was the thing to do, and I'm going to do what I think is the thing to do, and only time will tell who's right and who's wrong. If the Leafs had won the Stanley Cup last year, then defence-would-have-been-the-way; but Montreal won it and they won it with skating."

And . . .

"I don't think there's any pressure, really. It's the old story: when you take a job as a coach, you're expected to win, and its winning that relieves all the pressures."

And . . .

"We're not exactly the worst hockey team in the world, you know. There's a lot of talent here. And I'm not here as a part of a rebuilding program: hopefully we can make this hockey club a winner today, not tomorrow."

Smith's goal for this season is to get 100 points in the final standing. Or, perhaps it is more accurate to say that 100 points is his interim goal: the way he figures it is that any team that manages that has a pretty good shot at taking the Stanley Cup.

Smith is no stranger to the blue-and-white. He came to Toronto in 1967 from Detroit, along with Paul Henderson and Norm Ullman in what has become known as "The Mahovlich deal," and left in 1970 to become the first captain of the Buffalo Sabres, rejoining Punch Imlach for what may become a once-a-decade ritual. He was in Toronto long enough to come to understand what it means to be a Leaf and that, along with the basics of the game, as he sees them, are what he's here again to pass along.

"I felt it was a great honour," he says, "just to put on my equipment and go out on the ice here. Though my stay was short and I didn't achieve very much, it was still an honour.

"I would like my team to want to come to Maple Leaf Gardens – really

want to come – to play hockey, and I want them to be proud to come here."

Like the team hierarchy above him, from Imlach to Harold Ballard, Smith is convinced that he has the skaters and the shooters to play the kind of game that will not only please the fans on a day-in, day-out basis, but also challenge for the big trophy. He's just about certain that he can switch some of the more defensive-minded players, those who responded to the Neilson system, over to offensive roles. What he talks about, frankly, is good, old-fashioned hockey played (as much as skills and circumstances will allow) in the other guy's end of the rink.

In theory at least, it seems easier to develop effective defensive strategies than to create a workable offense. "What you're asking," Smith says, "is:

how do you generate a guy putting the puck in the net who's never done it before?

"Well, it's not going to be easy and it's not going to happen overnight, but remember this: everybody likes to score goals. And if I say to a guy that I want him to take more chances in the opponent's end and score some of those goals, he's going to say: sure! Getting them to try it is no problem . . . Getting them to try it and *do* it, well, that's something else again."

What Smith is aiming for, certainly hoping for, is a team in which each player, in his own way, is a leader on the ice, a team of Dick Duffs. "He was good offensively, he was good defensively, he could skate, and he was aggressive. What the hell else is there, to put it bluntly?"

The last time Floyd Smith signed on with the Leafs, he was kind of a forgotten man but now, in one of the most enviable and precarious jobs in hockey, he has a chance to remedy that *(Kent Jones)*

Return of the Native

The 53-year history of the Toronto Maple Leafs is distinguished by some of the greatest names in hockey, from Clancy and Conacher to Sittler and Salming. But in all those years, it can be said without too much fear of contradiction, nobody has typified what it means to be a Leaf more than Dick Duff. Nobody recognized that more than the fans, who retained their appreciation and affection for him whenever he returned to the Gardens with the Rangers, Canadiens, Sabres, or Kings. No matter whom he played for, he was always a Leaf, and while adjectives cannot truly describe what that means, hockey people just know it in their bones.

Punch Imlach, who brought Duff back to the team this season as an assistant coach, probably comes as close to providing that definition as anybody. "He's been a winner," Imlach says. "He was on winners here and he was on winners during his career with Montreal. It seemed that Duff used to be 20 per cent more effective under pressure situations like the Stanley Cup playoffs."

Those old enough to remember will never forget that spring night in 1962 when, late in the third period, Duff took a pass from Tim Horton, bypassed the Chicago defence and beat Glenn Hall

with the goal that would give the Leafs their first Stanley Cup in 11 years. Luck was a factor, of course, but to re-state the truism, the Duffs of this world make their own luck.

"I hope," Imlach adds, "that he can bring his kind of intensity to these Toronto Maple Leafs, and that the young people in our organization can learn from a champion like Duff."

Unlike some team leaders, who inspire only by words or only by actions, Duff inspires by both; he is a student of what it takes to make winners of also-rans, and he is quite articulate about it. "From the first day we came to training camp, we had one thing in mind – a great big picture in front of our faces of the Stanley Cup. For some of the other teams, that may be an unrealistic goal right now, but not for this team." And for anybody who immediately thinks of the Canadiens, or the Islanders, Duff replies: "You never know, boy. Some players may play way beyond what they thought they could, and beyond where we thought they could, and there can be a total effort beyond what we thought possible. Things can happen. In 1967, if Toronto had not been pushed to make fourth place, they'd never have seen the Cup."

The role that Duff wants to fulfil is

Dick Duff is happy to be home, and if a little of what he has manages to rub off on this new crop of Leafs, well, that's mostly why he's here *(John Maiola)*

that of motivator, the guy who can get that extra out of others that he always seemed able to get out of himself when the game was on the line. What he's saying to the young Leafs, in so many words, is: "Stand up and be counted. Let it be known that you didn't just come here to play hockey, but that you have the intention of becoming one of the very good ones." And while he recognizes that talent counts, he also maintains that it doesn't count for everything. What counts more is, for lack of a better word, doggedness, finding a reason to play flat-out every game. Duff recognizes, of course, that such things are not easily achieved nor always possible, but his simple theory stands: "You hope a greater percentage of your team will be higher up for the game than the percentage of their team." And try to make it so.

Having played for the Leafs for a decade until traded in 1964, and with the great Canadiens teams of the late

1960s, Duff believes that tradition, as much as anything, can be that motivator. "We can recall our past glories here and use them just like Montreal does. And if you can say you've been on a Stanley Cup team, well that's something that's retained forever."

In pro sports, Duff insists, winning is more than a pleasure, it's a necessity. He's convinced that the Stanley Cup the Leafs won in 1962 re-instilled meaning to his career and justified all the pain and disappointment that went into getting there. Another thing that matters, he says, is that the team itself be competitive, like this Leaf team, with the potential to win it all. "When it's not there, then things are difficult. And I think we see positive results when players come from a team that is not in contention to one that is.

"Some guys can only feel good about themselves if they can be a champion. Now maybe in other areas of life that's a negative thing, but in sports it's necessary, and yes, sometimes you have to become another person out there. It's nice to be a nice guy and all that, but in hockey there's intimidation involved – physical, emotional, and mental – and it has to be used. I mean, players come into this game knowing what the circumstances are."

As noted, Duff himself was a great pressure player, but what does that mean in a game? Simply: "I'm going to outplay the guy I'm up against. When he's tired, or letting up, I've got to sense it, sense that *this team can be beaten now*!" But surely that instinct cannot be taught? Yes, says Duff, it can.

The kind of player he was, and the kind of man he is, is probably illustrated best in a story he tells about himself, a story that is not in the least self-flattering.

He was with the Canadiens and he ran into the then-coach, Toe Blake, on the street. Did he like Montreal? Yes, Duff replied, very much. Did he like the other players? Again, Duff answered enthusiastically in the affirmative. "Fine," Blake said, "but if you don't start playing hockey the way we think you can, you won't be here next week."

And what was Duff's reaction? Did he sulk, or blame others, or bring up injuries? No. "I realized that I had to play better, that I was not playing well enough in Blake's estimation, and that was good enough for me."

Every Inch a Captain

When people started telling Darryl Sittler, before the season began, that the new Leaf system, geared as it is toward offensive hockey, would likely mean 50 goals and a scoring title for him, he refused to be caught up in the enthusiasm. He pointed out that in 1977-78, under Roger Neilson's stringent defensive game plan, he had his best scoring season ever – 117 points, including 45 goals and a team record 72 assists – and that his mere 36-goal, 51-assist performance last year was somewhat affected by injuries and a vicious abscessed tooth that drained his strength.

It wasn't that Sittler, the Leafs' captain and the leader of a team of leaders, wanted to rain on anybody's parade. It was just that he was not going to get caught up in predicting where his team would finish, or how far it would go; naturally he wants the Stanley Cup, and yes, maybe his team can win it, but it is simply not in his nature to make promises he can't keep. One of the problems of being Darryl Sittler is that every utterance gets etched in concrete, so he very, very carefully measures what he has to say.

He will say, for instance, that the Leafs of the past few years lacked consistency, and that unless this year's team can develop it, the style of play will become pretty irrelevant. "We all want to end up in first place and win the Stanley Cup," he says, "but next April it doesn't really matter whether you finish first overall or tenth. Look at the Islanders: they finished first and got knocked out. No, the idea is to play the season with more consistency and come up big in the playoffs."

He reminds us as well that in the playoffs, both last year and the year before, the Leafs did not exactly come up small, beating teams (Atlanta last year, the Islanders in 1978) that finished above them in the standings. Sure they were knocked out by Montreal, but then so was everybody else. Sittler pointed out during the season last year, and repeated before this season began, that for the Leafs to win, they had to get up for each and every game. "Other teams had more raw talent than we did to carry them over." And getting up for every game is, needless to say, impossible. "The body can only do so much."

Which brings us to mental attitude. The Leaf players, Sittler says, are happy to be with one another, to be on this team. "It's a team with a lot of character," he says, "a team without any prima donnas. We know what has to be done, we dig down and we work hard; and getting up for games has a

lot to do with the feeling we have for one another.'' There are those who think that the Leafs were overcoached by Roger Neilson and that maybe the easier hand of Floyd Smith will result in a happier club. Sittler, however, only talks about that in the abstract. ''A coach can keep things loose, or he can put a lot of pressure on you. If you get somebody down on you all the time, or giving you hell all the time, that can have a bad effect.'' But Smith, he says, is a ''Don Cherry-type'' of coach, who makes everything fun, including the practices. ''For him it doesn't matter if you win 6-5 or 2-1, as long as you win.''

With Neilson, Sittler explains, ''if there was ever a doubt about taking a chance, you didn't; you were supposed to back off.'' But with Smith, the attitude is: ''What better defence is there than to have the puck? So you go in and forecheck and make things happen.''

The other problem, under the Neilson system, was that he had the Leafs broken down into a team of specialists, and where that tended to fall down mostly was in the way that it allowed the opposition teams to pretty well dic-

tate the game plan. It meant, for example, that the Jimmy Jones-centred checking line, assigned to the other team's big scoring line, was often on the ice more than the Leaf scorers – Sittler and Lanny McDonald and whatever checker they had on their left side.

''With Smith,'' Sittler says, ''we just go out there and let the other team worry about us.'' Asked if goalie Mike Palmateer would suffer in the new regime, Sittler recalled that under the defensive system, the Leafs were still quite often out-shot and out-chanced, and ''it stands to reason that if you play in your own end, you increase the chances of being scored on.''

The other thing that he expected to happen was that lines other than his own would be given the opportunity and the mandate to score some goals. A lot will hinge, of course, on whether or not the fast young Leafs like Saganiuk and Anderson and Quenneville can come along this year (but, after all, it took Sittler and McDonald two seasons to become the stars they are today). Sittler was particularly impressed with Laurie Boschman, the team's first draft choice from the junior ranks. About

Darryl Sittler, wife Wendy, and the kids take no small pleasure in a composite painting of the captain himself in some of his more typical and memorable moments in hockey *(Sinclair/Arnett)*

half-way through training camp he was saying the kid ''reminds me of Bryan Trottier a little bit; he's strong on his skates,'' and predicting a rosy future for him.

As for personal goals for this season, Sittler, as usual, didn't set any. ''I play to the best of my ability each game, and by the end of the season the personal things take care of themselves. You want to come home from the rink after each game happy that you've done the best you can. And I think I'm a strong enough person, and hard enough on myself, to know when I have or haven't done that.''

The Way They Were

Wayne Lilley

Syl Apps, Governor General Lord Alexander of Tunis, Detroit's Sid Abel and Leaf president E.W. Bickle in 1947 *(Turofsky)*

By all that seems right, the Toronto Maple Leaf Hockey Club should have been perfectly attuned to the 1950s. The political and social conservatism that characterized the decade was almost a mirror reflection of the principles of the Maple Leaf organization, moulded as it was in the image of its crusty founder and guiding spirit, Conn Smythe. Hard work, loyalty, and pride in tradition, according to the Calvinistic credo of Smythe, would bring their own rewards. And he had ample proof that the ethos was right: he'd become wealthy in business, had built the most magnificent hockey facility in the world in the midst of a depression, and, by the start of the 1950s, had seen the hockey team he created win the Stanley Cup six times in 20 years.

The fifties too began successfully. But while the 1950-51 team coached by former star player Joe Primeau won the Cup for the seventh time in the Leafs' history, it failed to repeat the following season. Two years later Leafs finished ignominiously out of the play-offs – only the second time that had happened in 20 years. Furthermore, it was a harbinger of things to come. For three successive seasons leprecaun-ish King Clancy, another former Leaf star, guided the Leafs into the playoffs only to be beaten on each occasion in the semi-final round. Impatiently, Smythe brought in Howie Meeker, a player on the last Cup winner, but he lasted only a year and did worse than Clancy, missing the playoffs. So did his successor, ex-Montreal Canadien Billy Reay.

It was inevitable, of course, that other teams in the six-team NHL would from time to time grow strong enough to beat the Leafs. But when this had happened in the past the customary response had been a stoic analysis of the team's needs followed by a systematic filling of management holes with perfectly moulded plugs from Leafs' wealth of loyal ex-players. From 1952 on, though, a futility seemed to creep through the organization. Indeed, a faint whiff of panic emerged: not only was Billy Reay from outside the Toronto organization, but also he was the fourth coach of the Leafs in seven years; in the previous 20 years in Maple Leaf Gardens, there had been, to all intents and purposes, but five Leaf coaches.

To fans who saw the problems on the ice, the solutions effected by Leaf management seemed feckless. The formation of a seven-man policy-making committee in 1957, for instance, seemed to the more than slightly jaded, to be a characteristically unsubtle plot by Conn Smythe to employ his son Stafford and such friends as Harold Ballard and John Bassett within the Maple Leaf Gardens empire. Stafford had become chairman of the group, popularly known as the Silver Seven.

But the upshot of the move was that by the summer of 1958, fans had little reason to equate the arrival of one George "Punch" Imlach with the second coming of Syl Apps. For one thing, Imlach was made assistant general manager, an executive position, puzzling because since the Silver Seven had come on the scene, there was no shortage of front-office personnel in the Gardens. Indeed, observers suggested with equal parts of cynicism and justification that the question of the day was not "Who's Punch Imlach?" but rather, "To whom is Imlach assistant?"

By the Leafs' normal nepotistic standards of the day the appointment of Imlach was something of a departure. But while, like Reay, he'd come from outside the Leaf organization, unlike Reay he'd had broad experience as a player, coach, accountant, general manager, and part-owner of professional teams. His stint during the war as an army drill sergeant was an agreeable curriculum vitae item so far as the patriotic Conn Smythe was concerned. But the fact was, Imlach's experience had all been in the minor leagues; when the Silver Seven "discovered" him, he was completing his first season in major league hockey as director of player personnel for the Boston Bruins.

Still, there was something different about Imlach. He candidly admitted he'd hardly seen the Leafs play in the past seven years, but offered that he saw no reason why any team he was connected with should not reach the playoffs. In fact, he announced, tipping his trademark fedora to the back of his bald pate, there was no reason the Leafs couldn't win the Stanley Cup – that season.

The Toronto media loved this new, eminently quotable, frequently profane, and always cocky Leaf. And Imlach's brash confidence appeared to infect the harassed Silver Seven as well. Perhaps to save having to identify the immediate superior of the new assistant general manager, the committee promoted him to general manager. Within a few weeks of the 1958-59 season, Imlach made changes of his own: he fired Billy Reay and became coach and general manager of the Toronto Maple Leafs.

If the mercurial ascent within the organization of Canada's (and maybe the world's) best-known hockey team awed Imlach, little evidence showed on a face whose pallor suggested not only winters, but summers as well, spent in sunless arenas. Instead he went to work to fulfil his prophecies: with players bequeathed him, with others he bought or traded for, and still others culled from the minor leagues he knew so well, he added to the nucleus from the previous season; juggling line-ups, baiting opponents, his own players, and management alike, and driving his team relentlessly in practice, within six years he'd duplicated the feat of Hap Day and coached the Leafs to their second string of three consecutive Stanley Cups. Within eight years, he'd added a fourth Cup. And within ten years, he was fired by Stafford Smythe.

For better or (as some might argue) for worse his enormous influence would be felt throughout hockey for years to come: no fewer than 15 of the players who played for an Imlach-run Leaf team in the 1960s would go on to assume positions as coaches or managers in the highest ranks of professional hockey. Another handful would continue as developers of minor league talent. Following expansion, Imlach himself would move to Buffalo and create one of the most powerful of the new teams in the NHL. But the Imlach saga would have all been so much fought-over folklore, another chapter in the considerable mythology of the Toronto Maple Leafs, had Imlach not been hired once more by the Leafs in 1979 as general manager.

Naturally, no one had to ask, on Imlach's second coming, who he was. The Leafs' dramatic history could be roughly segmented into six ten-year acts and Imlach had written, directed, and performed in the fourth act of the 1960s. But the plot had gone awry when Imlach had left, so now he was being invited, as he had been 20 years earlier, to provide the Leafs with a workable script.

Though no one can say how successful he will be, it is worth noting that one of the criticisms of Imlach when he was fired was that he needed the right stage and cast of players to make his scripts work. Even if that is so, the future of the Toronto Maple Leafs looks bright, because there is an uncanny similarity between the 1959 Leaf team he turned into a Stanley Cup winner and the one he inherited in 1979.

No sports team in Canada (and few anywhere else in the world) has a greater or more picaresque mythology than the Toronto Maple Leafs. And few professional sports team builders have occupied a higher place for a longer time in the minds of sports fans than Conn Smythe. As a pugnacious 5-feet, 7-inch centre for the University of Toronto's teams in the 1920s, Smythe absorbed the fundamentals of building, coaching, and inspiring hockey teams to lofty heights. Interrupting his education in civil engineering to serve overseas in World War I, Smythe returned to Toronto, finished his degree, and went to work for the City of Toronto, before striking out on his own in a highly successful sand and gravel business.

But hockey remained his hobby and in 1927, he persuaded a graduating University of Toronto team to stay together so he could coach it to the Allan Cup, symbolic of Canada's senior hockey championship. A year later, the Varsity Grads, coached by Conn Smythe, won the Olympic Gold Medal for Canada.

But even before that, Smythe had become enamoured of trying his hand at professional hockey and had readily accepted the offer of Colonel John Hammond of New York to assemble and coach the New York Rangers, recently admitted to the National Hockey League. Calling on his knowledge of amateurs across Canada, Smythe had brought together a team that included Ching Johnson, Taffy Abel, Bill and Bun Cook, Frank Boucher, and goalie Lorne Chabot. When he failed to buy a star the Toronto St. Pats were trying to trade, however, Hammond fired him.

Typically, the feisty Smythe refused to let his fate upset his self-confidence. As a faithful University of Toronto alumnus, he bet his $10,000 severance pay from the Rangers that the Varsity team would beat McGill in a

football game and when Toronto won, he parlayed his winnings into a wager backing the Toronto St. Pats against the Ottawa Senators in an NHL hockey game. When that bet also paid off, Smythe persuaded two business associates, Peter Campbell and E.W. Bickle, that since the Toronto St. Pats of the NHL were for sale, the three should buy the team. When they came up about $40,000 short of the asking price of $200,000, Smythe went to work again: wouldn't it be best if the team remained in Toronto hands? he asked the St. Pats owners. Unaccountably, they agreed with the chauvinistic argument and Smythe and his partners bought the team for $160,000. As a final touch, the patriotic Smythe changed the name of the team to the Toronto Maple Leafs, the name it has played under since 1927.

The Maple Leafs were not quite an instant success. Under first-year coach Alex Romeril, they missed the playoffs. And in three years behind the bench, Smythe himself could only

Toronto Mayor Phil Givens congratulating Punch Imlach and his Stanley Cup winning Leafs (in the background) during the last great dynasty of the 1960s (*Graphic Artists*)

Another season underway in the 'Ted Kennedy Era' of the late 1940s and early 1950s as owner Conn Smythe performs the ceremonial faceoff between Kennedy and Hawks' Jim McFadden *(Turofsky)*

make the post-season matches once. But he'd been building his line-up carefully, and the cornerstone of the construction was his hiring of Frank Selke. For most of his life, Selke had been an electrician at the University of Toronto, but his hobby and obsession, like Smythe's, had been hockey. By 1928, he'd finally given up his job to manage the minor professional Toronto Ravinas and to coach the Toronto Marlboro Juniors. If Smythe knew hockey talent across Canada, Selke had an eye for what there was in and around Toronto. By combing rivers, ponds, and rinks in the city, he'd

assembled a Ravinas team that included Joe Primeau, Carl Voss, Red Horner, Charlie Conacher, and Harvey Jackson. Selke labeled them future stars. As would any savvy hockey man, Smythe agreed; he saw them as the perfect complement to Ace Bailey, Hap Day, Harold Cotton, Andy Blair, and goalie Lorne Chabot — the nucleus of his Leaf team. To get at Selke's mother lode of young talent, he hired the diminutive electrician as director of scouting, publicity, and programs. Such was the state of the Leafs' finances, however, that Smythe knew the Maple Leaf directors would flinch at the thought of another salary to cover, so he paid Selke out of his own pocket. But if the directors would have been upset at whatever Smythe paid Selke, it's hard to imagine what went through their minds when he informed them he planned to buy Francis "King" Clancy from Ottawa for the unheard-of price of $35,000. To get the money, Smythe had bet on a horse at the race track, and once again, gambling winnings would support his hockey habit.

The wheeling and dealing began to pay dividends in 1930-31, but as the Leafs reached the playoffs (only to be beaten in the quarter-finals) Smythe realized a new problem: the drafty Mutual Street Arena where the Leafs played was only a small step up from Ravina Gardens, a crater-like rink on a west Toronto hillside where Selke's minor pro teams often played on fog-shrouded ice. Not only was Mutual Street Arena unacceptable for the calibre of hockey Smythe saw in the NHL, but even if he filled every one of its 8,000 seats, the $200,000 in revenue that represented would hardly keep the team afloat. Smythe embarked on the most ambitious plan in the history of sports in Toronto: he put together a consortium to build the biggest and best hockey arena anywhere in the world.

His business contacts helped him get the project off the ground and their contacts, in turn, brought more local investors into the plan; these included one of the directors of Eaton's department store, which happened to own one of the prime pieces of property in the city. Smythe bought the parcel at the corner of Church and Carlton Streets for $350,000 and, amidst the greatest depression the world had ever known, set out to raise building funds.

It helped his cause that the Maple Leafs had become popular with Toronto hockey fans. When Smythe bought the St. Pats, he inherited Foster Hewitt, a young broadcaster whose nasal "He shoots! He scores!" was becoming as well known as the names of the Maple Leaf players. When Hewitt casually mentioned during a broadcast of a Leaf game that there was a book on the Leafs (prepared by Selke to help raise building money), the book sold a remarkable 90,000 copies.

But as the depression deepened, investors who might normally have been willing to share Smythe's vision and profits instead shied away. Again Selke came to Smythe's rescue. A former union man respected in labour circles, Selke made speeches pointing out the benefits of the Maple Leaf Gardens project in providing jobs for tradesmen. In return for Smythe's guarantee to employ only union labour, workers agreed to accept 20 per cent of their pay in shares of the publicly owned company. By June 1931, the project was underway and six months later on November 12, 1931, the building that became the shrine of hockey was host to 13,542 fans for a Leaf game against Chicago. (The Leafs, incidentally, lost.)

As it turned out, Maple Leaf Gardens was also the most highly leveraged of real estate in Canada at a time when foreclosures were not exactly rare. The building had mortgages totalling $2.1 million and the contractor was still owed $75,000. Convinced he now had the players to win – and that a winner would fill the Gardens seats – Smythe needed a coach to replace mild-mannered Art Duncan, a former Leaf, now seemingly lost among the likes of players with colourful nicknames like King, Ace, Hap, Red, Busher, and Gentleman Joe. Smythe recalled being beaten in the 1930-31 season by a Chicago team he felt was not as good as the Leafs. The team had been coached by Dick Irvin, a flinty individual given to quoting Knute Rockne's homilies and displaying an attitude toward work that parallelled Smythe's own Puritan ethic. When Irvin was fired by Chicago's eccentric owner, Smythe hired the Regina native to coach the Leafs. Inspired by a new coach and the surroundings of Maple Leaf Gardens, the Leafs won the Stanley Cup in their new home in 1932.

It was a feat the team would never duplicate under Irvin, even though he lasted until 1940 as coach. But perhaps no other individual could have ridden herd on the rambunctious Leafs of the 1930s nearly as well as Irvin did. Even the impatience of Smythe was somewhat appeased by the Leafs' record: not once did they fail to make the playoffs, and six times they reached the Stanley Cup finals.

Even without the coveted trophy, the Leafs of the 1930s became a Canadian institution. Names of the players rolled as easily off the tongues of fans as they did off Foster Hewitt's during game broadcasts. Newspapers reported on the stars' every move on

and off the ice. Conacher's predilection for fancy cars was as well known as his scoring prowess on The Kid Line, alongside Busher Jackson and Joe Primeau. When Hap Day married in 1937, some 3,000 fans turned up at the church to cheer the Leaf captain, his bride, and his team mates in the wedding party.

Hockey also became more commercial. Hewitt's Leaf broadcasts became the most popular radio program in Canada and Imperial Oil, Foster Hewitt, and the Maple Leafs became what writer Jack Batten called hockey's Holy Trinity. The Hot Stove League, the between-periods radio show hosted by Wes McKnight, became as popular as the game itself. St. Lawrence Corn Starch Co., which sponsored McKnight's nightly sportscast on another station, saw its product, Bee Hive Golden Corn Syrup, become synonymous with "energy" to the young fans who exchanged Bee Hive labels for pictures of the Leafs. And everywhere in Canada, shinny and road-hockey games featured "stars" wearing Toronto Maple Leaf sweaters — always the blue ones with white trim, which confused many a youngster on a first visit to Maple Leaf Gardens where the Leafs always played in white sweaters with blue trim. For some reason, the Leafs never sold facsimiles of their white sweaters to the public.

Of all the rivalries the Leafs had over the years, that with the Boston Bruins of the thirties was the fiercest. The feud began when Smythe felt he was bilked by Boston general manager Art Ross in a player transaction. Smythe did his best to incite Ross at every opportunity and at one point during a visit of the Leafs to Boston, even took out a newspaper ad implying that until the Leafs came to town, Boston fans had not seen a real hockey team; that quarrel, which produced some bitterly fought hockey games, came to a shocking climax in December 1933. King Clancy, as was his wont, slyly tripped Boston's truculent Eddie Shore and then took off down the ice with the puck. Shore, with blood in his eye, pelted down the ice, gunning for any Leaf in his path; it happened to be Ace Bailey. Caught unaware, Bailey was hurled into the air and he landed head first on the ice. Naturally, Red Horner, the Leaf enforcer, came to the defence of his fallen mate and proceeded to knock Shore to the ice, leading to an emptying of both benches. The warfare ended abruptly, however, when both sides realized that Bailey was seriously injured. He was taken to hospital where he remained near death.

On the way out of the rink the bellicose Smythe objected to a fan's suggestion that Bailey was faking, and his swing at the fan earned him a trip to the police station. Not until his old adversary Art Ross bailed him out at 2.00 a.m. was he able to request of Selke, who was back in Toronto, that arrangements be made to transfer Bailey's body. Fortunately, Bailey recovered in a couple of days, but never sufficiently to play hockey again.

As other stars of the 1930s began to age, the system of farm teams organized by the shrewd and tireless Selke kept the Leafs stocked with players. When Primeau and Clancy retired, players such as Nick Metz, Bob Davidson, and Gordie Drillon replaced them. Smythe, too, came up with his share of talent, often selecting players for their qualities of moral rectitude and competitive spirit as much as for their hockey ability. He found Syl Apps, for example, in a football game and was admiring, rather than impatient, at Apps' refusal to turn professional until he'd competed for Canada in the 1932 Olympics. Apps turned out to be not only a superb hockey player but also the epitome of what Smythe had always felt the typical Toronto Maple Leaf should be: modest, well conditioned, unselfish and clean-living to a point just short of saintliness.

But Smythe never forgot that he was in the business of hockey, nor did he let sentiment cloud his business judgement. When he discovered a corpulent young goalie named Turk Broda, he was so confident in the rookie that he sold veteran George Hainsworth to Montreal. When faithful Hap Day, Leafs' only captain for ten years, grew long in the tooth by Smythe's standards, he was sold to the New York Americans in 1937. When Conacher and Primeau retired, Busher Jackson, the last remnant of the Kid Line, was lumped in with other players and traded for Sweeney Schriner, a smooth winger from the same New York Americans, in 1939. But while Leafs were able to maintain their position as one of best teams in the NHL, they never seemed able to win the Stanley Cup. Finally, in 1939, Dick Irvin tired of always being the bridesmaid as

Leaf captain Hap Day looked pretty much the way he felt that day back in 1935 when a broken thumb took him out of the play for a while *(Alexandra Studios)*

well: he asked to move to Montreal and his wish was granted, closing the 1930s for the Toronto Maple Leafs.

By the opening years of the 1940s, the Leaf tradition had begun to tell. Hap Day was recalled to the Leafs to become the new coach, and after an initial year of adjustment in the job, Day accomplished what Irvin had been unable to for so many years: in 1941-42, the Leafs won their second Stanley Cup. Furthermore, they did it in grand style. After losing the first three games of the final series against Detroit, they roared back to take four straight.

But the war, declared in 1939, began to take its toll in 1942. Nine Leafs joined the Canadian forces and Smythe himself re-enlisted to command the Sportsmen's Battery overseas; the next season, Syl Apps and Turk Broda went overseas as well. Frank Selke, left behind to shore up Leafs' sagging roster, proved at least as capable as Smythe at managing a team. He traded for Babe Pratt, and obtained the rights of 17-year-old Ted Kennedy in a deal with Montreal. In the

meantime, Gaye Stewart and Gus Bodnar won the Calder Cup as rookies-of-the-year in successive seasons. Led by Kennedy and amply rearguarded by goalie Frank McCool, yet another Calder winner, the 1944-45 Leafs surprised everyone by winning the Stanley Cup. With veterans Apps, Broda, Nick and Don Metz, and Bob Goldham slated to return from overseas, the future of the Leafs seemed bright, perhaps dazzling.

Among the returnees, however, was Conn Smythe, and he was not as pleased as the Maple Leafs' directors with the way Selke had handled things in his absence. The thought that the directors might find him replaceable by the more affable Selke was not a pleasant one for the veteran commander. He began ensuring that it would not happen. In particular, Selke's trading of promising defenceman Frank Eddols to Montreal for the rights to Kennedy (a deal vetoed by Smythe from Europe but consummated by Selke anyway) had begun to look disastrous. Kennedy got off to a horrendous start in 1944 and then got hurt. The quarrelling between Smythe and Selke heated up until, at the end of the 1946 season, Selke left to join Dick Irvin in Montreal. The struggle also had a corrosive effect on the Leafs, as front-office affairs will: the team ended up out of the playoffs for the first time in Hap Day's coaching career.

For the next three years, however, nothing could stop the Leafs. Veterans like Apps and Broda blended perfectly with now experienced youngsters like Stewart, Bodnar, and Kennedy, and also with a covey of rookies from Selke's incubator teams. When the opportunity arose, Smythe involved Leafs in one of the biggest trades in hockey by sending five players to Chicago to obtain slick centre Max Bentley. With Apps, Kennedy, Bentley, and Broda down the centre, the Leafs had one of the strongest teams ever put together in the NHL. They closed out the 1940s with three consecutive Stanley Cups, something no other team in NHL history had accomplished.

Still, there was something ominous about the wins. The rebuilding of the Leafs had been carried out using Frank Selke's farm system, which had nurtured future Leafs at St. Michael's College and as pros with the American Hockey League team in Pittsburgh. Jim Thomson, Bob Goldham, Fleming

MacKell, Tod Sloan, and Harry Watson, all important cogs in the Leaf machine, had spent some time in the farm system. In 1949, it would deliver Tim Horton and George Armstrong to the Leafs as well. But in the absence of Selke's attention, the farm had gone to seed somewhat as Smythe concentrated on the Leafs.

Even so, the Leafs stumbled only for a season as they began the 1950s losing in the semi-finals of the Stanley Cup playoffs, After ten years behind the bench, Hap Day became assistant general manager and was replaced by his former team mate, Joe Primeau. And to begin the third decade in Maple Leaf Gardens, Leafs came up with one of the most powerful teams in their history. The 1950-51 team won more games than any other team, losing only 16 times over the season. In the

playoffs, it took them only ten games to win the Stanley Cup. Jim Thomson, Sid Smith, and Ted Kennedy all made the second all-star team and goalie Al Rollins won the Vezina Trophy. But never again in the 1950s would they play up to their form of the first year under Joe Primeau.

There are a number of explanations for the Leafs' grim slump during the 1950s and, not surprisingly, most bring Conn Smythe into the picture (where, in fact, he had always been). His prickly personality and uncompromising refusal to give up any of his iron-handed authority was beginning to develop severe ramifications. The farm system he'd left fallow no longer teemed with hot prospects, and furthermore his much-demonstrated prescience was beginning to appear questionable. Fleming MacKell and

Turk Broda (left) with his brothers Lou and Stan (who also worked at the Gardens) enjoying a drink out of the Stanley Cup in the great 1940s years *(Turofsky)*

Stafford Smythe (third from the right, front row) played for some long-forgotten teams like this one, but his fame would come, as far as hockey was concerned, in the executive offices *(Alexandra Studios)*

Fern Flaman, traded to Boston for Dave Creighton and Jim Morrison, both turned up as all-stars; Morrison played only adequately in Toronto and Creighton languished for most of his career in the minor leagues. Smythe also dumped Jim Thomson and Tod Sloan, two useful players weened in Selke's farm system to become stars with the Leafs. Smythe rationalized the latter trade on grounds that the have-nots of the NHL needed support if the league was to survive. But he'd never been noted for such magnanimity in the past. A more likely reason for the trade was that both players had become involved in the newly formed NHL Players' Association. Ironically, the labour movement that had helped Smythe build Maple Leaf Gardens was now viewed by the owner as a threat to professional hockey. Ultimately, though, it was Smythe's determination

to make the Leafs a monument in perpetuity to his memory that resulted in a change in the management style of the Maple Leafs' executive.

For years, Smythe had been trying to interest his son Stafford in becoming involved with the Leafs. But Stafford, along with his friend Harold Ballard, was content to operate the Toronto Marlboro Juniors. When Stafford finally consented to move to the Leafs, his interest in the job quickly surpassed even his father's wildest hopes; before he'd been chairman of the Silver Seven for a year, he acted for the hockey committee to make his father an offer of $4 million for the Toronto NHL franchise. The elder Smythe turned down the offer, but by 1961, Stafford, Ballard, and *Telegram* publisher John Bassett, acting as a troika, challenged his reign and successfully bought him out of Maple Leaf Gar-

dens. With 60 per cent of the voting stock, the three gained effective control of the Toronto Maple Leafs.

In itself, the change hardly represented a guarantee of success for the Leafs, given that Ballard and Smythe had been making most of the decisions affecting the team since the formation of the Silver Seven in 1957, and the team wasn't exactly going places. When they replaced Howie Meeker with Billy Reay in 1957, however, their instincts had been right: Meeker *did* lack the experience to handle the rebuilding required. While, as it turned out, Reay wasn't the answer either, the hiring of Punch Imlach in 1958 vindicated the Silver Seven. To begin the 1960s, the Leafs would be coached and managed by one of the smartest hockey minds in the business.

Although Reay didn't last long enough with the Leafs to reap the ben-

efits, two moves he'd advocated would serve the Leafs well. In one, he obtained Bert Olmstead, an intense dervish of a player who'd been a team leader and team mate of Reay in Montreal. He also played a part in obtaining the services of Johnny Bower, a well-travelled goalie playing in Cleveland of the American League after failing to stick in a number of NHL trials. Reay had also recommended that the Leafs pick up 33-year-old Allan Stanley, an accomplished defenceman whose deliberate style had made him the object of fans' ire in Boston. All three would play a major part in the reconstruction of the Leafs in the sixties.

Although Imlach's Leafs were generally characterized as playing conventional, albeit winning, hockey with an emphasis on hard work, there was nothing conventional about Imlach's personal style. To stir things up on the

Imlach, Tim Horton, Rudy Migay, and Ron Stewart in the late 1950s, attempting to prove, perhaps, that the team that plays together stays together (*Turofsky*)

Howie Meeker (no, he hasn't changed a bit) accepting a cheque for the Crippled Children from a couple of members of his fan club back in 1957, the one season he coached the Leafs *(Turofsky)*

ice, he created a line called The Rocks which featured Gerry James, a Winnipeg Blue Bomber fullback, and durable winger Johnny Wilson flanking centre Garry Edmundson, whose nickname was Duke. The opposition played against The Rocks trying to look over both shoulders at once.

Imlach might not have been steeped in Leaf tradition when he arrived at the Gardens, but as did almost anyone who went to work there, he quickly acquired all he needed through his assistant general manager and kindred spirit, King Clancy. When Red Kelly balked at being traded to New York by Detroit and retired instead, Clancy readily agreed that the Leafs could use anybody with a name like Kelly, especially if he had been an all-star defenceman for six of his 12 years in the NHL. While Clancy talked Kelly into joining the Leafs, Imlach made a deal to

send a very ordinary journeyman, Marc Reaume, to Detroit in payment. It was probably the best trade in Leaf history. Kelly, converted to centre by Imlach, helped Leafs beat Detroit in the semi-finals in 1959-60, but neither he nor anyone else could beat Les Canadiens, who won the Cup in four straight games.

The 1960-61 season was a lull in Leafs' climb while individuals established their credentials. That year, Frank Mahovlich scored 48 goals while his centreman, Red Kelly, had 50 assists. Bower and Mahovlich made the first all-star team and Allan Stanley the second. Rookie Dave Keon won the Calder Trophy, Red Kelly the Lady Byng, and Johnny Bower the Vezina. Although the Leafs lost to Detroit in the semi-finals there was a newly found confidence.

In 1961-62, the addition of Al Arbour,

Larry Hillman, and forward Eddie Litzenberger, combined with the all-star calibre play of Dave Keon and Carl Brewer, put all the pieces together and brought Toronto its first Stanley Cup in 11 years. In the next two years they would go on to win another two Cups, easily in 1962-63 with 4-1 series wins over both Montreal and Detroit, and with a great deal more difficulty the next season. The Canadiens and Wings each took them to seven games. There had been the hint of desperation in that 1963-64 victory. As the season developed Imlach realized he needed more scoring power than he had, so he traded popular Dick Duff, Bob Nevin, and three minor league players to New York for aging stars Andy Bathgate and Don McKenney. The trade paid off with a Stanley Cup, to be sure, but later it would be cited as a classic example of giving up youth for immediate rewards, a reputation Imlach has not been able to shake completely.

When the Leafs were beaten in the semi-finals the following two years, Imlach seemingly refused to concede his aging team was over the hill. Patching with rookies like Ron Ellis and veterans like Marcel Pronovost and Terry Sawchuk, he endured a 1967 season that featured the longest winless streak in Leaf history and a heart attack that hospitalized him. During Imlach's confinement, Clancy handled the Leafs, turning the team around. But by the playoffs, Imlach was back behind the bench to lead the Leafs to the Stanley Cup in Canada's Centennial year.

But hanging on too long to older players and his unbending refusal to coddle stars eventually would contribute to the downfall of Imlach's Leafs. The most celebrated of his difficulties with individual players was his almost studied misunderstanding of Frank Mahovlich, a bona fide star and perhaps Leafs' most talented player; Imlach persisted in calling him "Ma-ho-lo-vich." Finally Imlach packaged his moody winger with youthful Garry Unger and Peter Stemkowski and traded them to Detroit for Norm Ullman, Paul Henderson, and Floyd Smith. One of hockey's longest running arguments is: who got the better of the deal? In any case, it was difficult to determine the benefits for Toronto. The decay Imlach had been attempting to stem had finally taken hold and in 1967-68,

the Leafs finished out of the playoffs. In 1968-69 they rebounded to gain a playoff spot, but lost to Boston in the quarter-finals. Imlach was fired on the evening of the last game by Stafford Smythe, the man who'd hired him ten years earlier.

Imlach's departure from the Leafs was as controversial as his tenure. But the critics who accused him of sticking too long with veterans overlooked the fact that the NHL expansion in 1967 (endorsed by Leaf directors who reaped $2 million from it as their share of the new teams' entry fees) had swallowed up most of the good young players, including 22 that the Leafs owned on various farm teams. And the critics who suggested that Imlach depleted Leafs' farm teams overlooked the front office's decision to sell, at a profit, teams in Victoria and Rochester that Imlach had helped build.

On the other hand, Imlach's irascible coaching personality probably did hurt the Leafs. Besides his on-going problems with Mahovlich, from time to time he had clashes with Carl Brewer, Mike Walton, Jim McKenny, Bob Nevin, Bob Pulford, Jim Pappin, Eddie Shack, and Andy Bathgate as well as with his bosses. Though the pragmatic might have questioned Imlach's firing – and players who'd been declared over the hill before Imlach gave them a chance with the Leafs certainly did – there were few emotional tears shed in the dressing room by the younger Leaf players.

But for the Toronto Maple Leafs, the decade of the 1970s would become as stormy as that of the fifties prior to Imlach's arrival. And the tempest would encompass not only the dressing room but the front office, engulfing the entire organization.

Under the triumvirate of Smythe, Ballard, and Bassett there had been a gradual change over Maple Leaf Gardens. A lounge that sold liquor was added (souring Conn Smythe just about completely on the new regime), the seating capacity of the building was expanded to more than 16,000, prices for tickets were raised, and the Gardens became the venue for everything from evangelical crusades to rock concerts. In fact, it seemed that Maple Leaf Gardens had forsaken its purity of purpose – hockey – for the pursuit of money. What was left of those Smythe-era purists could not help but feel there was something

déclassé at having the ice, in the very cathedral of hockey, flooded by a machine that bore the paid-for message, "It's mainly because of the meat." But there were bills to pay, and hockey players were no longer available for the price of an NHL sweater and a new pair of skates.

The big Leaf story of the early seventies, however, did not take place on the ice or in the coach's office. It involved the spectacular indictments of Ballard and Stafford Smythe on a series of charges of tax evasion, fraud, and theft. Overall, hundreds of thousands of dollars, appropriated from the Gardens and from the Marlboro Hockey Club, were involved.

The tax evasion and false reporting charges actually were laid in 1969. Thirteen days before they were made public, board chairman John Bassett cast the deciding vote in ousting Stafford Smythe and Ballard as president and vice-president of the Gardens, thus dissolving their close, 17-year partnership. Life on the outside was short for Ballard and Smythe, as it turned out, because six months later they were back in their old positions, having blitz-bought all available Gardens stock. In December, 1970, Bassett declined to run again for board chairman (he eventually sold his stock, too) and Smythe replaced him.

Two years less a week after their original ouster, Smythe and Ballard found themselves in more serious trouble, charged with fraud and theft involving some $600,000-plus. Again, it was a case of misuse of corporate funds; in fact, it basically involved the same funds. The hard-living Smythe died of a severe bleeding ulcer before the matter came to trial, but Ballard was convicted for his part and served time in penitentiary, running the Gardens, which he then virtually owned (having beaten off attempts by the Smythe family to gain control after Stafford's death) from his cell.

Whether or not such front-office goings-on affected the team on the ice, no one can say with certainty. Under new coach Johnny McLellan, the 1969-70 Leafs failed to make the playoffs. The following two seasons, even with Jacques Plante and Bernie Parent sharing goaltending, and Dave Keon succeeding George Armstrong to become Leafs' 11th captain, and the presence of a rookie named Darryl Sittler, Leafs failed to get past the quarter-finals even in the expansion-weakened league.

In 1971, a new threat crippled the team that general manager Jim Gregory, Imlach's Leaf-tattooed replacement, had been patiently assembling. The World Hockey Association stole newcomers Rick Ley, Jim Dorey, Brad Selwood, Jim Harrison, and emerging star Bernie Parent.

In 1972-73, McLellan missed the playoffs once more with the line-up decimated by the WHA. Ulcers drove him into the front office and the hunt was on for yet another new Leaf coach. When Red Kelly left Pittsburgh, he was once again wooed by the Leafs.

Kelly appeared to have all the credentials: as a player, he'd been a star as both defenceman and centre; after leaving the Leafs, he'd gained management and coaching experience in Los Angeles and Pittsburgh and his image was impeccable; in the tradition of Syl Apps, his lips had never uttered a profanity or touched a drink. But like Imlach, Kelly could also be stubborn and intractable. Unfortunately for the Leafs, he could also be as unsuccessful as McLellan. He failed to get past the quarter-finals in three years with the team and not even an inspired performance before losing to the crude but powerful Philadelphia Flyers in a sometimes violent 1975-76 Stanley Cup quarter-final series could save his job. He was let go at the end of his fourth season as the Leafs' 12th coach.

Whatever Kelly's shortcomings as an inspiration behind the bench, he

There will never be another one like Eddie Shack, who generated more excitement missing the net – as he did here against Rogie Vachon of the L.A. Kings – than most players manage scoring a couple of dozen goals *(Norm Betts, Toronto Sun)*

had set an example of outstanding citizenship and he was uncommonly patient at times with Leafs' young players. Under his tutelage, stars like Darryl Sittler, Lanny McDonald, and Errol Thompson became scorers of the first magnitude. Borje Salming and Inge Hammarstrom, discovered by Leaf scouts in Europe, blossomed into first-rate NHLers as did Ian Turnbull, a brilliant rushing defenceman, and Brian Glennie, one of hockey's best body-checkers. Don Ashby turned into a 19-goal scorer in his sophomore year with the Leafs and 18-year-old Jack Valiquette at times showed flashes of the scoring ability that had made him one of the top junior players in Canada.

The stage seemed set for a move towards the top of the NHL and Ballard brought in Roger Neilson to coach. Touted by Ballard as a leading light among the new breed of brainy young coaches in hockey, Neilson had first come to Ballard's attention when his Peterborough, Ontario Juniors had repeatedly beaten the Toronto Marlboro Juniors. In a year with the Leafs' Tulsa farm team, Neilson had helped such youngsters as Randy Carlyle improve to the point that they became useful to the big team, and Ballard felt Neilson would understand the young Leafs better than some of the older coaches might. But Neilson tended more to the role of an analytical technician with a scientific approach to hockey, and his philosophy emphasized checking over offensive play. With Ballard's blessing (which was to become quickly more mixed), he proceeded to turn the team into a plodding, defensive-minded club. High scoring Errol Thompson was sent to Detroit for trudging checker Dan Maloney; Inge Hammarstrom, whom Ballard considered a timid player, was exchanged for Jerry Butler, a hard-checking winger from St. Louis; Carlyle and George Ferguson went to Pittsburgh for Dave Burrows, an excellent defensive defenceman; truculent Dave Hutchison replaced Brian Glennie; and Jack Valiquette eventually bloomed as a scorer – with Colorado – after his defensive shortcomings kept him on Neilson's bench in Toronto. Sadly, Don Ashby was sent to the minor leagues and eventually quit hockey in frustration, though he returned last season, to the Rockies in the deal that brought Paul Gardner to the Leafs.

Not surprisingly, Neilson's teams produced little in the way of exciting hockey. At the end of the regular schedule in his first season, in fact, the Leafs had done no better than Red Kelly's team the year before. But in the playoffs, they advanced to the quarter-finals against the heavily favoured New York Islanders and won the series with a classical display of checking. It hadn't been a pretty thing to watch, but it was a win; and although the Leafs lost to a fresh Montreal team to get knocked out of the playoffs, hope grew in Toronto.

Neilson's second year as coach, however, was tribulation from start to finish. For most of the season the Leafs teetered on the brink of a playoff spot and Ballard grew as frustrated as the fans. The Leafs not only lost frequently but did so with a display of dull hockey. Even opposing teams who beat the Leafs complained at the Toronto team's style which was often about as exciting as watching the ice freeze between periods.

At first the flamboyant Ballard's comments on the techniques of Neilson were humorous. But as the season wore on, they became caustically pointed. In particular, he criticized Neilson's devotion to a video-tape machine used to instruct the Leafs to correct mistakes made during games. But as the team continued to lose under Neilson, a former high school teacher, Ballard grew more agitated, as did hockey fans. Then, late in the season, Ballard had enough and fired Neilson.

Whatever Neilson's faults as a coach, real and perceived, he maintained his dignity in a situation in which its loss would have been excusable. His refusal to criticize Ballard thus made it easier for the team owner to hire him back a few days later when the players petitioned Ballard to do so. (For Ballard's version, see the interview with him.) But it was clear to everyone that unless Neilson could win a Stanley Cup – an unlikely prospect given the Leafs' season – his days were numbered as coach of the Toronto Maple Leafs. When the team lost in the playoffs, Ballard let Neilson's contract run out, and in July Neilson joined Buffalo Sabres.

Ballard too looked to the Sabres in the summer of 1979. He hired back Punch Imlach, recently fired as the Buffalo general manager. Imlach quickly surrounded himself with Floyd Smith (a short-term Leaf player and one-time Sabre coach) to coach the team, and long-time Toronto hockey favourite Dick Duff, to work as Smith's assistant.

Like the Leafs he took over in 1959 and made into the frequent toast of Toronto in the 1960s, the team Imlach inherited in 1979 has had its share of would-be deliverers. McLellan, Kelly, and Neilson all had their chances to produce a winner. But the core of the 1979 Leafs is at least as solid as the one Imlach built around 20 years ago, and in many respects it's much better. Darryl Sittler, for example, is every bit as respected as George Armstrong was as a team leader and Sittler is a much better hockey player besides, ranking among the top centres in the NHL. Winger Lanny McDonald is not only as good a scorer as Frank Mahovlich, but he's a dedicated checker and has nothing approaching a "star" complex. Dan Maloney, though hardly the whirlwind on skates that Bert Olmstead was, is nonetheless as effective in the corner, experienced, and a solid team leader in the dressing room.

There is, of course, no clutch scorer along the lines of Dick Duff; but there is a host of sturdy wingers with Duff's industry; and it remains to be seen whether Duff himself can inspire a Pat Boutette, or a Rocky Saganiuk to become more effective offensively with the consistency Duff gave Imlach – and every other coach he ever played for – in the past.

Among the veterans Imlach was bequeathed in 1959 there were some who were nonpareils, to be sure. But Dave Burrows is the equal of Allan Stanley in some very important ways; Ian Turnbull that of Carl Brewer; and Borje Salming, probably the best athlete to play for the Leafs in years, is more valuable to the team than even Tim Horton was to Imlach's Leafs of the 1960s.

In goal, Bower lifted the Leafs in the 1960s. But Mike Palmateer, tutored by Bower, has been doing the same thing for the Leafs through the late 1970s and he has a youth Bower never had, even when he started out with the Leafs in 1959.

All in all, it's not a bad cast to begin writing a script for. And while it's hard to believe on the basis of past performance in Toronto that Imlach won't change some of the characters, at least he knows how it feels when the plot develops as it should. The last time it did, he was the one who scripted most of it.

When the Livin' Was Easy

As a soccer star, Sittler proved himself to be a pretty good hockey player, as his team lost to (gasp!) girls *(Toronto Star)*

Hockey has always been known as "the winter game" but, let's face it, that has become more than something of a misnomer. Training camps begin in mid-September, before the first leaf has turned colour and before the sun gets safely south of the equator, and by the time the playoffs are over, most of the Canadian populace is looking for someplace to escape the summer's heat. The off-season has become shorter and that, combined with the fact that annual salaries ($92,000 was the NHL average in 1977-78), provide a pretty fair living these days, has all but eliminated the summer job as a way of life for professional hockey players. Rocky Saganiuk, for example, was virtually assured of a regular spot with the Leafs this year and, as a result, he was able to forgo the summer construction work he'd done with his father's company for the six previous years. It allowed him to relax, get in some water-skiing, and work on his physical conditioning. And, oh yes, he also got married.

Not everybody spent the summer doing nothing to fill the coffers, however. Ian Turnbull had to make sure things ran smoothly at his Toronto wine bar, Grapes, and when the popular spot needed a new patio, he went out and built it himself. He also managed time for golf, tennis, squash, and racquet ball, and for a new arrival in the Turnbull household, a son named William.

And young John Anderson, while taking two weeks off in Florida and another in Barbados, joined Turnbull in the entrepreneurial food business with a take-out spot called, appropriately, John Anderson's Hamburgers in Toronto. "A lot of public relations had to be done," he said. "And my being in the store was a big part of it." Anderson also got in some tennis, golf, and water-skiing.

Tennis and golf, it seems, are the off-season games of choice for the Leafs. Jerry Butler didn't do much else, he says, other than that and lying around his pool; he also started playing squash and he and his wife did get down to Jamaica for a week with Jim Jones and his wife, and Paul Harrison and his wife. Jones "played a lot of tennis and spent a lot of time conditioning, getting in shape for the season." He was also working on the home he bought last year in Kleinburg, just north of Toronto.

Dave Hutchison also had a new

house to work on – a full paint job plus the cultivation of a garden – but he also played about 40 games on a slow-pitch softball team that went to the Canadian finals after winning the Ontario championship. He also played the seemingly-mandatory tennis and golf and generally filled up the time. "I'm an active person, so I like to be doing something all the time. Even if I don't have anything to do I'll just put on my shorts and run; I have to do something every day."

A number of the Leafs, of course, spend chunks of their summertime working at various hockey schools. Paul Gardner did a week with former coach Roger Neilson's Trinity school, but his two main operations over the summer (aside from golf and tennis, naturally) involved spending five weeks in Denver saying a long goodbye to his former team mates, and searching the Toronto area – unsuccessfully – for a house.

Joel Quenneville worked in a couple of schools around his home town of Windsor, played some T&G (or G&T – the initials should be sufficient from here on in) and worked out as he does every summer. He also spent some time in Florida, and headed into Northern Ontario for some fishing, "but the fish didn't like my line."

Ron Wilson, also a hockey instructor, bought a house in Providence, Rhode Island, where he spent four years as a college player, and where he plans to live permanently when his career ends. He also golfed and "went to the beach a lot."

Although he did do some instructional work, and played a bit of golf, Lanny McDonald says: "My real off-season job is spending a lot of time with my family; I don't get to do it much in the wintertime." He and his wife also spent four days in the Bahamas for the players' association meetings and followed that up with a two-week stay in a cabin in Montana.

Speaking of cabins, Dave Williams filled up part of his summer building one on Diefenbaker Lake in northern Saskatchewan. As is typical, Williams spent another off-season atypically. "I've been going to the Yukon every summer for the past three. I'm into remote areas, and I've never been anywhere as a sightseer. I do a little bit of everything – hiking, canoeing – none of it related to hockey. I just don't play golf and tennis like the bulk of the players in the league."

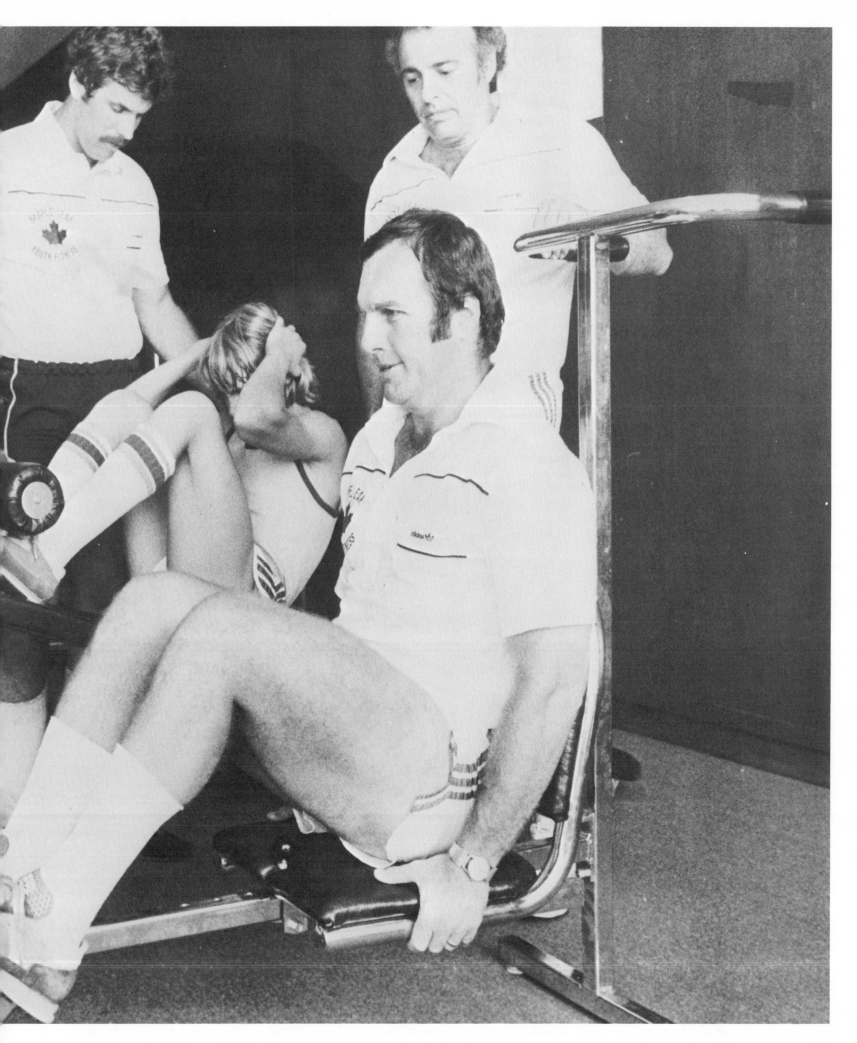

Ron Ellis in action at his youth fitness project at York University *(Barry Gray, Toronto Sun)*

Like Hutchison and Jones, Dan Maloney had a new home to work on this past summer, an older place in nearby Oakville. Also, in keeping with his established pattern, he went someplace warm (the Bahamas this year) and someplace to fish (the North West Territories) with his wife.

For bachelor goalie Mike Palmateer, summers are there strictly for the fun of it. "I take a three-and-a-half month holiday every summer." He spent two months in Florida this past off-season, snorkelling and fishing and playing T&G. Then he was off to Europe for another month, doing it the way he has been doing it for the past few years – with a knapsack on his back.

His back-up, Paul Harrison, on the other hand, spent six weeks in various hockey schools – a nice change from the Timmins gold mines of his youth – and managed some golf and fishing. He and his wife were also in Jamaica for two weeks with the Butlers and the Joneses.

And the third goalie, Jiri Crha, had a more eventful summer than most people. What started out as a Bavarian vacation for him and his family ultimately turned into a defection to Canada and the Leafs from Czechoslovakia and the Parbudice team. It could be said that he "spent his summer travelling."

Aside from a couple of weeks getting familiar with San Francisco, Pat Boutette spent most of his time around his Windsor area home base, indulging in T&G, swimming, boating, and water-skiing at St. Clair Beach. Also: "I usually work at a few hockey schools and try to relax as much as possible."

Walt McKechnie did some hockey teaching, golfed, water-skied and swam some, but as the half-owner of a Pro Hardware franchise in London, Ontario, he also took care of business. He also managed to get to California for 10 days, as he had done the year before.

As befits young fellows, rookies Laurie Boschman, Mark Kirton, and Greg Hotham all had some kind of summer work, although Boschman laboured for only two weeks in a bakery before taking it easy with T&G, swimming, and waterskiing, and a small amount of travelling. Hotham worked as a maintenance man at a swimming pool in Aurora, Ontario, as he'd done the two previous summers, after a three-week vacation in Florida; he played T&G, fastball, and (would you believe it!) hockey two nights a week. Kirton put

Old buddies Darryl Sittler and Bobby Orr having themselves a ball *(Jerry Hobbs)*

in five weeks in hockey schools, in Leamington, Ontario, and in Peterborough, where he'd played as a junior. He also spent three weeks in Florida, and went camping on a number of weekends. Kirton, who came to the 1978-79 training camp exhausted from five hours a day of Roger Neilson's training program, cut back last sum-

mer and came in fresh.

Ron Ellis spent the off-season working on a program of summer hockey conditioning at York University, and on the co-authorship of a book on the subject. He was also on hand at Teen Ranch, one of his major interests as a Christian, and, whenever he could, got in some horseback riding.

All Walt McKechnie seems to be worrying about here is whether or not he should have taken that pitch (*Jerry Hobbs*)

Borje Salming returned, as he always does, to Sweden with his wife and family and spent most of his time at his cottage in the northern town of Gavle. He also visited for a week in his home town, and managed a week of skiing. And, like his Canadian counterparts, he indulged in G&T.

Dave Burrows also spent most of his summer at his cottage, fishing and water-skiing, and being with his kids. "I like to keep my summers for my family because the kids are kind of robbed of their dad a lot of time during the winter." He and his wife were in Myrtle Beach, South Carolina, for a week, and he taught at a hockey school for two weeks.

Captain Darryl Sittler's summers tend to be almost as busy as his winters, what with constant demand for his presence at a myriad of functions, and promotions. But he did find peace in the Lake Couchiching cottage he bought from Mike Walton, and he did work on his personal biography with Brian McFarlane of Hockey Night In Canada.

Sittler, of course, is a year-round captain, and during the off-season he and a number of other Leafs rejoined forces to play some charity softball, and for a benefit soccer game against a Scarborough girls' team. As soccer players, the likes of Sittler, Turnbull, Jones, Ellis, Gardner, and Hutchison left a lot to be desired, losing 4-3 to the women, but softball was another matter. The ProStars, staffed largely by Leafs such as Sittler, Turnbull, Palmateer, Hutchison, and Gardner, played seven games in the Molson's Charity Softball series, and thereby added $50,000 to the coffers of the Ontario Society For Crippled Children. They also acquitted themselves well on the field, winning six games and tying one. (The tie, in the last game of the series, was the result of Gardner's mammoth three-run homer in the bottom of the ninth.) The team was so formidable, in fact, that one Leaf fan who'd endured last season's tedium at the Gardens told Ian Turnbull: "You guys should play baseball instead of hockey."

And, as usual, Maple Leaf Gardens itself tended to be nearly as busy in the summer as in the winter. When it was strictly a hockey palace, under Conn Smythe, the Gardens was dark for most of the year. But after Harold Ballard arrived, with partners Stafford Smythe and John Bassett, it became a

Pressure? Ron Ellis laughs at pressure *(Jerry Hobbs)*

Pete Mahovlich of the NHL ProStars may be thinking of going, but John Anderson is playing him tight *(Jerry Hobbs)*

The Oilers' Wayne Gretzky, a future perfect *(Jerry Hobbs)*

Mike Palmateer, never out of demand *(Jerry Hobbs)*

centre for conventions and concerts as well, in use some 260 nights (or days) a year. This past summer was no different.

Rod Stewart packed the place in May, as did Steve Martin in late July. Just after Martin's show, the rock group KISS held the floor for one of its extravaganzas, and at the end of August the BeeGees drew 18,500 people for a one-night stand that was a scalper's dream, with seats in the golds going for $70 apiece. On the other hand, advance ticket sales were so disappointing for scheduled performers like Peter Frampton and groups Chicago and Kansas that their shows were cancelled.

In terms of conventions, it was a fairly quiet year for the Gardens. The Kiwanis International was there on the first weekend of July, about 4,500 of them, and they took the occasion to reaffirm, 3,731-to-702, their male chauvinist policy on membership. And in late August some 9,000 members of the Church of The Latter-Day Saints took over the place for their annual convention.

Beyond the ice surface and the seats, it was a working summer, as they all are, for the Leaf and Gardens management (although Harold Ballard and King Clancy did get out a few times, notably for Hamilton Tiger Cat games, and for the fifth anniversary of

the Metropolitan Toronto Zoo, an event they attended, naturally, in safari suits). It was a case of out-with-the-old and in-with-the-old, as Punch Imlach, Floyd Smith, and Dick Duff returned to Carlton Street, and they, along with incumbents Ballard, Clancy, John Bower, John McLellan et al., had to spend their time trying to build a hockey team.

Sure Ian Turnbull's happy. His team had a seven-game unbeaten streak (*Jerry Hobbs*)

Twenty Against One:
A Guide to the Opposition

Frank Orr

Rocky Saganiuk appears to have Hawks' Tony Esposito beaten, but Greg Fox got to him before the rebound *(Barry Gray, Toronto Sun)*

In a small banquet room of the slightly decaying Warwick Hotel in New York on a warm, March, 1979 afternoon, the armistice in the Great North American Hockey War was signed. The generals who led the two armies – National Hockey League president John Ziegler and Howard Baldwin, president of the World Hockey Association – sat at a table, all smiles and good will, faced a mountain of microphones, and launched a typhoon of superlatives about the greatness of the event in hockey history.

That day, the NHL board of governors had voted to accept the four surviving teams from the WHA – Winnipeg Jets, Hartford Whalers, Edmonton Oilers, and Quebec Nordiques – in an expansion package for 1979-80 season, increasing NHL membership to 21 teams. A three-quarters majority was required for the NHL to expand. The vote was 14-3. Toronto Maple Leafs, Boston Bruins, and Los Angeles Kings opposed the accommodation with the World Hockey Association.

One word not heard from anyone in either league on that historic day was "merger," although all indications were that the NHL and WHA had merged. The news media referred to the joining of the two leagues as a merger. The NHL and WHA folks called it an "expansion" because merger was a word that might have attracted the chaps who monitor violations of the United States anti-trust laws. "It's not a merger," Ziegler insisted. "The WHA ceased operations and the NHL accepted four teams that had been members of the WHA as expansion clubs."

The benevolent old NHL didn't take in the four WHA orphans in an enormous outburst of largesse. The four WHA teams paid, oh, how they paid, to gain admittance to the establishment lodge. The teams from the WHA shelled out $6 million each for membership in the NHL. They paid for the funerals of the two WHA teams not involved in the merger – $3.5 million to Cincinnati Stingers and $2.85 million to Birmingham Bulls – and looked after the "clean-up" of any WHA business, including the contracts of players and officials who lost their jobs because of the merger . . . ahem . . . expansion.

The NHL view is that the end of the skirmish between the leagues, which caused an enormous escalation in the cost of operating a team, grants the opportunity to concentrate on upgrading the skills of the players and calibre

of hockey they play, something ignored, for the most part, in the past seven years.

"If we'd been able to use the money we've spent on legal action alone in the battle between the two leagues on player development and coaching clinics, the game would be much better," said NHL president John Ziegler.

"The one-league concept will give us a chance to work on such areas. It's not something we'll be able to do overnight because we still have many problems to sort out – there always is when a league expands – such as parity among our teams. But not having a second league to divert our attention is a big step in that direction."

To Canadian hockey fans, the best part of the merger of the two leagues is that it adds three Canadian teams to the NHL. Edmonton, Winnipeg, and Quebec City are good hockey cities where capacity crowds are expected for most games.

The NHL's terms for expansion were harsh. The four WHA teams were allowed a priority protected list of two goalies and two skaters from their '78-79 rosters and the NHL clubs reclaimed the players from the WHA clubs to whom they held NHL rights. However, in a mind-boggling assortment of deals, the WHA clubs were able to retain some front-line players.

The league will play a "balanced" 80-game schedule in the '79-80 season. Each club will meet the other 20 teams four times. Sixteen clubs will participate in the Stanley Cup playoffs. The first-place team in each of the four divisions qualifies automatically plus the 12 teams with the highest point totals.

The divisional line-up for the 1979-80 season.

Adams Division: Boston Bruins, Buffalo Sabres, Toronto Maple Leafs, Minnesota North Stars, Quebec Nordiques.

Smythe Division: Chicago Black Hawks, Vancouver Canucks, Colorado Rockies, St. Louis Blues, Edmonton Oilers, Winnipeg Jets.

Patrick Division: New York Islanders, New York Rangers, Philadelphia Flyers, Washington Capitals, Atlanta Flames.

Norris Division: Montreal Canadiens, Pittsburgh Penguins, Los Angeles Kings, Hartford Whalers, Detroit Red Wings.

The NHL plans to play a balanced schedule for at least one season, then

an attempt will be made to work out a divisional re-alignment and an unbalanced schedule which takes advantage of extra matches between divisional rivals to boost interest.

"Geography must be considered in a re-alignment to try and reduce travel costs, which have soared in recent years," Ziegler added. "It's going to be very difficult to reach an agreement on the way the league should be re-aligned. Just about every team owner has a different idea on how it should be done."

Thus, the NHL enters a new era in the 1979-80 season. Here's a look at the clubs that will supply the opposition for the Maple Leafs.

Atlanta Flames
Masterminded by general manager Cliff Fletcher, one of hockey's best executives, the Flames supply strong evidence that expansion teams don't have to be long-range sad sacks. Careful drafting, both from the expansion pool and the amateur crop, made them respectable very quickly after their NHL entry in 1972.

The Flames earned a playoff spot in their second season and attained the .500 plateau in their third term. In the past five years, they've been one of the NHL's best half-dozen teams during the schedule.

But the playoffs are another story. The Flames have participated in five preliminary rounds and one quarter-final and they've won one of 13 Stanley Cup playoff matches. The Flames' playoff woe is easy to explain. They've been excellent in producing goals – third-best offensive club in '78-79 with 327 goals – but ordinary in the prevention of same. The Flames yielded 280 goals last season and a 3.50 goals-against average is too high for a team to be a serious contender.

Thus, the target for new Flame

coach Al MacNeil is an upgrading of the club's defensive performance.

"There's no reason why we can't be a sound defensive team with no major sacrifice on the attack," MacNeil says. "Because the team has size, strength and speed, improving that goals-against total becomes a matter of discipline, working hard at the defensive side of the game."

MacNeil has turned down more job offers over the past seven years than any man in hockey. He coached Montreal Canadiens to a surprise 1971 Stanley Cup championship and, as a reward, was replaced by Scotty Bowman. MacNeil was then made coach-general manager of Canadiens' productive farm team, the Nova Scotia Voyageurs, where he developed the assorted star workers for the NHL club. He'd been the Canadiens' director of personnel for the past two seasons.

He inherited a Flame team with excellent forwards, led by winger Bob MacMillan (108 points last season) and centre Guy Chouinard (50 goals, 107 points). Eric Vail and Ivan Boldirev (35 goals each) and Jean Pronovost (28 goals) are strong shooters.

Atlanta's Dan Bouchard won this struggle with the puck *(Norm Betts, Toronto Sun)*

The Flames plucked a prize in the NHL-WHA merger when they reclaimed Swedish centre Kent Nilsson, 23, from Winnipeg Jets. One of hockey's fastest skaters, Nilsson is a superbly skilled player who produced 107 points in each of his two seasons with the Jets.

Late '78-79 additions, Phil Russell and Bob Murdoch, two good veterans, plus young Brad Marsh and Dave Shand, form a respectable defence.

Goalie Dan Bouchard, however, remains an enigma. When he's hot, Bouchard is among the best. But he's inconsistent and has yet to produce a really strong playoff. Bouchard did play a league-leading 64 matches in '78-79, a too-heavy workload made necessary by the lack of an adequate back-up. Pat Riggin, who at 18 played 46 games for the WHA Birmingham Bulls, was a Flame draft choice and he could solve that problem.

The potential for a heavy contender appears to be present. Turning it into production is MacNeil's big challenge.

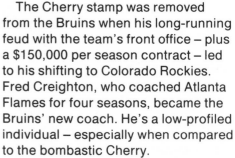

Boston Bruins

For the past five seasons, the Bruins really haven't been the Bruins. They've been "Don Cherry's team."

Volatile, outspoken, controversial coach Cherry called his club the "lunch-pail" team, a dedicated pack of grinders who performed with maximum effort and superb discipline. That approach worked, too, because the Bruins won the Adams Division pennant the past four seasons, advanced to the Stanley Cup final in '77 and '78 and lost a seven-game semi-final last spring in overtime to Montreal.

The Cherry stamp was removed from the Bruins when his long-running feud with the team's front office – plus a $150,000 per season contract – led to his shifting to Colorado Rockies. Fred Creighton, who coached Atlanta Flames for four seasons, became the Bruins' new coach. He's a low-profiled individual – especially when compared to the bombastic Cherry.

Creighton takes over an aging club (eight players are in their 30s) and several key men have injury problems. Defenceman Brad Park, goalie Gerry Cheevers, and winger Bob Schmautz have serious knee woes; winger Wayne Cashman has a chronic sore back.

One of the NHL's great players, Park missed much of the '78-79 campaign. At 31, there appears to be little chance of his avoiding a premature end to his career. "My knee situation is the same as Bobby Orr's," Park says. "All the cartilage has been removed and the only thing preventing the bones in the joint from grinding together is a very thin lining over the end of the bones. When that lining wore out in Orr's knee, the grinding produced bone chips that locked up the knee. I'll be the same when the lining wears out."

Cherry's "lunch-pail" tag made it appear that the Bruins had very little talent and succeeded only by out-working their opponents. In reality, the team has some first-rate players.

Most NHL clubs look at the Bruin wingers with envy – Schmautz, Rick Middleton, and Terry O'Reilly on the right side, Cashman, Stan Jonathan, Don Marcotte, John Wensink, and young Al Secord on the left. They're tough, bruising forecheckers who win most of the battles in the corners. Add centres Jean Ratelle, still excellent at 39, Peter McNab, and Bob Miller, and the Bruins own a splendid attack. Eight shooters topped the 20-goal mark last season.

Park, of course, anchors the backline when he's sound. On paper, the remainder of the defence cast doesn't appear to be much – Gary Doak, Rick Smith, Mike Milbury, and Dick Redmond. On the ice, it's a different story. "Every time I hear it said that we don't

Boston's Bob Miller discovers that even with a stick as equalizer, it is still no easy matter to get around the Leafs' Dave Hutchison *(Norm Betts, Toronto Sun)*

have a very good defence, I laugh,'' says Bruin general manager Harry Sinden. "It's an advantage for us to have opponents think that way. Night after night, our so-called weak defence gets the job done." The Bruins drafted two excellent young blueline prospects in Raymond Bourque and Brad MacCrimmon.

A frequent occupant of Cherry's doghouse, goalie Gilles Gilbert will receive much more work under Creighton. Gilbert took over the Bruin net from Cheevers in the third game of the 1979 series against the Canadiens and almost backboned a major upset. Cheever's surgery-ravaged pins have placed him, at 38, in the doubtful category.

The Bruins' major problem is the lack of good young talent to replace the aging, sore-legged stars. The team has had poor fishing in the amateur draft pool, claiming several players who were excellent juniors but flops as professionals.

Buffalo Sabres

When Scotty Bowman decided that there had to be more to life than winning the Stanley Cup every spring and shifted from the coaching chair with Montreal Canadiens to run the Buffalo Sabres' operation as general manager and head coach, he stated that he would initiate a "coaching staff approach" with his new club. Bowman hired Roger Neilson, who coached the Maple Leafs for two years, as associate coach of the Sabres, and Jim Roberts, a player on Bowman-coached teams in Montreal and St. Louis for a dozen years, as assistant coach.

That inspired Bowman's good friend and long-time rival, Don Cherry, to take a few potshots: "Scotty wants several assistants so he'll have somebody to share the blame if things go wrong," Cherry chortled.

That isn't quite the inspiration for Bowman's team approach to the coaching job: "I agree with the Europeans," Bowman says. "They can't understand why NHL teams have figured one coach could do the job. It's just too complex for that now. I plan to try a batch of new things with the Sabres, both in coaching technique and the style of hockey the team will play. Roberts and I may both be behind the bench with one of us in communication with Neilson in the press box, passing along suggestions from the spotter's vantage point, the

Jim Schoenfeld of the Buffalo Sabres wonders if the officials have seen what Toronto's Joel Quenneville has just done to him *(Bill Sandford, Toronto Sun)*

way football teams operate."

Bowman's contribution to the Canadiens' success often has been downplayed, even though the club won the Stanley Cup five times in his eight seasons as coach. He's one of the very best, a forward thinking man who, with his assistant coach Claude Ruel, did a big job in upgrading the skills of Canadiens' players.

Bowman's ability and patience will be tested by the often uninspired Sabres, a puzzling team during the past four seasons. The Sabres were the last team to win a playoff series from the Canadiens, ousting the Montreal club in the '75 semi-final before losing the final to Philadelphia Flyers. Since then, the Sabres have failed to win a Cup series, although the team has owned some of the finest pure hockey talent in the NHL. That floundering led to the demise of Punch Imlach as Sabre general manager in December, 1978. Imlach had built the club from an expansion team in '70 to the finals in only five seasons. For some reason, the Sabres never have transformed all that ability into positive results. Bowman's big challenge is to discipline the Sabres into some semblance of consistency.

Any club that has Gil Perreault, Richard Martin, Rick Dudley, Don Luce, Danny Gare, Ric Seiling, and Craig Ramsay on the forward lines, Jim Schoenfeld and Jerry Korab on defence and two superb youngsters, Don Edwards and Bob Sauve, in goal, should be a hot contender. The Sabres have many of the same attributes that made Bowman's Canadiens unbeatable over the past four years – scoring punch, puck control, and speed. Thus, the '79-80 Sabres will be perhaps the most interesting team in the NHL.

At least a great many people will be watching to see if Bowman's coaching genius, which made St. Louis Blues the early expansion success and the Canadiens the dominant team of the '70s, can push the disappointing Sabres around the big corner and into contention.

Chicago Black Hawks

Back in the 1960s, when Bobby Hull and Stan Mikita were in their prime, the Black Hawks were an exciting, freewheeling team that created big demand for tickets everywhere they played. Crowds of more than 20,000 fans jammed their way into Chicago Stadium to watch the team.

But that's been a distant memory for the past few seasons. Last year, crowds dipped below 10,000 for some Hawk home games and it's easy to understand why the Windy City fans have found the team easy to ignore. The Hawks have been about as exciting as watching paint dry.

In '78-79, they produced only 244 goals and fans aren't too willing to pay their money to see a team that often appears to be trying for a 1-0 win in every game. Only two NHL clubs, the woeful Vancouver Canucks and Colorado Rockies, produced less offence than the Hawks. As well, the Hawks had only three players who topped the 20-goal mark – Tom Lysiak, a late-season trade acquisition from Atlanta Flames, Ted Bulley, and John Marks.

The Hawks' general manager, Bob Pulford, surrendered the coaching segment of his portfolio to Eddie Johnston, the long-time NHL goalie who did a good job in his coaching debut with New Brunswick of the American League last season. In the off-season, the Hawks tried to bolster their puny attack. They reclaimed two solid forwards from Winnipeg Jets – a good centre, Terry Ruskowski, who had 86 points in the WHA, and winger Rich Preston (28 goals).

Quite obviously, the team's No. 1 asset, goalie Tony Esposito, will seldom work with much of a cushion. But then, he's accustomed to trying to stretch a few goals a very long way. The 63 games in which Esposito, 36, played last season were his lightest workload in six campaigns. Tony O likes to play a great deal but at his age, and on a team that was seven games below .500, anything more than 50 starts would seem to be too many. However,

the team doesn't have an established back-up goalie and there will be little rest for Esposito. Although Esposito explored the free-agent market during the summer and several teams were interested in his services, the matter of compensation and his contract demands scared them away.

The Black Hawks tried to boost hockey interest in Chicago by re-acquiring the services of Bobby Hull. He'd bolted from Chicago in '72 to Winnipeg Jets of the WHA. Last fall, he retired from hockey because of personal problems, then changed his mind.

Hull didn't want to play in Winnipeg and the Hawks wanted him to hype their gate. The Jets figured they had a deal with the Hawks that would allow them to retain Ruskowski in exchange for Hull's services. Then the Jets claimed that the Chicago club reneged on the arrangement and reclaimed both Hull and Ruskowski.

When the Hawks didn't protect Hull, the Jets claimed him in the expansion draft.

Colorado Rockies

During the past five seasons, the best travelling road show in the NHL has been The Don (Grapes) Cherry Follies, a.k.a. the Boston Bruins.

Cherry has had a profile approximately as high as Mount Everest. In a game sadly lacking in controversial characters, Cherry is pure show business. He has an opinion on any subject and he's one of the few coaches who's not afraid to throw a few darts at his opponents. Cherry has called the other teams "chickens" and made fun of the way other coaches dress. "For

heaven's sake! Can you believe it? Scotty Bowman wears hush puppies!'' said Cherry, who has a large wardrobe of three-piece suits. In Boston, Cherry made his beloved bull terrier, Blue, a popular figure with her own fan club. Cherry claimed that Blue ignored him when the team lost and that he often consulted his dog on strategy matters.

However, Cherry also happens to be a fine coach, a firm believer in hard work and sound fundamentals. He's one of those rare men in sport coaching who can turn every game into an event, a mini-war for his team; and the

Bruins responded to his approach. Part of that approach is to isolate himself and the team on a dressing room island and to regard the front office as the enemy.

When Cherry's contract expired at the end of '78-79 season, the Bruins' management had had enough. Cherry figured that his record with the team qualified him for the top pay bracket among NHL coaches. The Bruins offered him $90,000 on a new deal. When Cherry figured that wasn't enough, he went shopping in the job market.

Rockies' captain Wilf Paiement has ideas about where that bouncing puck should be that are somewhat different from those of Ian Turnbull, Paul Harrison, and Dave Burrows *(Toronto Star)*

The Colorado Rockies, badly needing a shot in all their arms, especially the publicity vein, offered Cherry $150,000 per season and Grapes took his show to Denver.

Hockey interest in Denver, hardly a Rocky Mountain high in the team's first three seasons there, increased immediately. The Rockies' season ticket sales, a trickle before Cherry, moved up at least to a dribble.

"I just love the challenge of working with a team that doesn't seem to have much going for it," Cherry enthuses. "Last season, the team wasn't very good [42 points in 80 games] but the players always worked hard. That's all I ask."

Surprisingly, the Rockies do have some fine talent. Defenceman Barry (Bubba) Beck, 22, at 6-feet-3 and 220 pounds, is a superb young player, strong, mobile, and smart. And the team's '78-79 disaster had one benefit. It earned the team the first selection in the entry draft. They claimed Rob Ramage, another exceptional defence prospect, who was a '78-79 WHA all-star with Birmingham Bulls, although still eligible for junior hockey. Beck, Ramage, ex-Leaf Trevor Johansen, Mike Kitchen, and Mike Christie give the Rockies the raw material for a strong defence.

Right winger Wilf Paiement would be a decoration for any NHL team. Only 24 and a swift, powerful skater, he has 50-goal potential. He did score 41 goals in the '77-78 season.

The remainder of the cast falls into categories of "promising" and "some potential." Although Cherry's discipline and enthusiasm will make a large difference, the Rockies sit at the bottom of the hockey hill, the equivalent of the mountains that surround Denver.

Detroit Red Wings

The future was all shiny for the Red Wings, back there at the conclusion of the 1977-78 season; they had been the NHL's most improved team, jumping from 41 to 78 points in one season, the first for "Old Scarface," Ted Lindsay, as general manager and for Bobby Kromm, who earned NHL coach-of-the-year honours.

The Wings were young; hockey interest was revived in Detroit; plans were set for a new arena as part of the city's downtown development; and when the team signed free agent goalie Rogie Vachon from Los Angeles Kings, their direction appeared to be up.

Well, a funny thing happened on the way to the top: the Wings headed back to the bottom. They sagged to 62 points in '78-79.

One of the league's premier goalies for a half-dozen seasons, Vachon defected to Detroit from L.A. for a long-term, $300,000 per season contract, only to see his 2.78 career goals-against average soar to 3.90 with the Wings.

The addition of Vachon also triggered the much-publicized Dale McCourt case. Under NHL rules when the Wings signed free agent Vachon, they were obligated to compensate the Kings. When the clubs were unable to agree on that compensation, the matter went to binding arbitration. The Kings asked for – and received – centre McCourt, the Wings' leading scorer in '78-79 as a rookie. McCourt challenged the compulsory shift to L.A. in court and received a temporary injunction that allowed him to remain with the Wings in '78-79. A three-judge panel ruled in May, '79, that McCourt was indeed a King because the compensation rule was the product of collective bargaining between the NHL owners and the players' association.

Detroit Red Wings' Dan Labraaten and the Leafs' Dave Hutchison share a pained expression as the both pursue that elusive puck (Toronto Star)

McCourt continued his fight against a move to Los Angeles and launched an appeal of the lower court's ruling that appeared to be headed for the U.S. Supreme Court. But after McCourt turned down an offer from new King owner Jerry Buss, a deal that would have paid him $3 million for six seasons, the clubs settled the matter with a trade. In exchange for McCourt's NHL rights, the Wings sent centre Andre St. Laurent and two future draft choices to the Kings.

One quantity the Wings do have is speed. Swedish winger Dan Labraaten and Czechoslovakian centre Vaclav Nedomansky (38 goals last season) are two of hockey's fastest skaters. Ex-Leaf Errol Thompson, Paul Woods, Dan Bolduc, and Reed Larson also are swift and top draft pick Mike Foligno from Sudbury Juniors is a good one. Three WHA refugees – Thommie Bergman, Perry Miller, and Barry Long, all of whom played for Kromm in Winnipeg – are on the defence. However, the Wings' brightest prospect is backliner Willi Huber, who made rapid improvement in his rookie season.

A comeback by Vachon, of course, would be a big boost for the team. If Rogie can't rediscover his fine edge, the Wings will lean heavily on Jim Rutherford, who played extremely well late in the '78-79 season when Vachon became the NHL's highest priced benchwarmer.

Somehow, trips to Motor City won't be the same when the games aren't played in the old Olympia, where the best hot dogs in the NHL were served. The Joe Louis Arena, named for Detroit's most famous athlete, is the Wings' new home. The team, though, just doesn't seem ready to deliver many kayo punches.

Edmonton Oilers

On every step he's taken up hockey's ladder from pee wee to pro, Wayne (The Great) Gretzky has heard the same statements: he's moving too fast, he's too young, and *that* league will be too much for him. Gretzky is hearing it all again as he leads the Oilers into the NHL as one of the four surviving WHA teams joining the establishment as expansion clubs. The hockey know-it-alls are claiming that the NHL stars will overpower him.

You see, Gretzky is only 18 years of age but he's already had more publicity than most players acquire in their entire careers. From the time he was a nine-year-old pee wee in Brantford, Ontario, with a point total that resembled the national debt of a small country, Gretzky has been in the spotlight.

Gretzky's career was advanced quickly to earn him some competition in proportion with his talents. When he hit Junior B hockey at 14, some figured he was being pushed too fast, but he scored at a heavy pace. The same things were heard when he moved to Major Junior with Sault Ste. Marie Greyhounds at 16, but he produced 182 points and was named all-star centre in the world junior championships. When he turned pro at 17 with Indianapolis Racers of the WHA in '78-79, the predictions of doom were even louder. His contract was sold to the Oilers early in the season, just before the Racers folded, and guess what: Gretzky produced 110 points, third best in the WHA, and he led all playoff scorers with 10 goals and 10 assists in 13 games.

"People have always said that I was moving ahead too quickly," says Gretzky, a slender 5-feet-11-inches and 170 pounds. "But I haven't done badly so far. I know it's going to be tough in the NHL because I'll be going against so many good players."

The attendance leader in the WHA, the Oilers could repeat the feat in the NHL before long. The team sold 14,600 season tickets in 11 days for their first season in the NHL. The remaining 1,600 seats and standing room spots will be sold on a game-to-game basis. The beautiful Edmonton Coliseum, opened in 1974, has room for expansion of the seating capacity to 19,000. That additional seating is planned for the '80-81 season, and will make it the biggest rink in the NHL.

Gretzky supplies the splendid young star around whom the Oilers will construct their future. Coach Glen Sather has high hopes for young Swedish forward Bengt Gustavsson, as well as for some youngsters the club was able to retain in the expansion draft – forwards Blair MacDonald, Brett Callighen, Ron Carter, and Dave Hunter.

The Oilers have no worries in goal where the incumbent is Dave Dryden, the older brother of Ken Dryden.

In the expansion draft, the Oilers concentrated on defencemen and landed Lee Fogolin, Colin Campbell, and Pat Price, none of whom ever has been considered for an all-star team.

Owned by free-spending zillionaire Peter Pocklington, and with the resources available from sell-out houses, the Oilers should move to the front ranks of the NHL very quickly – unless, of course, The Great Gretzky finally has encountered a step too big for him to make. But no one is betting on it.

Hartford Whalers

Early in 1980, the Whalers will move into their reconstructed arena in downtown Hartford. The building was erected to replace the original arena which collapsed in 1976 under the weight of a heavy snowfall.

The building will be new but the team the Whalers take into it won't be. Granted, the Whalers will have a few young players of promise when they make their NHL debut after seven seasons as a cornerstone of the WHA. But they'll also have some of the game's oldest active players on their roster.

The greybeards are led by Gordie Howe, 51, on right wing and former Maple Leaf captain Dave Keon at centre. Then there's centre Andre Lacroix, 34, the leading scorer in WHA history. Lacroix holds the pro hockey record for playing on teams that folded. He was a member of the Philadelphia Blazers, New York-New Jersey Raiders, San Diego Mariners, and Houston Aeros before joining the Whalers, a team which has no immediate plans to pack its tent and vanish.

The incredible Howe, who retired from Detroit Red Wings in 1971, then launched a comeback with the Houston club to play with his sons, Mark and Marty, decided to return for one last fling in the NHL, his 32nd pro season.

"I had a special 'grand-daddy' clause in my contract," Howe says. "That meant I didn't have to decide to play another year until just before training camp. I figured why not? There might be a few old friends kicking around the NHL arenas and this gives me a chance to see them." While the fans in NHL cities will want to take one last look at a genuine legend, another Howe, Mark, also creates great interest. At 24, he's one of the very best young players in the game. He built a 42-goal, 65-assist point total last season on left wing.

The Whalers will experiment with Mark Howe on defence, a transition coach Don Blackburn feels Mark will make with ease, considering the large amount of natural ability he possesses. If the Whalers can afford to drop Howe back to the rearguard, he'll join veteran Rick Ley, the WHA's best defenceman last season, and two good youngsters, Alan Hangsleben and Gordie Roberts, on a competent blueline.

The team is solid, if not spectacular, in goal, with Al Smith and John Garrett.

They're also sound at the bank. Much financial backing for the club is provided by the several insurance companies based in Hartford. The insurance folks view the arena and the Whalers as important in the redevelopment of downtown Hartford. The Whalers will fit right in because several of their players are monuments to hockey greatness.

Los Angeles Kings

The most interesting rookie in the NHL this season has never scored a goal. In fact, there's doubt if he's ever been on skates. His name is Jerry Buss. Buss, who can carry a "Doctor" in front of his name – a Ph.D in physical chemistry – is the new owner of Los Angeles Kings. In a $67.5 million deal, Buss bought the Kings, the basketball Lakers, and the L.A. Forum from Jack Kent Cooke. The purchase also includes a 13,000 acre ranch in the California Sierras.

A real estate wheeler-dealer who drives a $127,000 Rolls-Royce Camargue, Buss is renowned for the large number of beautiful ladies he dates, including many who were *Playboy* magazine centrefolds.

Buss has a realistic view of the Kings' financial picture. After all, the team's average home attendance at the Forum dropped by 1,800 last season to 9,992 per game. "There's a big question that must be asked about the Kings: can hockey ever be a west coast sport?" Buss says: "The team has lost money every year – $200,000 in their best year, $1.5 million in their worst. We must sell another 3,000 season tickets to make money regularly."

The Kings did participate in an unusual happening in the off-season. For only the second time in their history, they made a first round selection in the amateur draft. In the past, the Kings have traded away those selections, sacrificing a field of tomorrow's wheat for a loaf of yesterday's bread. The '79 choice wasn't the Kings' own. It was one obtained in a trade with Montreal Canadiens. The Kings employed the pick to land defenceman Jay Wells.

The Kings do have an excellent young coach in Bob Berry, a fine winger for seven seasons with the team. A psychology major at Sir George Williams University in Montreal, Berry made no promises when he was named Kings' boss for the '78-79 season. He said that a .500 season was his goal and that's precisely what the Kings accomplished.

The Kings can score goals (292 in '78-79) and much of that attack springs from three excellent forwards. Centre Marcel Dionne is one of the premier players in the NHL, a second team all-star last season when he had 130 points on 59 goals and 71 assists. Winger Dave Taylor produced 43 goals and 48 assists and quick little centre Butch Goring had 36 goals and 51 assists. Big Charlie Simmer, playing left wing with Dionne and Taylor, counted 48 points in 38 games.

When Rogie Vachon bolted the Kings as a free agent to Detroit Red Wings, the club was left with no established goalie. They did acquire Ron Grahame in a deal from Boston Bruins, but their net answer turned out to be young Mario Lessard, who had been kicking around the Kings' farm system for three years. The chubby little Lessard played in 49 games and built an enviable 3.10 goals-against mark on a team which wasn't too strong defensively.

Minnesota North Stars

During his ten-year career as a player with the North Stars, Lou Nanne was known as "The Duke Of Discount." The word was that no matter how good a price you'd got on something, Lou could find a better deal. "Let's just say that I never figure that the price marked on anything I want to buy is the final one," Nanne smiles.

Of course, a graduate in marketing from University of Minnesota should be qualified to make a good deal and when the opportunity to make one for himself arrived, Nanne was ready. The North Stars were going nowhere in the '77-78 season when the owners asked Nanne to give them a report on the way he figured the team could be improved. Nanne's presentation was of such quality that he was named general manager of the team, probably the first time in hockey history that a player jumped directly from the ice to the front office in mid-season. Since

Rookie-of-the-year (1978-79) Bobby Smith of Minnesota was in pretty good position to complete this play – at least until Borje Salming's left leg unsettled him just a little bit *(Toronto Star)*

then, Nanne hasn't stopped making deals in his effort to rebuild the Stars into an NHL contender. In fact, he had a role in a deal of epic proportions – the one in which the North Stars acquired an entire hockey team, Cleveland Barons.

That shotgun wedding happened in June, 1978, when the ultra-wealthy Gund brothers, George and Gordon, who were losing large amounts of money in Cleveland, bought the Stars and merged the two teams.

It would have been a sad reflection on the already sad state of affairs in the NHL if the combination of the two teams, albeit two weak ones, had failed to produce an improved club. The Stars didn't set the world aflame in '78-79 but the club *was* better, and it does have some future.

A large part of that future rests on centre Bobby Smith, the NHL's '78-79 rookie-of-the-year. Smith is an extra-ordinary prospect with size (6-feet-4-inches, 210 pounds), speed, and a splendid variety of skills with a hockey puck.

The North Stars added two excellent young players in the '79 entry draft — defenceman Craig Hartsburg, who played with Birmingham Bulls of the WHA last season, and Tom McCarthy from the Oshawa Juniors, a 19-year-old who had 69 goals among his 144 points. Al MacAdam, Glen Sharpley, Tim Young, Mike Fidler, Steve Payne, Kris Manery, and Ron Zanussi supply a good batch of young forwards.

Nanne was able to inject two solid, experienced defencemen into the Star's cast. Paul Shmyr, a WHA all-star, was reclaimed from Edmonton Oilers, and Bill Nyrop added in a trade with Montreal Canadiens.

A Minnesota product who attended Notre Dame University, Nyrop had matured into a first-rate backliner with the Canadiens when he retired from hockey at 26 during the '78 training camp. He returned to Minneapolis where he spent the winter studying the real estate business. Nanne acquired his services in exchange for a second-round draft choice. So at the most important position — defence — Nanne has assembled an admirable corps, a good balance of youth and experience. Hartsburg, Greg Smith, and Brad Maxwell are strong youngsters; Shmyr, Nyrop, Gary Sargent, and Fred Barrett give poise and wisdom.

The North Stars' goaltending is in good hands with Gilles Meloche and Gary Edwards.

Montreal Canadiens
When Sam Pollock departed from his position as general manager of the Canadiens in the summer of 1978 to pursue other business interests, a tremor of hope ran through the NHL that the loss of the man generally regarded as hockey's finest executive would mark the end of the Canadiens dynasty. Or, at least, the start of a slide.

It didn't. Plagued by injuries, the Canadiens did lose the overall pennant during the '78-79 season by one point to New York Islanders, but they won their fourth consecutive Stanley Cup, their 15th in the past 24 seasons.

This season, hope rises again that defections from hockey's seeming paradise will knock the Montreal club from its pedestal. Coach Scotty Bowman no longer could co-exist peacefully with general manager Irving Grundman and used an escape clause in his contract to take a high-salaried job as head man in the Buffalo Sabres' operation. And Al MacNeil, director of personnel for the Canadiens, joined Atlanta Flames as coach.

Then the club lost two splendid players: centre Jacques Lemaire, the club's leading goal scorer in the playoffs, announced that he had accepted a job as general manager, coach, and player with the Sierre team in Switzerland; and then Ken Dryden, the NHL's best goaltender, retired from hockey at 32 to pursue one of the many alternate avenues the possession of a law degree opens to a person.

However, no opponent would predict that the Canadiens' reign was at an end. The club simply has too much talent, tradition, and pride to fall apart. Granted, there are some holes in the roster now but the Canadiens, as always, have the players to fill the gaps.

For the past six years, Dryden's understudy has been Michel (Bunny) Larocque, who had a 2.84 goals-against average in 34 games in the '78-79 season. At 27, he's very ready and able to get the job done. The Canadiens added depth and experience to their goaltending when they acquired Denis Herron from the Pittsburgh Penguins in a deal. Herron had a 3.37 goals-against average in 56 games for the Pens in '78-79.

Lemaire was the No. 1 centre on a club which, unlike many great teams, hasn't had overwhelming strength down the middle. But Pierre Mondou, 24, scored 31 goals last season and has the potential to become an all-star.

Assorted names were kicked around as candidates for the coaching job but it wasn't until just before training camp opened that the Canadiens hired their grand old right winger Bernie (Boom-Boom) Geoffrion to replace Bowman. Boomer had successful stints as coach of New York Rangers and Atlanta Flames, where he's been vice-president for the past two years, but ulcer outbreaks forced him out of both jobs.

A big reason for Bowman's success with the Canadiens was the presence of Claude Ruel as assistant coach and he'll continue in that job under Geoffrion. He works long hours on skill-upgrading with the young Canadiens. Toe Blake, who coached the team to eight Stanley Cups in the '50s and '60s, assumes a much more active role in the team's operation this season than the unofficial "adviser" he's been since his retirement in 1968.

"It's not the first time the Canadiens' organization has lost key people but it always survived and thrived," Grundman says. "Rocket Richard retired. Toe Blake retired as coach. Jean Beliveau retired. But the team continued to win."

Guy Lafleur is still around on right wing. He's merely the NHL's finest talent who grinds out 50-goal and 125-point seasons with incredible regularity. Larry Robinson, Serge Savard, and Guy Lapointe are there, too, giving the Canadiens the NHL's best defence. No team in NHL history, including other great Canadiens teams, has ever had three of the league's six best backliners at the same time.

Bob Gainey, tabbed by Soviet Union national team coach Victor Tikhonov as "technically the best hockey player in the world," is on left wing again. He's been the NHL's best defensive forward; now he's blossoming as a scorer. And the team still retains people like Gilles Lupien, Rod Langway, and Brian Engblom on defence, as well as forwards Doug Jarvis, Steve Shutt, Mario Tremblay, Rick Chartraw, Yvon Lambert, Mark Napier, Rejean Houle, and Doug Risebrough.

Danny Geoffrion, the son of coach Boom-Boom, was reclaimed from Quebec Nordiques of the WHA and he'll want a job. Draft choice defenceman Gaston Gingras, a young man with great raw potential, will want one, too.

If decay has set into the Canadiens' organization, opponents might have problems finding it.

Getting past Mike Palmateer and Borje Salming individually is tough, but when they're in tandem it's nigh impossible, even for the great winger of the Habs, Bob Gainey *(Hugh Wesley, Toronto Sun)*

New York Islanders

The Islanders appear to have it all — strong management and coaching, fine individual stars, and a strong supporting cast of good players. They supply a textbook model on the way an expansion team can be constructed in seven years from birth (1972) to excellence, winning the overall pennant in the NHL in '78-79, one point in front of the Canadiens.

But the Islanders' '78 and '79 playoff failures have dimmed considerably their remarkable accomplishments and led to the occasional use of the word "choke" to describe the team. In a '78 quarter-final, the Islanders lost to the Maple Leafs; in '79, New York Rangers eliminated them in the semifinal.

There have been assorted explanations for the Islanders' failures in the Stanley Cup tournament. One analysis is that the team relied too heavily on talent and discipline, not enough on emotion. "We have a very intelligent group of men on this team and, I think, more pure ability than any club in the NHL," says defenceman Denis Potvin. "Perhaps we try to get the job done on ability and intelligence instead of sometimes playing on sheer emotion, being on a 'high' the way a few other clubs operate. Maybe we need a player or two who makes no sense at all but gets all cranked up for the games."

The Islanders dominated the NHL's individual awards in '78-79. The league's finest player during the 80-game schedule was centre Bryan Trottier, 23, who was named most valuable player and all-star centre and won the scoring championship with 134 points. Right winger Mike Bossy, 22, led the league with 69 goals and was a second team all-star, only six points behind Canadiens' Guy Lafleur in the vote. Left winger Clark Gillies (91 points) was a first-team all-star; Potvin won his second consecutive Norris Trophy as the league's best backliner and counted 101 points, the only de-

fenceman other than Bobby Orr to top the 100-point total. Islanders' Al Arbour was named coach-of-the-year; goalie Chico Resch was a second team all-star.

The Islander management refuses to panic over the playoff failures. The rapid climb to the top was the result of a carefully conceived and executed construction plan. The team is sticking to that approach. "Of course, our playoff losses were a bitter disappointment, but after carefully analyzing our team, we knew that a major shake-up wasn't the answer to anything," says Islander general manager Bill Torrey. "We feel our team hasn't reached its peak because we are still very young. We're a team which still has considerable growing up to do. We just have to play with more toughness and intensity in the playoffs."

This season, the only Islander who has reached his 30th birthday is goalie Resch. The team's core of excellent young players are all 26 or younger.

The Islanders made only minor alterations in their roster for the '79-80 season. They reclaimed strong young defenceman Dave Langevin and drafted a prize rearguard prospect, Thomas Jonsson from Sweden.

The team's success, especially in the playoffs, will hinge on how much the maturing process has worked on all those young players.

New York Rangers

A few NHL team owners don't have high regard for Sonny Werblin, the head honcho of New York Rangers and Madison Square Garden, which are part of the enormous Gulf-Western

---

If Borje Salming is proud of the goal-scoring efforts of his countryman, Ulf Nilsson of the New York Rangers, he's not showing it here *(Toronto Star)*

conglomerate. The view is that Werblin, backed by all the G-W loot, has no concern for costs in his effort to make the Rangers a winner, and many other teams simply lack the resources to compete with the New York club.

"The rest of us are like the little corner store operator trying to compete with the huge supermarkets, which is what the Rangers are with all that Gulf-Western money to spend," snorts Leaf owner Harold Ballard.

Evidence does exist that Werblin hasn't exactly aided the NHL's attempts to lower operating costs. He hired Fred Shero away from his coaching job with Philadelphia Flyers and paid him in excess of $200,000 per season as manager-coach of the Rangers. That led to the escalation in the salaries of managers and coaches and helped such chaps as Scotty Bowman and Don Cherry to earn gigantic contracts when they changed teams in 1979.

Many NHL clubs made an offer for the services of those magnificent Swedish forwards, Ulf Nilsson and Anders Hedberg, who had escape clauses with the WHA Winnipeg Jets at the conclusion of the '77-78 season. Then the Rangers blew the other NHL clubs off the street in the Swede-hunt. They paid Hedberg and Nilsson signing bonuses of $600,000 each plus $200,000 annual salaries to shift from Manitoba to Manhattan.

But the less provincial thinkers in the NHL are Werblin backers because they know the publicity value to the NHL of having a top contender in New York. When the Rangers executed a major upset of the heavily favoured New York Islanders in a '79 playoff semifinal and faced the Canadiens in the final, the NHL received enormous exposure in the New York-based national media.

"The Ranger-Islander series was the best thing to happen to the NHL in a long time," says one NHL team owner. "It revved up that town about hockey and the publicity earned for the NHL can't be measured. For heaven's sake! The *New York Times* ran hockey pictures and stories on the front page of the bloody newspaper, and when did that ever happen before?"

Of course, the Canadiens didn't cooperate, blowing the Rangers' doors off in a five-game final. But the New York club is a sound young team and seems set for a good run in the NHL's upper echelon.

Shero's timing in his move from Philly to New York was perfect. He took over a club well-stocked with good young talent plus Hedberg and Nilsson. Freddy the Fog (who loves to create the impression that his mind is somewhere in the twilight zone), and his long-time trusty assistant, Mike Nykoluk, turned a collection of players into an exciting, well-disciplined team.

Hedberg (79 points) and Nilsson, who had 66 points in 59 games until a broken ankle shelved him, turned out to be even better than anyone expected. Old (37) Phil Esposito bounced off the trading block to an excellent 42-goal season. The Rangers' bright future is further supplied by a talented group of players, all under 25 – goalies John Davidson and Doug Soetaert, defencemen Ron Greschner, Dave Maloney, Mario Marois, and Mike McEwen, forwards Ron Duguay, Lucien Deblois, Ed Johnstone, and Don Murdoch, who scored 15 goals in 40 games after serving an NHL suspension imposed when he was convicted on a drug possession charge.

Philadelphia Flyers
Bobby Clarke had his 30th birthday in August, 1979, and, as a birthday gift befitting a player of his stature, Philadelphia Flyers named him as a playing assistant coach to head coach Pat Quinn.

Not that the transition from captain to the coaching staff represents such a big change for Clarke, the Flyers' spiritual leader for the past decade, but the 30th birthday and job elevation certifies Clarke as an NHL senior citizen and marks a milestone in the Flyers' NHL history.

The Flyers do hold an important spot in the league's modern annals. They were the first club in the NHL's ambitious expansion program, started in 1967, to win the Stanley Cup. The "Broad Street Bullies" was the tag granted the Flyers during the Cup

glory years in '74 and '75 when they established team penalty records. The Flyers were scorned by the hockey purists, who claimed the club in those years used intimidation as part of its tactics. The Flyers, an increase in NHL violence, and Ontario attorney-general Roy McMurtry's crackdown on hockey antics, inspired the NHL to initiate tough anti-brawling legislation.

The Flyers, however, won those Cups on more than their fists. Hard work, team discipline, and devotion to coach Fred Shero's system of play, all of it with captain Clarke cracking the whip, had a large role in the club's success.

Time, albeit a short five years, has broken up that old gang of Bobby's. Shero shifted his "Fog" act to New York as general manager-coach of the Rangers. Dave (The Hammer) Schultz, the man who, to many, typified the Flyer approach, has toured the NHL – Los Angeles to Pittsburgh to Buffalo. Goalie Bernie Parent, the most valuable Flyer in the Cup years, never really came back to top form after neck surgery in '75. An eye injury ended his career in '79. Gary Dornhoefer, whose specialty was dancing on goalies, took his battered knees into retirement.

A few of the old gang remain on the roster – defencemen Jim Watson and Moose Dupont; forwards Clarke, Bill Barber, Reggie Leach, Bob Kelly, and Rick MacLeish. The old gang plus some good new faces had enough to build the fourth-best record in the NHL in '78-79. And the Flyers have some fine young players for their reconstruction program. Defenceman Behn Wilson was one of the top rookies in '78-79, and feisty little centre Ken Linseman has demonstrated some Clarke-like attributes, including aggressiveness.

The Flyers acquired goalie Phil Myre, an NHL veteran, from St. Louis Blues to replace Parent. Their first-round draft pick, left winger Brian Propp, produced 94 goals and 100 assists for Brandon Juniors last season. The Flyers would settle for 30 per cent of that production in Propp's rookie season.

Pittsburgh Penguins

A hockey cliché claims that building a good team through trades is impossible, but the Penguins took a large shot at it in the '78-79 season.

General manager Baz Bastien wheeled and dealed and although he didn't produce a legitimate contender, the Penguins, at least, were an improved club, acquiring 85 points, the second-best total in their 11-year history.

The Penguins dealt a '78 first-round draft choice to Philadelphia Flyers for forwards Orest Kindrachuk and Ross Lonsberry and defenceman Tom Bladon; they dispatched defenceman Dave Burrows to the Maple Leafs for backliner Randy Carlyle and centre George Ferguson, and added defenceman Dale Tallon (Chicago), forwards Rod Schutt (Montreal), Gary McAdam (Buffalo), and Gregg Sheppard (Boston) in an assortment of deals. Of course some time was required for the players to be introduced properly to each other. But, by the second half of the season, the Penguins had jelled into a solid hockey team.

"Because we added experienced players, our club was able to jell much more quickly than if we'd picked up the same number of rookies," says Penguin coach Johnny Wilson. "We added some guys, like the three players from Philadelphia, who had played on winning clubs, and they were able to give us a very positive attitude. They knew the price that had to be paid for a club to be a winner."

The big question that must be asked about the Penguins is: how much can a veteran club improve?

"Really, our roster isn't that old and we do have some young players who will become front-liners," Wilson adds. "We feel we have an intelligent, flexible team that will become much better. We have the experienced players who won't kill us with mistakes."

One player on whom the Penguins pin large future hope is defenceman

If the Penguins' Russ Anderson does not seem sufficiently impressed by Rocky Saganiuk, it's probably because he had more important things to worry about here, like the puck *(Hugh Wesley, Toronto Sun)*

Carlyle, 23. He never earned a permanent first string berth with the Leafs, although he did deliver two admirable performances during injury-induced emergencies in the playoffs. Carlyle had a splendid season with the Penguins, counting 47 points in 70 games. Greg Malone (35 goals), swift Peter Lee (32 goals) and another ex-Leaf, Rick Kehoe (27 goals), give the team some attack. When they traded goalie Denis Herron to Montreal Canadiens, the Penguins gave their goaltending job to two promising but green youngsters – Gord Laxton and Greg Millen.

The Penguins did improve their attendance in Pittsburgh last season but the team's operation is far from cancelling its order for red ink. They face a major problem in the first half of this season in attracting much media attention. The baseball Pirates are perennial contenders; the football Steelers, the '79 Super Bowl champs, and several bowl-bound college teams in the area are tough competition for the sports ticket dollar.

Quebec Nordiques
The Flying Frenchmen!

That title has been the exclusive property of Montreal Canadiens from the time they entered the NHL in 1917, in reference to the great flair and speed with which their French-Canadian stars played the game.

Now the Canadiens' ownership of the "Flying Frenchmen" tag is challenged. Quebec Nordiques, one of the NHL's four expansion teams from the WHA, enter the league with an assortment of Quebec-born players who have speed and offensive skills as their combined major asset. "We feel we will have an attack in our first NHL season that's better than many of the established teams," says Nordiques' coach Jacques Demers. "The Nordiques will be an exciting attraction in the NHL cities because we play what they've always called 'firewagon hockey,' a wide-open, attacking style."

Driving the Nordique firewagon is right winger Real (Buddy) Cloutier, 23, one of the game's finest young players. Swift and superbly skilled, Cloutier won the '78-79 WHA scoring title with 75 goals and 54 assists. That raised his five-season WHA total to 283 goals and 283 assists, equalling 566 points. "It wouldn't surprise me if, before long, the NHL all-star right wing spot is a battle between the two great French-Canadian players, Cloutier and Guy Lafleur of the Canadiens," Demers adds.

Left winger Marc Tardif, 33, has been one of the WHA's premier players for the six seasons since his defection from the Canadiens. Tardif had 41 goals among his 96 total points in '78-79.

The Nordiques made a key acquisition in landing centre Robbie Ftorek from Cincinnati Stingers, one of the WHA clubs not included in the expansion. Perhaps the best American-born player in the game, Ftorek was runner-up to Cloutier in the scoring race with 116 points. Serge Bernier (36 goals, 46 assists) and Richie Leduc (35 goals, 41 assists) are two useful veter-

ans, and the Nordiques drafted a splendid young winger in Michel Goulet, 19, who had 28 goals and 30 assists for Birmingham in the WHA last season.

The Nordiques managed to retain two good young defencemen, Paul Baxter and Gary Lariviere. The expansion draft yielded a pair of competent rearguards – Gerry Hart, 31, a seven-year regular with the New York Islanders, and Dave Farrish, 23, who was made expendable by New York Rangers' depth of young defence talent, not his own lack of ability.

One place the Nordiques will be successful is at the box office. The "House That Jean Beliveau Built," the Quebec Coliseum, will be expanded by 6,000 seats from its capacity of 10,004 over the next two years. The rink was built during Beliveau's days as a junior and senior demi-god there. "If we had those seats this year, we would have sold them because the demand for season's tickets was high," says Marcel Aubut, Nordiques' president. "We'll be sold out for every game because the people in Quebec City have wanted – and deserved – the NHL for many years."

Or as one NHL owner said: "I'd love to have a fist-full of tickets to scalp in Quebec City the first time the Canadiens visit the Nordiques. I could retire."

St. Louis Blues
In recent seasons, the team's name had described accurately the hockey situation in St. Louis. It had been very, very blue.

Once the crown jewel of the NHL's expansion showcase, Stanley Cup finalists in their first three years of existence, the Blues have fallen on hard times. In fact, in the summer of '77, the team came within a dish of dog food of folding its tent. Then the huge Ralston-Purina company, a leading manufacturer of pet food, rescued the franchise by buying the Blues and the St. Louis Arena, which promptly was renamed "The Checkerdome" to pro-

mote one of the new owner's products.

Now the team, under president-general manager Emile (The Cat) Francis, is trying to regain the glory and fan interest of the late 1960s. "Back in '77, things were so bad with our franchise that we were down to three employees in our office – me, my assistant general manager, Dennis Ball, and a secretary," Francis says. "I was paying the secretary out of my own pocket and we didn't have enough money in the bank to pay the bills for our pucks. The uncertainty of it all cost us some draft choices who signed with WHA clubs because they didn't like the look of our situation. Fortunately, those days are well in the past because we have great owners now. The Ralston-Purina people felt that the Blues were good for St. Louis and couldn't be permitted to move. Our owners are in for the long haul, which means we can make long-range plans. When a team gets down as this one did, there's no miraculous recovery possible. Building with young players is the only way to do it."

Although the Blues had a miserable '78-79 season with only 48 points in 80 games, they did make some progress in the talent department.

The team's move upward is led by an outstanding young forward line of centre Bernie Federko, 23, who had 95 points; left winger Brian Sutter, 23, who scored 41 goals, and right winger Wayne Babych, 21, who scored 27 goals in 67 games. As well, the Blues landed one of the '79 entry draft's prizes in right winger Perry Turnbull, who scored 75 goals for Portland Juniors. He's big (6-feet-2-inches, 205 pounds), fast and tough.

The return of experienced winger Chuck Lefley, after a two-year defection to play in Europe, supplies a steadying influence.

Missing from the Blues' line-up this season for the first time is centre Garry Unger, who started the season as the NHL's "iron man" with a string of 883 consecutive games. But he didn't start it with the Blues. Unger wanted out of St. Louis because he didn't feel he could play his best there. He played out his option and moved on as a free agent.

The prevention of goals remains the big problem for coach Barclay Plager. The Blues were the worst defensive club in the NHL in '78-79, yielding 348 goals, approximately 100 more than a contender should surrender.

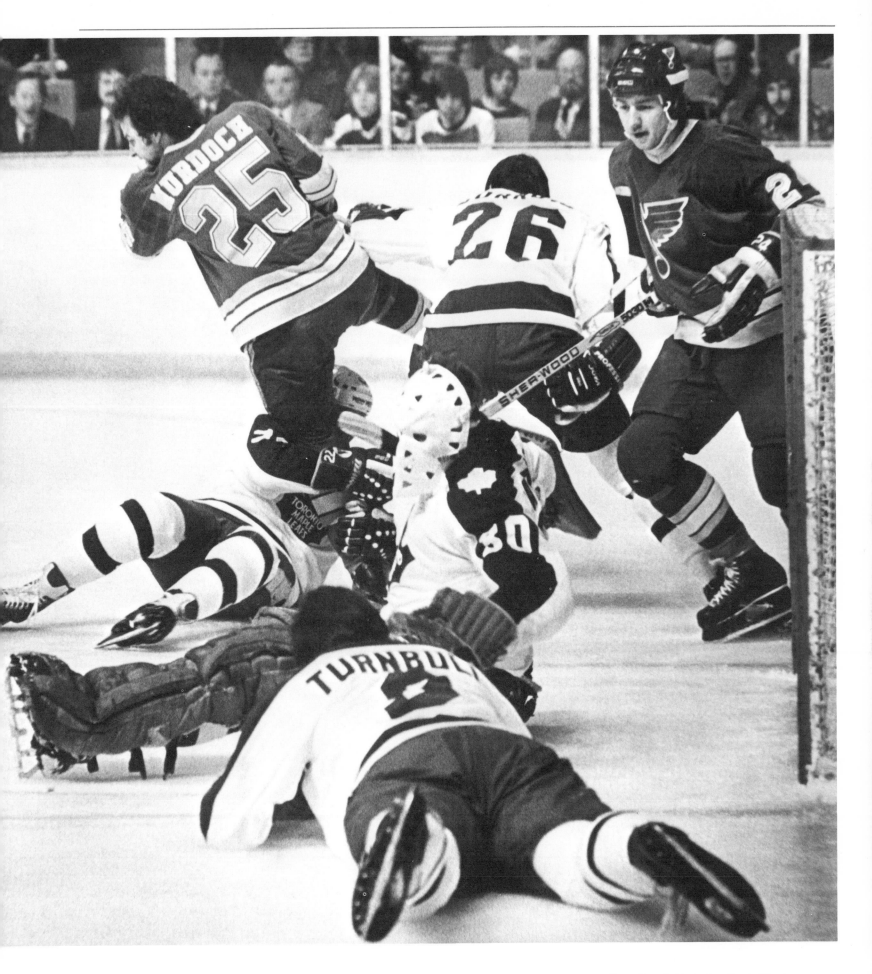

Even Bernie Federko, the brilliant young St. Louis centre, can't extricate the puck from this gaggle of Leafs, and Bob Murdoch can't help 'cause Dave Williams has just tackled him *(Bill Sandford, Toronto Sun)*

Vancouver Canucks

Harry Neale is highly rated as a hockey coach, strategist, and teacher of the game's skills. As a comedian, he's in the No. 1 spot among NHL coaches, a man who always has a few choice lines about himself and the team's fortunes.

The '78-79 season, Neale's first with the Canucks, wasn't especially successful as the team finished 17 games below .500 and earned a playoff spot only because it resides in the woeful Smythe Division. But those Canuck struggles failed to dim Neale's wit. Here are a few examples:

"We had trouble winning at home; we didn't do very well on the road. My failure as a coach was that I couldn't think of any other place to play our games."

"Often with the Canucks, our best system of forechecking was to shoot the puck into the attacking zone – and leave it there."

"We didn't have much rushing from our defencemen. In fact, we had a couple of defencemen who would make a rush up the ice – and then we'd have to replace the pucks."

Fortunately for the Canucks, there's much more to Neale than a few one-liners. He took over a club that has floundered through its first decade after joining the NHL as a 1970 expansion team. In only two seasons has the club been above the .500 mark, and Neale is the sixth man who has held the coaching job.

Attendance at Pacific Coliseum has reflected the club's long-running record of mediocrity. When the team entered the NHL, a city long hungry for big league hockey supplied a huge demand for tickets. But in the late 1970s, that interest had dwindled. The Canucks drew solid crowds but lately there have been sizeable numbers of "no shows," fans who purchase season's tickets but stay home if the visiting club isn't a top attraction.

"Our big aim is to supply an entertaining team, one that gives the fans in Vancouver their money's worth in pep

and effort," Neale says. "We feel the way to do that is to go with young players and build on them. We're on the right track, too, because we have a good nucleus of kids now."

Goalie Glen Hanlon, 22, heads that youth movement. He had a 3.10 goals-against average in 31 matches in '78-79 as a rookie, although a knee injury sidelined him for a long stretch at mid-season.

Swedish centre Thomas Gradin (20 goals), defenceman Lars Lindgren, and wingers Stan Smyl and Curt Fraser had sound rookie seasons. The top '78 draft pick, forward Bill Derlago, had his first NHL year wrecked by a knee injury but he remains a splendid prospect. The Canucks' first-round pick in '79, Rick Vaive, is another lad with a big future. He spent the '78-79 season with the Birmingham Bulls of the WHA where he scored 26 goals and earned 248 penalty minutes, the skill-aggressiveness combination pro teams use as a measurement of potential.

Back in the early 1970s when Neale was coaching Hamilton Juniors, he predicted a big hockey future for a 17-year-old winger, Ron Sedlbauer. In the '78-79 season, Sedlbauer, 25, realized that potential when he scored 40 goals.

Washington Capitals

There's been one bright side to Washington Capitals' five years of floundering since their 1974 NHL entry as an expansion franchise. Their low ranking has granted them the one privilege of have-nots – early selections in the NHL's entry (formerly amateur) draft.

The Caps' Robert Picard, despite his big-league credentials, just can't get no respect from Mike Palmateer; and as for Dave Burrows, he's ignoring Picard completely *(Toronto Star)*

As a result of making all those picks from the elite portion of the draft field, the Capitals, at last, appear to have sufficient talent to launch a move towards the Valhalla of expansion clubs, the .500 mark.

The break-even point, however, is 17 points away for the Caps. But the team improved its effort by 15 points last season and the presence of all those good young players, plus some useful veterans, supplies a faint bit of hope.

The few times the Caps have performed consistently in the past, the crowds at their beautiful arena, the 18,190 seat Capital Centre in Landover, Maryland, have increased. "We have a solid group of devoted fans who attend every game but the big crowds seem to be pegged to our club's performance," says Cap general manager Max McNab. "We have no doubts that we'll consistently draw crowds in excess of 15,000 when we are playing steadily above the .500 mark."

The Caps did make an unusual move just before the start of the '78-79 season when they sacked coach Tommy McVie, who had guided the team for almost three seasons. Danny Belisle, who had built an enviable record in the minor leagues, took over on the eve of the season's opener. Understandably, the team staggered in the first half of the season while Belisle learned the ropes, both about his own team and the NHL. But when Belisle completed his indoctrination course and the club ended its shuffle of players, the Caps finished the season strongly, totalling 63 points, their best mark in five seasons. However the Caps employed 40 different players during the season, hardly the roster stability demanded in a contender.

Important in that strong finish was goalie Gary Inness, who was added to the Caps when the Indianapolis Racers of the WHA folded. Inness had a 14-14-8 won-lost-tied record with the Caps, an excellent mark on a struggling team. Adding veteran Wayne Stephenson from Philadelphia Flyers gives the Caps strong goaltending.

Although the Caps made some bad choices in the draft – defenceman Greg Joly was a flop as a pro – they do have some splendid prospects. Defenceman Robert Picard had 21 goals and 44 assists last season and owns all-star potential. Rick Green, 23, is another outstanding young backliner,

and Swedish import Leif Svensson had a good rookie year. Winger Ryan Walter had a fine rookie season in '78-79 with 55 points, and the team landed two good wingers in the '79 draft – Mike Gartner from the WHA Cincinnati Stingers and Errol Rausse, a 65-goal junior.

The Caps own two excellent offensive centres in Dennis Maruk (31 goals, 59 assists) and Guy Charron (28 goals, 42 assists).

Winnipeg Jets

The merger of the WHA and NHL really came two years, or maybe only one year, too late for Winnipeg Jets, the WHA champs in the league's final two seasons. Had the Jets been allowed to enter the NHL with the roster of their '77-78 team intact, they would have gained quick parity in the old league.

That season the Jets, the first North American big league team to make full-scale use of European players, had the splendid line of Ulf Nilsson, Anders Hedberg, and Bobby Hull, defencemen Lars-Erik Sjoberg and Thommie Bergman, forwards Kent Nilsson, Willi Lindstrom, Dan Labraaten, and Peter Sullivan. Only Sjoberg, Sullivan, and Lindstrom will enter the NHL with the Jets.

"I'll always be disappointed that we didn't have the chance to take the '77-78 Jet team into the big buildings of the NHL," says Hull. "Not that we would have beaten all those NHL teams but we would have showed them the calibre of entertainment that I thought was hockey at its best."

The defection of Hedberg and Nilsson to New York Rangers and Labraaten and Bergman to Detroit Red Wings plus Hull's "retirement," forced the Jets into a rebuilding job last season. Under the guidance of general manager John Ferguson and coach Tom McVie, the Jets were the WHA champs again.

The Jets were hit hard by the rules of the expansion draft that permitted them to protect only skaters and two goalies: Atlanta Flames reclaimed Kent Nilsson; Rich Preston will be a Chicago Black Hawk; and Barry Long was taken by Detroit.

Now the fans in Winnipeg can watch a club which employs a much different approach than the slick, fast, clean hockey the WHA Jets, with their many Europeans, produced. Ferguson, who joined the Jets after he was sacked by New York Rangers, was the prototype of the hockey enforcer-policeman during his excellent playing career with Montreal Canadiens. Coach McVie, sacked by Washington Capitals two days before the start of the '78-79 season, is a man who likes strong physical conditioning in his players.

Thus, the Jets will feature muscle and belligerence.

"Sure, we'd love to have players with great skill who can play slick offensive hockey," Ferguson says. "But it's funny. The NHL clubs didn't make many of those available to us in the expansion draft. We don't plan to build any sort of goon team that uses fighting as its main asset, but we do want a team that can play strong, physical, defensive hockey."

The Jets salvaged a few of their shooters – tough little winger Morris Lukowich (65 goals), Sullivan (46 goals) and Lindstrom (26 goals), and the team claimed winger Peter Marsh, who had scored 43 goals for Cincinnati Stingers.

Sjoberg, one of the game's most knowledgeable players, missed most of the '78-79 season with an ankle injury, but he anchors the club's defence. Big backliner Scott Campbell was a player the Jets protected. He's a blue-chip prospect who had 248 penalty minutes last season. Ferguson also secured Barry Melrose (222 penalty minutes) and Craig Norwich from Cincinnati to give the team some respectability on the backline.

Many Are Called:
Few are Chosen

Frank Orr

Floyd Smith, Leafs and would-be Leafs get acquainted (*Toronto Star*)

A Training Camp Diary

Sunday, September 16
DAY ONE

Several Leaf players confessed that it had been an "uneasy" summer because of the large changes in the team's front office – the ousting of general manager Jim Gregory and coach Roger Neilson and the hiring of Punch Imlach as general manager, Floyd Smith as coach, and Dick Duff as assistant coach.

"I guess having a new coach always creates a little feeling of unrest because you wonder about the style of hockey he'll want the team to use and how you'll fit into it," said Leaf candidate Ron Wilson. "But no matter who the coach is, it all comes down to one thing: you have to show him that you deserve a job."

Not only were Imlach and Smith new with the club but some statements they made weren't exactly flattering to the players. When he was hired, Imlach called the Leafs a .500 hockey team and said that they lacked speed and talent. Smith, too, made a few remarks about the club's lack of speed.

Then came the great Showdown Caper in which Imlach and owner Harold Ballard tried to block team captain Darryl Sittler and goalie Mike Palmateer from participating in the filming of the Showdown, the television competition between top NHL players. The Leafs even sought an injunction in the Supreme Court of Ontario to block them, but the judge turned them down.

"Everyone wondered just what the hell was going on with the team all summer," said one Leaf player. "The new guys Ballard hired to run things really bad-mouthed the club and made it sound as if we weren't up to much. Then the Showdown thing, when they tried to stop Sittler and Palmateer, who

mean so much to this team, from going on Showdown, something the board of governors and the players' association had approved. We wondered if it was going to be a horror show around here with hassles about everything."

When the veteran Leafs plus 17 players from the 36-man rookie camp arrived for the main training camp, they discovered that everything was remarkably normal. They had medicals in the morning and a light skate in the afternoon.

Smith is a low-key man who laughs a great deal. He's an "old school" hockey man who takes a traditional approach to coaching a team.

"Montreal Canadiens haven't exactly been a flop in this league and they have the players do a great deal of skating and scrimmaging in their workouts," Smith said. "The style of hockey we want to have the team play requires much skating so that's what we'll be doing. We'll have specific drills in various areas of the game – forechecking, moving the puck out of our end, and the specialty teams, penalty-killing and power-play.

"One of the advantages of having an assistant coach is that Duffie [Dick Duff] can help me spot areas of skill where a player is lacking and then we can drill him on it."

When the players arrived, they discovered that the club had purchased new hockey pants for them to wear and there were some minor complaints about the trousers. The pants have high waists which extend to the players' rib cages and make them appear to have fat backsides. Defenceman Borje Salming immediately grabbed a pair of scissors and removed several portions of padding from his pants.

A pre-camp story in a Toronto newspaper had pointed out that some Leaf forwards lacked good speed and might have trouble fitting into the plans for an offensively oriented team. Centres Walt McKechnie and Paul Gardner were listed as two players with offensive skills but a lack of quickness.

"This is the slow-poke section of the dressing room over here," said McKechnie, indicating the corner of the Leaf room where he and Gardner both sit.

"Speed isn't the only thing that counts in this game, is it?" McKechnie added. "If they give me and Paul some wingers with speed, think of all the tricks we'll be able to do in getting the puck to them."

"Remember the story of the hare and the tortoise," winger Lanny McDonald offered.

Monday, September 17
DAY TWO

Laurie Boschman, the Leafs' first selection in the amateur draft, discovered during the rookie camp that in a town where a team is covered in the media as closely as the Leafs are in Toronto, a fellow must be careful in his statements.

Boschman, who's 19 years of age and fresh from Brandon Wheat Kings Juniors, was talking with Leaf trainer Danny Lemelin and a Toronto sportswriter when he mentioned that the Brandon team wasn't exactly large in its largesse with money. Boschman said that the Brandon players often had to buy their own 47-cent skate laces, that they received only $7 per day in meal money on the road, and that he had only $105 per month clear from his pay after taxes.

His statements appeared in the paper and Boschman was upset because he didn't want to appear to be a big shot, poor-mouthing his junior club. The sportswriter told Boschman that if he wanted something to be off the record, then to say that it was the next time. Boschman replied that there wouldn't be any next time.

Boschman hadn't signed a contract with the Leafs although his agent Bill Watters, an associate of Toronto hockey lawyer Alan Eagleson, claimed that a deal was close. As an underage junior, Boschman will become a professional this season only if he sticks with the Maple Leafs. Under the draft rules, the 19-year-olds must be retained on the major league roster or be returned to junior hockey. They can be farmed out to minor pro hockey only if the junior teams don't want them back.

"Because of that we'll be taking a very good look at him in the exhibition games," Floyd Smith said. "But he's showed us plenty in the rookie camp and our early drills at the main camp. He's a fine skater, smart with the puck, and he can handle himself physically."

The Leafs got down to the serious business of training camp starting with a physical training program off the ice supervised by former pro wrestling great Fred Atkins. Atkins is 67 years of age but he's in superb condition. He appears to be so hard that if you slapped him on the back you'd hurt your hand.

Because most players have been skating for several weeks and working on their own conditioning programs all summer, the drills reached a high tempo very quickly. As always, the great players excel all the time. Darryl Sittler and Borje Salming, the men who carry the Leafs, are in peak form the day they arrive in camp and work as hard as the rookies who are trying to earn jobs.

Salming's nickname is "King" and when he's in high gear, the Leaf players say "The King is dancin'." Salming was dancing in both drills, skating miles and carrying the puck end-to-end repeatedly. On one play he was moving up the ice at top speed and big defenceman Dave Hutchison had him lined up for a devastating bodycheck, by slipping in on Salming's blind side as he cut toward the middle of the ice. Salming saw Hutchison just a split second before the collision and, with his incredible agility and balance, veered away from the check.

"The Swede is like Muhammad Ali," Smith said. "It's very difficult to get a good piece of him. I don't know if there's any one else in hockey with the ability to slip off that check."

The Leafs' shooters faced excellent goaltending in the two drills, which limited the number of goals scored. The competition for goalie jobs is stiff. Only Mike Palmateer, the Leafs' number one man, is certain of a job even though he's heading into the option year of his contract and he's involved in a tough hassle with Leafs because he wants $200,000 per season on his new pact.

Paul Harrison was Palmateer's back-up but he's being challenged for that role by Czech defector Jiri Crha, Don (Smokey) McLeod who's 33 and spent five seasons in the WHA, and draft pick Vincent Tremblay.

Tuesday, September 18
DAY THREE

Jim Dorey made his debut as a National Hockey League defenceman with the Maple Leafs back on October 16, 1968, against Pittsburgh Penguins. The Leafs needed some muscle at the time but not quite as much as Dorey volunteered in that game.

In one of the NHL's truly magnificent displays of lunacy, goonery, or whatever it's called, Dorey placed himself solidly in the NHL record books. In less than two periods of action, Dorey earned nine penalties – four minors,

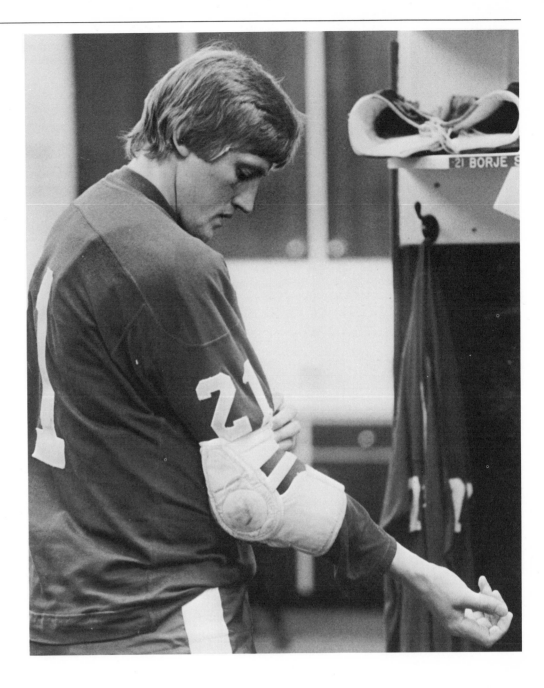

Just another opening, another show for Borje Salming *(Toronto Star)*

two majors, two 10-minute misconducts, and a game misconduct – 48 penalty minutes, a mark that still stands.

Jim "Flipper" Dorey is 32 now and he's been around the horn – New York Rangers, New England Whalers, Toronto Toros, and Quebec Nordiques. When he recovered from back surgery last season, Nordiques employed him very little. He asked Punch Imlach for a tryout with the Leafs.

Dorey always was a man of style. He dressed well and liked to dine in good places with the right wines. He's always been a physical fitness bug and he showed up for camp in splendid shape, still carrying the big shoulders and small waist.

"I asked for a chance to come to camp and show what I can do – no promises, no guarantees," Dorey said. "I've kicked around a little over the

years but I still think I can help an NHL team."

Floyd Smith plans to carry six defencemen and the top five appear to be set. Borje Salming, Ian Turnbull, Dave Burrows, Joel Quenneville, and Dave Hutchison have a lock on jobs. Ron Wilson can play defence plus all forward positions and that versatility could earn him employment. Greg Hotham has spent three seasons in the Leaf chain and every year at camp he makes few mistakes. He's not very flashy and appears capable of playing in the NHL. Dorey will have to beat them out for the sixth job.

John Bower tells how to Vince Tremblay and Bob Parent (*Toronto Star*)

In each day's scrimmages, Smith changes his forward lines and defence pairs. The pace of the drills continued to be swift and, at times, produced very entertaining hockey.

The coach is encouraged by the attitude he's seen in the first two days of camp.

"Some camps are dull; there's just no life among the players," Smith enthused. "But that's no problem here. It's a big advantage when the top players are tramping, really moving. That's how it's been with Borje Salming, Darryl Sittler, Lanny McDonald, the guys who really have nothing to prove. They've been setting a high standard of play in the scrimmages and the other players have to follow."

Jiri Crha is called "George" by the Leaf players. That's what his name means in English. He'd asked the Czech hockey people if he could head

west to play hockey and they said that perhaps he could in six years or so. Because he's 29, Crha decided that would be a trifle late for a pro career.

The Czechs did allow him to go to West Germany with his wife and two daughters for a vacation and that's where he defected. Crha contacted another Czech defector, centre Vaclav Nedomansky, who bolted in 1974 to join Toronto Toros of the WHA and now plays for Detroit Red Wings. Big Ned contacted his friend, George Gross, sports editor of the Toronto *Sun*, himself a defector from Czechoslovakia back in the late '40s. Gross told Imlach about Crha and the Czech goalie was granted a tryout. The Leafs sent him a set of goalie equipment to work out with in Europe, bought him an airline ticket, and arranged a visa for him.

Crha began studying English five months ago and although he's hardly Sir Laurence Olivier with the language, he can get by in it.

Crha is remarkably athletic, an excellent skater, and in the net, he's extremely quick. But his basic style of playing goal is European, and that means staying well back in the net. The good NHL shooters feed on goalies who don't move out to challenge them. Crha realizes this and is moving well out, often too far.

"He's got good basics," said Johnny Bower, the superb Leaf goalie of the 1960s who's a scout and goalie coach for the team now.

"But he needs work on playing the angles and challenging the shooters. He's eager to learn and when we have some time, I'll work with him on it."

Bower is well into his 50s now, and when he instructs the goalies, he dons full equipment and shows them how it's done. He was a master at the techniques of the profession, playing the angles to reduce the net openings available to the shooters.

Wednesday, September 19
DAY FOUR
Because the Leaf camp was being conducted at a rather swift pace, tempo was a subject kicked around the coaches' quarters. Smith's declaration that he wanted the club to play offensive, attacking hockey has opened things up and even the plodding skaters on the team are swarming to the attack.

The style of hockey played in the NHL often is dictated by the championship team. When Philadelphia Flyers muscled and brawled their way to two consecutive Stanley Cups in the mid-1970s, most NHL teams went looking for a few tough guys. Fortunately, the league – and Ontario attorney-general Roy McMurtry – stamped out the goons: then Montreal Canadiens took over as the kings of the hill with four Cup victories, speed and puck control their big assets. The wipe-out by the Soviet Union national team of the NHL all-stars last winter drilled it home: speed and pure, basic skill was the way the game should be played.

"Tempo is the key," Smith said. "All the good teams play with a constant tempo – the Russians, New York Islanders, Montreal Canadiens.

"Canadiens establish a tempo and hold it. They don't go up and down, faster and slower, in their pace. They don't send out any players who can't keep up the tempo. The Islanders don't play at quite as fast a pace as the Canadiens but they seldom vary from the tempo they establish at the start of the game. They're so consistent they force the other team out of their tempo and when you lose your own pace, it means the other team is dictating things.

"This season, we want the Leafs to play at a good tempo. But the key to it is not so much how fast your pace is, it's how consistent you are with it. But in the NHL now, skating is back in so we'll have to be able to set a fairly quick pace."

Dick Duff played on Cup teams in two towns – Toronto and Montreal – in the 1960s.

"Tempo was the key with both teams although the approach was different," Duff said. "With the Leafs in the early '60s, we played very disciplined, tough hockey. Teams hated to come into the Gardens to play us because they were in for a frustrating night. We'd check them hard both ways, force them into mistakes, and then pounce on those blunders to get our goals.

"When I was with Canadiens, we played a skating game based on puck control. I loved playing for the Canadiens because their style suited me – head-man the puck and skate.

"These days, the Canadiens have a few guys like Guy Lafleur and Steve Shutt to score the goals and a batch of players who can really skate and hold the tempo of the game. They just keep coming at you with speed. They never give you a second to coast."

Is Floyd Smith happy to be back in Toronto? You betcha! *(Toronto Star)*

Because the emphasis is on speed with the Leafs, the hopes of some young players have been raised, although John Anderson and Rocky Saganiuk would have qualified for first-string jobs even if the coach – and the club's style – hadn't changed.

Saganiuk had scored 47 goals for the New Brunswick Hawks and had a shot at the American League record of 55 when the Leafs recalled him late last season. Saganiuk is only 5-foot-8, but he weighs 185 pounds. His assets are quickness, a splendid shot, and a thoroughly combative attitude.

His given name is Rocky Ray Saganiuk.

"My father was a boxing fan and at the time I was born Rocky Marciano was his favourite boxer and Sugar Ray Robinson his second favourite," Saganiuk said. "That's why I was named Rocky Ray."

Fortunately for Saganiuk, his father wasn't a fan of Ishmael Laguna.

Because of the players' association legislation, Saganiuk wasn't obliged to attend the Leaf rookie camp but he did.

"I want to make the team very badly and the rookie camp was the chance to improve my conditioning and get in some work in the scrimmages," Saganiuk said.

Thursday, September 20
DAY FIVE

The fourth day of scrimmages was a fairly large one in the Leaf training camp. Laurie Boschman signed a contract with the Leafs, a four-year deal that will pay him more than $400,000. Tiger Williams, who'd been fairly docile to date during the camp, was embroiled in three minor fights.

And, perhaps most important, the Leaf players were starting to believe in Floyd Smith and his approach, a major breakthrough for a new coach. Of course, that view can change when the serious shooting starts, but the apprehension about Smith has vanished. He's been remarkably low-key all week and, slowly, that has loosened things up and produced a peppy, flat-out attitude in the scrimmages.

"It's been a good way to start a camp because it gets everybody moving fast," said defenceman Borje Salming, who's been the quickest man on the scene.

"I like scrimmages starting off because the season is long enough for the other stuff. Over the next couple of weeks, once the camp is down to the regular size, we'll be able to work on our passing and timing."

Until the club tests itself in a game against an NHL opponent, the players are a trifle reluctant to express any heavy optimism about the season ahead. But the feeling seems to be this: the Leafs have had two seasons of intensive coaching in specific skills and defensive tactics under Roger Neilson; the roster contains many experienced, mature players who know what has to be done for the team to be successful, and Smith's approach likely will be to allow the players to play within a loosely defined system.

Because he was exclusively a defensive player under Neilson, Jerry Butler admitted that his summer was "iffy" when he heard that the club planned to swing to the attack this season.

Neilson had told Butler not to worry about scoring goals, that his job was defensive play. Butler went through one streak of 30 games last season without scoring a goal, but he never missed a shift.

"I was used as an offensive forward by Rangers and St. Louis," said Butler, who's had two 17-goal seasons.

"I feel I can play attacking hockey. But after two seasons with Roger, everyone on this team knows how to play defensive hockey. When the puck changes hands and the other team has it, we can go to defence and get it back with no problems. Defence is second nature to us."

"Smith has created a good atmosphere in this camp because everything has been low-key," Darryl Sittler said. "One thing we've had on this club is a fine team feeling. The guys are really close as a group. It's a mature group of players who know the price we have to pay to be in top conditioning and to make it work."

When many NHL clubs sign their first-round draft pick, they make a little fuss about it with a press conference. Because he detests talking about contracts and salaries, general manager Punch Imlach avoids press conferences when he can.

Thus, the signing of Boschman had no fanfare. The writers weren't informed of the signing until they'd returned to their offices after the drill.

"We don't reveal the length or the numbers of contracts," Imlach said. "That's between us and the player. Of course, if players' agents want to shoot off their yaps about it, we can't do anything to stop them.

"Boschman is only 19 years old and we want to keep as much pressure off him as possible. We like the way he's conducted himself in this camp. Every scrimmage he gets at least one goal and makes good plays. He's a good passer, especially to his left. That's his backhand side and not all that many centres are strong that way. When I saw that kid [Boschman] passing so well to his left, I said that I'd bet that kid in Brandon who had all the goals [Brian Propp, Boschman's left winger last season who scored 90 goals] was on that side and I was right."

Tiger Williams, the NHL's penalty-leader last season and by far the league's busiest fighter, has concentrated on hockey throughout this camp. He's been mentioned as strong trade bait if the Leafs decide he's not fast enough for their new style of play. In fact, last spring when Jim Gregory

was still the Leaf general manager, there had been serious trade talks with Philadelphia Flyers involving Williams.

On this day, Williams was embroiled in three scuffles. Two of them were in the morning session with Alain Belanger, who's been called Bam-Bam ever since he demolished celebrated minor pro tough guy Steve Short with two punches a couple of years ago in the Central League. In the afternoon drill, Williams and Saganiuk administered some stick to each other, then wrestled briefly. No serious damage was done in any of the bouts.

"It feels like camp now, having a couple of little battles," Williams said. "But we're ready to play a game. We've been playing each other long enough."

Friday, September 21
DAY SIX

Ian Turnbull is a man with a rather engaging perspective on life. He plays defence for the Leafs but that's only part of his existence, not the be-all and end-all. He owns Grapes, a wine bar-restaurant near the Gardens and has studied the guitar, which he plays quite well.

One night in Minnesota after the Leafs had lost a game to the North Stars to keep a losing string alive, Turnbull stood in the dressing room, looked upwards, and asked: "Do you think there's life after hockey?"

Turnbull and Roger Neilson butted heads a few times because they had views at variance on the game of ice hockey. To Neilson, hockey was life and he devoted every waking minute to it. To Turnbull, the game is a way to earn a living but it's not everything.

"There was no personality clash between Roger and I," Turnbull said. "In fact, I think we rather liked each other. But we did have a philosophical difference on how the game should be played. Roger was a defensive specialist and that was the style he wanted us to play. I'm an offensive defenceman who likes to ramble a bit with the puck. So we disagreed on that point."

When he looks ahead to the 1979-80 season under Floyd Smith, Turnbull claims that a combination of the two styles – Neilson's defence and Smith's offence – will provide the Leafs with an opportunity for improvement.

"No club can be at the top without playing some defence, and playing it well," Turnbull said. "Everyone seems to think we're going to throw away the

Jiri Crha showing he's learned a little baseball, too *(Jerry Hobbs)*

defensive side of the game and just attack all the time. Now that's fine, except there will be times when the other team has the puck and wants to do a little attacking of its own.

"Well, we've spent two years with Neilson learning the defensive aspect of the game and no one teaches it better than he does. I think now we can combine it with some offensive prowess.

"Basically, I think we got too defensive-minded in the past couple of years. People talk about Neilson placing restrictions on my rushing but it was the system we played that did it. I had no more halter on me than Borje Salming or some other players did. We had guys who were designated defensive specialists who can be productive on the attack. I know because I see them in workouts every day.

"Four years ago we were the fourth-highest scoring team in the league; last season we were the fourth-highest

defensive team. To really move up, we have to combine the two. I think if we can score another 50 or 60 goals and maintain the same defensive record we can be among the top four teams in the league."

Like many other Leafs, Turnbull has compiled some lofty individual achievements in his seven seasons with the club – a record five goals for a defenceman in one game and a club record of 22 goals in one season.

"The individual things are nice when you're young but after seven years, I want to play on a winner. I want to be on a team that's in the Stanley Cup finals. We have a team now with a mature attitude and enough talent."

There were few surprises when Smith named his line-up for the next night's opening exhibition game against Boston Bruins at the Gardens. Laurie Boschman and Greg Hotham were the only players in the line-up who weren't with the team last season.

Saturday, September 22
DAY SEVEN
The Maple Leafs decided they'd seen enough good things by Jiri Crha in the week's drills, signed the Czech goalie to a contract late in the afternoon, and gave him the starting assignment in the opening "pre-season" game of the year, a match at Maple Leaf Gardens against Boston Bruins.

Years ago, games that weren't part of the regular schedule in sports were called "exhibitions." But when teams like the Leafs started to include these mean-nothing contests as part of the season ticket package, the title was switched to pre-season.

The Leafs play a dozen pre-season games this fall, jammed into a space of 16 days. The agreement between the league and the NHL Players' Association limits the number of pre-season games to 11 but the Leafs have an extra one – a match in Calgary against the Canadian Olympic team.

Pre-season games supply the chance for coaches to examine young players in combat against big-league opposition, and give the veterans a chance to tune up for the season ahead. Most coaches claim that they place little stock in the outcome of the matches but that's not exactly correct. Sometimes a bad record in the exhibitions can lead to a poor start to the season, something the Leafs experienced in 1978.

Thus, Smith employed mostly an experienced cast in the opener against the Bruins. Ian Turnbull, bothered by a sore back, and Walt McKechnie, who has an ankle injury, weren't used against the Bruins.

When the Bruins arrived for the game, their executives had long faces. Their remarkable defenceman, Brad Park, who missed half the '78-79 season because of recurring knee problems, was shelved again. He reported to camp below his playing weight and in fine condition but when he placed weight on his knee in camp, the old grinding started again in the joint.

Park was hospitalized and the bone chips were flushed out of the knee. He'd be off skates for three weeks.

Crha appeared tense and a trifle jittery for his first start in the west. He showed a tendency to fall to the ice too often but he had several tough stops among the 14 shots he faced in the first 30 minutes of the game.

He also surrendered two scores, but neither was his fault. After Darryl Sittler gave Leafs the lead early, Bruins tied the score late in the first period. Crha made a good save on Bruins' promising rookie defenceman Raymond Bourque but the rebound struck Borje Salming and bounced back into the net.

In the first minute of the second period, Bruins' Bob Miller, killing a penalty at the time, broke away against the Leaf power play. Crha moved out to meet him but Miller beat him with what Crha called "a shovel shot."

Paul Harrison took over the Leaf net half-way through the game and the Gardens' crowd gave Crha a good ovation when he skated off.

Ron Ellis tied the score for the Leafs from a faceoff on the first shot Leafs had against Bruins' second-half goalie Gilles Gilbert. But Gilbert played superbly over the duration of the game and Miller's second goal of the match in the third period gave Bruins a 3-2 victory.

After the game, Smith sat quietly in his little office off the Leaf dressing room. He'd wanted a win to start his Leaf coaching tenure on the right foot, but he wasn't unhappy with the team's effort. "We tried, and had scoring chances we didn't finish off," he said.

Sunday, September 23
DAY EIGHT
The 3,000 fans in Ottawa's Civic Arena booed when the announcements were made of the deletions from the Leaf line-up: Mike Palmateer, Paul Harrison, Ian Turnbull, Lanny McDonald, Ron Wilson, Paul Gardner, Darryl Sittler, John Anderson, Walt McKechnie.

The appeal of pre-season matches in non-NHL towns is the chance to see the big stars in action and the Leafs were playing minus many of theirs. The fans feel gypped when that happens.

Greg Hotham cavorted like a major star in the match against Boston Bruins, a shoot-out which the Leafs won 6-5, but he's barely a household word, except perhaps in his mother's kitchen. Hotham scored two goals, had an assist, and stated rather strongly his case for heavy consideration as a Leaf employee this season.

Hotham, from Aurora, Ontario, played junior hockey with the Kingston Canadians, and was the Leafs' fifth-round selection in the 1976 amateur draft, the 84th player claimed. He spent two years with Saginaw Gears in the International League and, in '78-79, played for New Brunswick Hawks in the American League. Along the way, he's built up points as a solid and efficient, but unspectacular, worker.

In '78, he made a surprise appearance with the Leafs for a game against a touring Czechoslovakian team, Brno. The Leafs created considerable controversy that evening by sitting out several regulars and Hotham was called from Saginaw to fill in.

Last season, Hotham's work in New Brunswick earned some good reviews. Eddie Johnston, the New Brunswick Hawk coach then, and now with the Chicago Black Hawks, said Hotham was ready for the NHL.

Through the Leaf scrimmages and in the opening exhibition, Hotham has made few mistakes. He's a disciplined defenceman who patrols his own patch of ice, moves the puck quickly, and places roadblocks in attackers' paths.

"We're going to take a good look at him in the pre-season games because he's getting the job done from the first day of camp," Floyd Smith said.

"He's a kid [23] who's worked his way up the ladder, improving all the time. You have to have time for that type of player."

Hotham is a lad with no illusions about the facts of hockey life. "I've been patient for three years," he said. "I've worked towards this chance at the Leafs and all I can do is play as well as I can. If I don't make it, well, I'll know I've given it everything I could."

It was a good night for the Leaf youngsters as Rocky Saganiuk also scored twice and Mark Kirton, a second year pro centre, had a goal and an assist. Jerry Butler had the other goal.

But it wasn't a good night for Smokey McLeod, the WHA refugee goalie who didn't play last season and, at 33, is trying to get his career on the rails again. He surrendered four goals in the half of the game he played. Young Vincent Tremblay, who's only 19, played the second half and impressed the club's brass.

"We skated well, much better than in the first game, and we were moving the puck well," Smith enthused.

The other Leafs had a morning workout and the remainder of the day off. Sittler then drove to his cottage on Lake Couchiching with his family for the afternoon and took along a passenger – goalie Jiri Crha.

"Sunday can be a long day when you're alone in a new city," Sittler said. "It's tougher for Jiri because his wife and children are still in Europe. He seemed to enjoy the day."

Small things like that make Sittler one of the NHL's best team captains.

Monday, September 24
DAY NINE
Walt McKechnie limped into the Leaf workout, wearing a cast on his injured ankle. The ligaments in the ankle were damaged and it can be a slow-to-heal injury.

"I'd been hurting for a couple of days and I hoped it would correct itself," he said. "Instead, it got worse and the pain was so bad that I couldn't sleep. I'll have to have the cast on for ten days, at least, and you always hate to have an injury in training camp."

McKechnie, 32, has been around the horn in the NHL and pro hockey. His record reads like a guided tour of North America – Minnesota, Phoenix, Minnesota, Iowa, Cleveland, Oakland,

Boston, Detroit, Washington, Cleveland, and Toronto. The Leafs picked him up the eve of the '78-79 season and he delivered an excellent season with 25 goals and 61 points.

Because there's some competition for Leaf centre spots, McKechnie doesn't like not being on hand to stake a claim on one. Darryl Sittler, of course, is certain of work at centre. McKechnie really doesn't need to worry because the Leafs need his experience. Paul Gardner, Jimmy Jones, Laurie Boschman, and Mark Kirton, who's having an excellent camp after a strong rookie pro season at New Brunswick, are also seeking jobs.

The Leafs reduced their roster by nine players, who shifted to the camp of the New Brunswick Hawks. The Leafs share that farm club with Chicago Black Hawks and 16 candidates checked in from the Chicago camp.

Goalie Don McLeod and defenceman Bob Neely were the veteran pros assigned to the minors along with Bob Halpin, Alain Belanger, Bob Warner, Bob Parent, Dan Eastman, Dave Simpson, and Jean-Gaston d'Ouville.

Neely has been one of the Leafs' major disappointments of the 1970s. They drafted him from Peterborough Juniors in 1973 where he'd been a tough, high-scoring defenceman. Neely was unable to maintain his toughness level against the pros and only in flashes has he demonstrated some of what seemed to be big potential.

Last season with New Brunswick, he was playing extremely well through the first half of the season, but when the Leafs bypassed him and called up other players during the injury emergencies, Neely's performance level sagged. He's heading into the final year of a contract that pays him more than $100,000 per season.

The Leafs didn't scrimmage in their workouts. Instead, they took skating and passing drills, high speed efforts aimed at preparing the team to play a quick-hitting offensive game.

There also was specialized instruction. Rookie Boschman had some trouble with faceoffs in the weekend games. After a workout, Boschman and Sittler spent 20 minutes taking faceoff draws while assistant coach Dick Duff dropped the puck.

Goalie coach Johnny Bower had a session with rookie Vincent Tremblay, who's eligible for junior but likely will become a pro goalie this season.

For Bob Neely, just one more year that isn't his *(Toronto Star)*

Bower is fabled as having the best pokecheck of all NHL goalies. He was a master at lunging out of the net to knock the puck away from incoming attackers. He taught the trick to Mike Palmateer and Paul Harrison, and was passing it on to Tremblay.

Tuesday, September 25
DAY TEN
Just about every year, the Maple Leafs play an exhibition game against the Minnesota North Stars in Kitchener and it's always a special night for team captain Darryl Sittler.

Sittler's hometown is St. Jacobs, a small village a few miles outside of Kitchener, and every time the Leafs play there he supplies a block of tickets for relatives and friends from the area.

"Yeah, there is something a little special for me to play in Kitchener because a great many people I know and quite a few relatives will be there," Sittler said. "I remember very well those NHL exhibition games in Kitchener when I was a kid. I'd bug my father for weeks to take me to the game and then I'd hang around the dressing rooms after the game to get the players' autographs.

"I'd take those autographs and trace them on other pieces of paper and give them to my friends. That's a big reason why I try to sign as many autographs as possible for kids. I know how much any NHL player's autograph meant to me."

In the morning, Floyd Smith was joking about the game that night. "If I wanted to commit suicide, I have the perfect way to do it," Smith said. "I'll take this team to Kitchener and I won't dress Sittler. The folks from that little town of his probably would take me right there and hang me in the town square."

North Stars are an improving NHL club, one the Leafs might have to battle in the overall standings, and that produces considerable curiosity about them among the Leafs. The match doesn't produce much curiosity among the hockey fans of Kitchener. In the past, NHL exhibition games have attracted at least 8,000 spectators but this one draws only 4,087.

Paul Harrison, who's had an outstanding camp, started in goal for the Leafs and continued that level of play. The game was in a 1-1 tie when Harrison left half-way through the second period and Sittler had scored the Leaf goal to a rather large cheer.

Jiri Crha replaced Harrison in the Leaf net and he had a rough time. North Stars popped two quick goals behind him, and in the 30 minutes he played, Crha was often out of position and had to scramble to stop several shots.

Twice the Leafs battled back from two-goal deficits to earn a 5-5 tie. Dan Maloney had a large hand in the outcome of the game. The Leaf left winger isn't an especially pretty player but no one in the game gives any more effort. His digging produced the puck for Paul Gardner to cut the Stars margin to 5-4. Then in the final minute of the game, with Crha on the bench for an extra attacker, Maloney tied the game with a tip-in of Ron Wilson's pass from deep in the corner.

"One thing I really like about this team is that there's no give-up on it," Smith said after the game.

In most rinks that they play in over the season, the Leaf players have a fairly clear path from the dressing room to the bus. It wasn't that way in Kitchener and a large group of youngsters, maybe some Darryl Sittlers of tomorrow, went home with a large number of autographs.

Mike Palmateer, trying to remember how the thing works *(Toronto Star)*

**Wednesday, September 26
DAY ELEVEN**

Goalie Mike Palmateer made his first '79 exhibition game appearance against the Montreal Canadiens and established, in his 30 minutes of work, that the Maple Leafs simply can't get along without him.

Palmateer is not only an exceptional goaltender – as he demonstrated with several dazzling stops against the Canadiens – but the Leafs play their best hockey when he's in the net.

For 30 minutes of the match the Leafs delivered the type of hockey Punch Imlach and Floyd Smith have been talking about since they were hired during the summer. They skated well, moved the puck quickly and, with strong forechecking, forced the Canadiens into some blunders in their own zone. Two goals by Rocky Saganiuk and one by Borje Salming supplied the 3-0 lead.

At the half-way point of the game, Palmateer was replaced by rookie Vincent Tremblay. Now young Vincent is an excellent goaltending prospect, but his sense of timing can be questioned: unfortunately he moved into the Leaf net against hockey's finest team at the time when the Leafs were running out of gas.

The Canadiens pumped four goals behind Tremblay and added one into an empty net for a 5-3 victory.

"We found out a few things in that game," Smith said. "To be successful, we have to maintain our intensity and skating for 60 minutes. We got that 3-0 lead and then eased up. We quit skating and forcing the play, which allowed the Canadiens to get their game into gear. When you have them down, you have to keep them there.

"But we had the chance to see some of our young players in a pressure situation. We also found out that we need a great deal of work on our power-play. We had five chances to use it and we didn't get a goal."

Despite the four goals he surrendered, Tremblay viewed the game as a big night in his young hockey career. He grew up in Quebec City and the Canadiens were his heroes.

"Oh, sure, it was a very big thrill for me to play against them," Tremblay said in his broken English. "Those Canadiens, they don't fool around when they shoot the puck. All their shots are serious.

"As a little boy, I dream of playing for the Canadiens. But I was happy when the Maple Leafs drafted me. I figured they had some need for goalies and I'd get a good chance. I've had that chance and I think that in a couple of years, I'll be with the team."

Tremblay will take the first step in that direction this season with New Brunswick Hawks of the American League.

Thursday, September 27
DAY TWELVE

Because the fans in Moncton heartily supported the New Brunswick Hawks, the American League farm team shared by the Leafs and Chicago Black Hawks, last season and turned the club into a money-maker, the Leaf brass wanted to run no risk of upsetting them.

When the Leafs played Chicago in an exhibition at Moncton, they took only the players who were on the Leaf NHL roster last season. The other candidates for employment remained behind in Toronto and practised with the Hawks, still training in Ontario.

The Black Hawks, too, brought the varsity roster but the Leafs counted a 5-3 win before a packed arena. Again, Mike Palmateer was exceptional. He played the second half of the game and held the Leafs together in the third period when the Black Hawks had a 15-5 edge in shots on goal.

Dan Maloney scored two more goals for the Leafs. Ian Turnbull, Tiger Williams, and Ron Wilson had the others. But Wilson also ripped up his knee and his hopes of earning a first-string spot with the Leafs must be postponed indefinitely.

Floyd Smith turned the bench coaching duties over to his assistant, Dick Duff, and watched the game from the press box where he could get a long-range view of his team.

"Watching a game from well above the action is good for a coach every so often," Smith said. "You get a good overall perspective on the way your team is going.

"I found out one thing again that I've known all along: this club simply must skate and move the puck to have any chance. We did it for two periods and were in control of the game. But in the third, we started to hang back and that's no good.

"Palmateer bailed us out in the third period but we can't expect him to do that every game. I have to drum into this club that we must skate for the whole game. When we do, we can give any club trouble but when we ease up and allow the other team to carry the puck to us, we get into trouble."

For Ron Wilson, it's a long flight by chartered plane back to Toronto and a trip to the hospital. He had high hopes that the swing to attack this season would give him a big chance of a regular spot because he has excellent offensive skills. He's been a spot skater for the Leafs for two seasons, and a regular during several stints in the minors.

But the knee, that fragile hinge that often appears to have been built for anything but contact sports, has chopped down those hopes.

Friday, September 28
DAY THIRTEEN

Few players in the history of the Maple Leafs have attained the popularity that Dick Duff enjoyed with the spectators at Maple Leaf Gardens during his near-decade, 1954-64, with the team.

Duff was a nifty little left winger who had good skill and always gave the game a big effort. He was noted as a player who could produce big goals under pressure, such as that of the Stanley Cup playoffs. He played on the first two of Leafs' three consecutive Cup teams in the early 1960s, then was traded to New York Rangers late in the '63-64 season, the deal that brought Andy Bathgate to the Leafs.

Duff wound up with Montreal Canadiens where he played on three more Cup teams in the late '60s. He finished up his career with Los Angeles Kings and, for a brief time, with Buffalo Sabres when Punch Imlach was the general manager-coach there. Since his career ended, Duff finished a college degree in political science, made an unsuccessful bid for a federal government seat, coached junior in Windsor briefly, and whipped a small drinking problem.

Imlach hired him to be Floyd Smith's assistant coach with the Leafs.

"Duffie was a winner, a player who knew how to pay the price to achieve good things," Imlach said. "Maybe he'll be able to teach some of our players how it's done."

Through the Leaf camp, Duff has maintained a very low profile, feeling his way slowly into his role with the Leafs. He worked on the ice with Smith during drills, gently offering small tips to the players. During the games, he worked as a spotter, passing on his findings to Smith between periods.

"It's a new role for me and I'll have to grow into the assistant's job," Duff said. "But it's great to be back in the game. Hockey's been a big part of my life."

"I was fortunate when I played this game to be with two outstanding teams and two great groups of men – the Leafs and Canadiens. Those clubs were successful for many reasons – talent and ambition – but they really won because they worked at it.

"I like to think I was good in tough situations because I really worked at it. I'd spend hours analyzing the other teams trying to figure out weaknesses in their style of play and their character too, something that would give me and my team a little edge.

"Henri Richard (Canadiens' centre) is a player I'll never forget. He never said much but boy did he play when things were tight. He'd just shove everything else out of his mind but the game. I can remember the nights before big games in the playoffs when Henri knew he'd have trouble getting to sleep. He'd spend the evening in his room reading or watching television, then he'd do a large number of push-ups until he was tired. That helped him get to sleep."

The Leafs were carrying a large roster and, with the large number of pre-season games, the team had little time to work on specifics in its drills.

"We're starting to get a line, though, on the players' strengths and weaknesses," Duff said. "Now we know the areas that need work in their game."

Saturday, September 29
DAY FOURTEEN

Roger Neilson, who had coached the Leafs for the past two years, returned to Maple Leaf Gardens as associate coach of Buffalo Sabres and claimed he received a warm welcome.

"The ushers and usherettes, a couple of Leaf players I bumped into, the cops, the girls in the concessions, all

The first thing to learn is how to stand very still ... *(Toronto Star)*

made me feel welcome," Neilson said.

Leaf general manager Punch Imlach, however, refused to allow Neilson to sit in the press box and no one could figure out the reason behind that decision.

The Sabres are trying some new wrinkles this season. They'll employ a three-man coaching set-up – head coach Scotty Bowman and assistant Jim Roberts behind the bench, associate Neilson in the press box or some spot high above the ice. Neilson will be in communication with Roberts via a new "walkie-talkie" hook-up. But they didn't plan to use the electronic link at the Gardens.

"If Neilson wants to coach, let him coach behind the bench," Imlach snarled. "He won't be able to do it from our press box."

Assistant coaches and scouts are

perched in the press box for most games. Neilson watched the game from the radio booth from which CKO-FM broadcasts the games.

"I guess the Leafs were trying to drum up some ink for this game, which wasn't on the subscribers' season ticket list," Neilson said. "We'll just get a ruling from the NHL on space for our spotter – me – to be located.

"Can you imagine one National Football League team keeping another team's assistant coaches out of a spot in the press box where they work as spotters?"

The Sabres' quickness gave the Leafs problems in a rough, chippy game but because of Mike Palmateer's goaltending the game was in a 1-1 tie when he departed at the half-way point and Paul Harrison took over the Leaf net. Harrison had been sharp all through camp but he had a rough time as the Sabres won the match 7-3, scoring four times in the third period. At least three of the six goals that beat him were soft ones.

For Leaf defenceman Dave Hutchison, the evening was a lost one. He became embroiled in a scuffle with Sabres' Larry Playfair. It was no large-scale battle but because they persisted in trying to continue the fight, they each wound up with major, 10-minute and game misconduct penalties.

Hutchison has a tendency to be a blow-top and, last season, it placed him in trouble. When an NHL player earns his third game misconduct of the season, he's automatically suspended for two games and additional game penalties earn increased suspensions.

Game misconducts acquired in a pre-season game count in a player's total and, in a pre-season game, Hutchison wasted one of his allowable sentences.

Sunday, September 30
DAY FIFTEEN
Paul Harrison established beyond any doubt that he would be the Leafs' back-up goalie, despite the rough time he had in Toronto against the Sabres the previous evening.

The Leafs travelled to Chicago and in the first period of a game against the Black Hawks, Harrison faced 21 shots, as the period ended in a 1-1 tie. Harrison and Mike Palmateer, who worked the second half of the game, faced a total of 43 shots as the Hawks won, 3-2.

"I was just awful against Buffalo," Harrison said. "I'm not wild about splitting games, especially having to play the second half. Sitting on the bench that long cools me out or something. If I have to play a half-game, I much prefer it to be the first half because that gets me right into the action.

"It's all in my head, I guess, but those 30-minute stints just seem weird. If I play the first half, after five or six minutes of the second period I start to watch the clock and hope that I don't have any shots until it's time to leave."

Harrison was acquired by the Leafs from Minnesota North Stars in the summer of '78 for a fourth-round draft choice. He's a pleasant man who played junior hockey for Oshawa Generals, then divided two seasons between the North Stars and the minor leagues.

Harrison realizes that if Palmateer

has no injuries, the back-up goalie's action will be 20 games at the most; but he's prepared to fill that role. Harrison is only 24 and being a back-up in the NHL is a better life than playing first-string in the minors, including, as it does in the NHL, a big league salary and bonuses, first-class living conditions, and no long hours on the bus.

"The secret of the back-up goalie is being ready all the time," Harrison said.

"I never know when I might have to go into a game because of an injury to Mike. I have to work hard in practice every day because that's how I stay sharp."

Surprisingly, perhaps, to some people, Harrison and Palmateer are good friends. They're roommates on the road much of the time and they share information on opposition shooters.

"Mike is the best goalie in the league," Harrison said. "There's just no doubt about that. So I have a role to fill: I play the games he doesn't.

"I've learned a great deal from Mike about playing goal and, during games, we give each other little tips all the time. I might be hanging back in the net a little or the other team might be doing something new. Mike will tell me and I can adjust. I do the same for him.

"Mike's incredible, really, because nothing ever seems to bother him. He has enormous confidence in his own ability."

Monday, October 1
DAY SIXTEEN
Lanny McDonald flew west the previous day, the advance party for the Leafs' exhibition match against the Canadian Olympic team in Calgary. His wife Ardelle and daughter Andra had spent the month of September in Medicine Hat, the town 170 miles from Calgary where McDonald played junior hockey – and also met Ardelle.

"Our little girl has been sick with tonsil problems and the doctors don't want to take them out quite yet," McDonald said. "Also, we're going to have another baby in January and Ardelle gets very, very tired. Because of training camp and the heavy travel in the pre-season games, she stayed with her folks in the Hat.

"I had permission to fly out Sunday morning to see them but my flight was delayed in Toronto and I missed the connection to the little airline that flies to Medicine Hat from Calgary. I had to rent a car and drive the 170 miles. But

it was good to see them. My little girl stuck to me like glue all the time I was there.

"We're moving into a new house in Toronto in early December so it's going to be a little hectic with the new baby and everything."

McDonald is an Alberta native, from the small farming community of Craigmyle in the northern part of the province. He needed 32 tickets to the game against the Olympic team because a large contingent of friends and relatives are making the trip to Calgary for the game.

The match against the Olympic team, a group of college players, is one the Leaf management didn't want to play. But the commitment to play it was made before Punch Imlach was hired.

The fans in Calgary, many of them Leaf supporters because of television, were upset because the Toronto team didn't bring Mike Palmateer, Borje Salming, Ian Turnbull (who's bothered by a back injury), Darryl Sittler, and Ron Ellis for the game. The team was booed loudly much of the evening because of the deletions from the line-up, and the way they played didn't help.

The Olympic team opened camp in early August, played in a tournament in Czechoslovakia, then built a good record in exhibitions against NHL clubs. The team's assets are abundant speed and discipline.

The Leafs played a chippy, sometimes silly, game against them, delivering a few cheap-shot fouls. They did take a 3-0 lead early in the game but wound up losing, 6-5, despite a fine three-goal performance by McDonald.

The Olympic team's quickness had exposed some Leaf flaws, especially when the club didn't have all its big shooters in the line-up. The lack of overall speed was the main one.

"There are some holes in our team, aren't there?" said Floyd Smith, who was looking slightly down as he walked around the bus after the game, waiting for the players to board.

"I'm glad I came out for this game," Imlach said. "I found out a few things I needed to know. At least, I had them confirmed for me in that game."

Imlach wouldn't elaborate on his discoveries.

Tuesday, October 2
DAY SEVENTEEN
Perhaps the biggest disappointment to the Leafs in the 1970s was the failure

of Bob Neely to develop into a competent, consistent NHL player.

The Leafs claimed him in the first round of the 1973 amateur draft – a crop that yielded Lanny McDonald and Ian Turnbull. Neely was a big junior hockey star with the Peterborough Petes, where he was coached by Roger Neilson; he was a swift defenceman who played tough, physical hockey.

But despite large numbers of chances to click with the Leafs, Neely never was able to make the step through to front-line status. The aggressiveness he displayed in junior hockey never surfaced in the NHL. But Neely had great physical talent. Few men his size (6-feet-1, 220 pounds) could move with his speed and agility.

Red Kelly gave Neely plenty of chances to make it in his four years with the team. Roger Neilson tried to draw performances from him that resembled his junior play but failed. The Leafs even sent him to the player-poor Colorado Rockies for part of a season but they cut Neely adrift.

Neely spent the '78-79 season with New Brunswick Hawks of the American League. He was the best defenceman in the AHL in the first half of the season, according to Hawks' coach Eddie Johnston, but when the Leafs never recalled him in injury emergencies, Neely's play suffered.

Because the Leafs are obligated to pay him on a long-term contract, Neely tried again this season. He was dropped back to the New Brunswick roster during camp but the Leafs used him in games at Chicago and Calgary.

On this day, big, gentle, sad-eyed Bob Neely was returned to New Brunswick on a permanent basis. The Leafs reduced their roster to 24 bodies and, accompanying Neely to Moncton were centre Bruce Boudreau and winger Reggie Thomas.

The axe also fell on veteran defenceman Jim Dorey. He returned to his home in Kingston, his future up in the air.

"I only promised Dorey that I'd give him a chance and he had his tryout," Punch Imlach said. "He wasn't going to help the team."

The Leafs had picked up Thomas from Edmonton Oilers and the solid little forward played well in camp and the exhibition games. Thomas had played for Floyd Smith with Cincinnati Stingers in the World Hockey Association in '78-79.

"He gives us a good back-up player who we can call up if we have some injuries," Smith said.

When the Leafs returned from Calgary, they worked out for an hour and Smith outlined some basic systems he wanted the team to use this season, especially in moving the puck out of their own zone.

"Because of all the exhibition games, we haven't had any time to work on specifics," Smith said. "Now that we have the roster down to 24 players, we'll be getting our systems going in practices."

Wednesday, October 3
DAY EIGHTEEN
Just before some rather severe despondency set in with the Leafs' administration over the team's ordinary work in the pre-season matches, the Leafs produced a calibre of all-round performance for which Punch Imlach and Floyd Smith had been waiting all fall.

The Leafs belted Chicago Black Hawks 5-0, with a splendid display of efficiency in all areas. Granted, the Hawks aren't a top rated team but they've been trouble for the Leafs in the past couple of seasons.

Mark Kirton, Laurie Boschman, Lanny McDonald, Rocky Saganiuk, and John Anderson had the Leaf goals.

"The best thing about the win was the fact that we got some goals from the players who have to produce for us to have much success this year," Imlach said. "We need goals from young players like Kirton, Boschman, Saganiuk, and Anderson to help out our big shooters. It was a very encouraging evening for us."

"What I liked about it was that we didn't allow them to get settled in our end of the rink," Smith said. "Much of the time, we went at them pretty well in their zone and we didn't allow them to keep on any pressure in our zone.

"Yesterday, we worked a little bit on some system of play, especially in moving the puck out of our zone. Well, the players executed that system very well.

"We've taken a look at a great many players in our camp but now that we're getting the roster down to a workable size, with more of a set line-up, it's good to see some cohesion developing with the team."

The steady improvement of Boschman was another bright spot for the Leafs. Boschman was awarded the first star in this match, counting a goal

and setting up Anderson for his.

"I think I'm gaining a little more confidence, especially in my ability to do things against NHL players, and it's making it easier," Boschman said.

Mike Palmateer, who has done very little incorrectly in the pre-season, earned the shutout, although he had five minutes and 38 seconds of surprise relief from Jiri Crha late in the second period. The rather comical mix-up was produced by Crha's lack of understanding of the English language.

Palmateer had skated to the bench to allow an extra attacker to go on the ice while the referee was calling a delayed penalty to the Hawks. As Palmateer reached the bench, he saw Crha standing up with his mask and gloves on, ready to play.

"I asked him if he was going in and he said yes," Palmateer said. "I thought it was a bit unusual because I was supposed to play the entire game, but I took a seat and Crha went in."

Smith was a trifle surprised by the switch.

"It was a case of George [Crha] not understanding because I told him that Mike was going all the way," Smith said. "George isn't too familiar with the rules over here and when he saw Palmateer skating flat-out for the bench, he just assumed that it was for a goalie change."

Crha stopped only one shot in his stint, then Palmateer returned for the third period and continued on to his shutout.

Thursday, October 4
DAY NINETEEN
Throughout the three weeks of the Leafs' pre-season schedule, the weather in Toronto was magnificent, warm and sunny, more suggestive of golf than hockey.

Floyd Smith had promised the troops an off-day to stage a club golf tournament at the tough National Golf club in suburban Woodbridge, and the entire team showed up at the course – at the same time as the rain arrived. A dozen players slogged through the wet to play nine holes before heading for home.

Rocky Saganiuk was one Leaf eager to play golf.

"Incredible, isn't it?" Saganiuk said. "Great weather all through camp when we can't play golf, and a flood when we can. Just the same, it's good to get a day off the skates. It's been a tough grind."

Saganiuk was leading the Leafs in goals with five at this point of the exhibition schedule. He's a peppy, hard-driving kid who makes things happen on the ice.

He's one Leaf player who wasn't disturbed by the coaching change from Roger Neilson to Floyd Smith.

"Look, I have nothing but great respect for Roger's coaching ability and I learned a great deal from him in the time I was with the Leafs last season," Saganiuk said.

"But when I heard that Floyd was going to be the coach, I felt I'd have an easier time proving myself with Smith because he wants to stress offence this season. Goal scoring is my strong point and Roger wanted me to put more emphasis on defence.

"I know I had to improve defensively and I think I did last season with New Brunswick. I learned how to play much more strongly in my team's end of the rink.

"Sure, I'm happy to have the goals I've got so far but I've been missing too many chances. I want to score 30 goals this season and if I'm going to get that many, I just can't miss as many good chances as I've botched up this fall."

While the Leafs were on an off-day, Punch Imlach was on the telephone trying to drum up some deals. He conceded that he was interested in free agent Garry Unger, who wanted to escape from the St. Louis Blues. Several NHL clubs wanted Unger but were unable to work out a trade with Blues for him.

Unger was free to sign with any team but that team had to compensate the Blues for his services, and that compensation would be settled by binding arbitration unless a previous agreement was reached between the two teams.

"I'm always interested in adding a good hockey player and I suppose that guy in St. Louis [Unger] qualifies as a good player," Imlach said.

"I'd never sign any free agent unless the compensation was worked out before we signed him. I'd never, under any circumstances, risk arbitration. The costs could be just far too high."

Friday, October 5
DAY TWENTY
The Maple Leafs flew west to play their first ever game against a club from the old World Hockey Association, Edmonton Oilers, one of the four survi-

Okay, Palmateer's here, so bring on the shooters! *(Jerry Hobbs)*

vors that joined the NHL this season. Leaf owner Harold Ballard was the NHL's leading opponent to any accommodation with the WHA.

And because of Ballard's opposition to their entry into the NHL, the Oilers' administration feels the team has some modest ambitions this season: "Our fans want to see us beat the Leafs every time we play them," said Oiler general manager Larry Gordon. "Because Mr. Ballard opposed our league and team so strongly, our fans don't like him or his team very much."

The Edmonton fans certainly turned out in large numbers to see the Oilers play the Leafs. Exhibition games weren't part of the Edmonton club's season ticket package but a capacity crowd of 15,415 fans was on hand for the game.

They didn't get their wish. The Leafs won the game 7-6, as the Toronto club enjoyed its finest offensive game of the pre-season.

"It was good to score seven goals, not so good to give up six, even though two of those Edmonton scores came late in the game," Floyd Smith said.

"But overall, the best part was the fact that our power-play produced

three goals. We've been concerned about it in the pre-season but maybe we're starting to click. Not having Ian Turnbull to play the point in many games, because of his back injury, has hurt."

The Leafs discovered something they've known all along – when their big guns, Darryl Sittler and Lanny McDonald, are cookin', the club is trouble for anyone. Sittler scored a goal and assisted on three more; McDonald scored three times. Laurie Boschman, Paul Gardner, and Joel Quenneville had the others.

Earlier in the camp, a few Leaf observers expressed concern over Sittler's lack of his accustomed snap. He was coming off an ordinary year – 87 points is superb for most players, ordinary for Sittler – a season when he fought some minor illnesses and a knee injury.

But as the camp progressed, the Leaf captain slowly rounded into form and appeared ready for another big season.

The Leafs had their first look at 18-year-old Wayne Gretzky, the Oilers' awesomely talented young centre, and they had to be impressed. Gretzky was credited with only two assists but his clever work led to five goals by his wingers, three by B.J. MacDonald and two by Brent Callighen.

Saturday, October 6
DAY TWENTY-ONE
The date of November 17, 1976, really wasn't a big one in hockey history except to the Maple Leafs. That night, goalie Mike Palmateer, playing his fifth NHL game, blanked Montreal Canadiens 1-0, at Maple Leaf Gardens.

Since then, the Leafs have played the Canadiens 25 times in pre-season, regular schedule, and playoff matches without earning a victory. The Canadiens have been the monkey on the Leafs' back, the club the Leafs want to defeat more than any other. In the past two playoffs, the Canadiens have swept the Leafs aside in two four-game series.

Conditions for the Leafs heading into their second meeting of the pre-season against the Montrealers weren't exactly ideal: after their game the previous evening in Edmonton, the Leafs caught the "red-eye" flight home to Toronto, a little over-night delight which arrives in Ontario at 7.00 a.m.

"It was 8.15 when I got to my house," Lanny McDonald said. "But I was up at noon, watched the baseball playoff game, and came to the rink. My old legs didn't have much life in them but, fortunately, I found a little."

In their earlier meeting with the Canadiens, the Leafs built a 3-0 lead in the game's first half with Palmateer in goal, then lost 5-3 after young Vincent Tremblay took over the net.

This time, Palmateer went all the way and the result was a landmark of sort in the Leafs' pre-season: a convincing 3-1 victory over the Stanley Cup champs. Palmateer needed to be brilliant as the Canadiens held a 29-24 edge in shots on goal.

Ron Ellis, McDonald, and Tiger Williams scored the Leaf goals.

"That win was tremendously important for this team for several reasons," McDonald said. "The Canadiens are the champs, the big number one club,

so beating them under any circumstances shows us that we have the potential to do something when we play intelligent hockey.

"Also, we haven't beaten them for so long that it was getting a little bit frustrating to the guys who have been around for a few years. It really was a sweet night, especially when we had to reach down for a little extra after that flight home."

But problems with the team's power-play continued. Canadiens' Mario Tremblay drew a major penalty for high-sticking Leafs' Dave Burrows in the first period and the Leafs couldn't score with the advantage.

"But our penalty-killing was good," Floyd Smith said. "We had three consecutive penalties in the third period and they couldn't score a goal. Also the fact that we gave them a 1-0 lead, then came back with three goals to win it was a good sign. Things are looking up around here."

Sunday, October 7
DAY TWENTY-TWO
There's really only one point to the absurd grind of training camp and pre-season games to which the NHL subjects its teams: the chance to make some money from a heavy exhibition schedule.

The Leaf training camp allowed five days of scrimmages, then a dozen pre-season games in 16 days. There were few times for Floyd Smith and Dick Duff to work on systems for their team to employ, and less chance for individual instruction on the players' weak points.

"If there's any way we can cut back to nine or ten games next season, we're going to try to do it," Punch Imlach said. "The players' association limits us to the amount of time we can devote to camp and it's too short. The two trips west [to Calgary and Edmonton] were arranged before I got here and we won't do that again."

For the Leafs, however, the training camp and exhibition games have been a time of familiarization with Smith, Duff and Imlach. Smith's low-key approach, his easy-going manner throughout the pre-season, has won most of the players into his corner.

"We're a loose team," Rocky Saganiuk said. "Smitty's a guy who seems to try to keep the pressure off as much as possible. Sure, he'll have to tighten the screws a little when the season starts for serious, but so far the

guys have enjoyed playing for him."

The Leafs finished their pre-season schedule on the up-beat, wrapping up the 12-game ordeal with a 4-2 win over Buffalo Sabres, their fourth consecutive triumph. They had six wins, four losses and a tie in 11 games against NHL foes plus, of course, a loss to the Canadian Olympic team.

The statistics of the Buffalo game indicated that the Sabres should have blown the Leafs out of Memorial Auditorium. The "official" shots on goal were 37-14 in favour of the Sabres but one of the longest-running NHL jokes is the low total of shots awarded visiting teams in Buffalo. The Leafs' own count showed they had 29 shots.

The Leafs received a superb goal-tending job from Paul Harrison, who has had an excellent pre-season except for his one appearance against the Sabres in Toronto. Harrison's work, plus the fact that Palmateer played the equivalent of four full games in pre-season and surrendered only five goals, guarantee that goaltending won't be a Leaf problem.

Another encouraging sign was the strong work of defenceman Dave Burrows. The Leafs paid a high price for Burrows prior to the '78-79 season when they dealt centre George Ferguson and promising young backliner Randy Carlyle to Pittsburgh Penguins for him.

Six games into his first Leaf season Burrows sustained a knee injury, missed 17 games and never really regained top form. He had a slow start in the exhibition games but in the final week of play he was the solid, efficient veteran Leafs needed.

After the win over Sabres, Smith said that the team planned to make no cuts before the season's opener three days away against the New York Rangers. They had 24 players, including the injured Ron Wilson and third goalie Jiri Crha, on the roster.

The showing of three youngsters – Laurie Boschman, Mark Kirton, and Gret Hotham – had earned them a look under fire during the regular schedule.

"The best part of the camp was the players' attitude; it was extremely positive towards the things we tried to do," Smith said.

"The effort was there, too, and it's going to be there during the season. Sure, we could strengthen at a few spots, but we're going to be heard from this season."

A Game of Individuals

John Gault and George Horhota

Sittler, Salming, and McDonald, the Leaf representatives on the NHL all-star team for the 1979 Challenge Cup (*Toronto Star*)

John Anderson

HEIGHT: 5'11" **WEIGHT:** 195 lbs **BIRTH:** 28 March 1957 **HOME TOWN:** Toronto, Ont.

MARITAL STATUS: single **PETS:** Abby, Ritchie (dogs)

Why did you become a hockey player? "My dad played and at first it was more of a fun thing. When I was 16 or 17, I saw the chances of becoming a player were better, especially when the new league was opened. Aside from money, being a professional hockey player is what everyone thinks of when they're young."

What would you have been if you did not turn pro? "I probably would have been in something to do with sports; I love participating in sports. I just like to play."

Sports celebrity pro and con: "I like the hours; it's not a nine-to-five job. You have the summers off to do what you want and, of course, the money isn't bad. You can make a lot when you're young and it gives you quite a few more opportunities; I could never have opened my hamburger business if I hadn't played hockey. It's getting to the point where a lot more people recognize me. It's unbelievable when I'm in a store and people follow me; they're not really sure if I'm the right person. Although it gets a bit tedious sometimes, it's when they don't recognize you that you're in trouble."

Lifestyle: "I like getting away in the summer. I like to dance, but I'm not an addict. I have no trouble spending my money."

Favourite people in hockey: "I like Sittler. Sittler, Lanny, Borje, and Turnbull are kind of my idols, the guys I'd like to be like. They're leaders by their actions, especially Darryl, who I kind of watch in awe."

Favourite and least favourite opponents: "No, I don't have any favourite opponents because, actually, I always think that I'm better than the guy I'm playing against. If I don't take that attitude, I become in awe of the person and then he'll take advantage of me. I'm out there to beat them."

Are you superstitious as a hockey player? "Sometimes I have superstitions. Last year I took my helmet off just to score a goal; I scored two and so I left it off for a couple of games. But a girl who did my horoscope said I'd get banged on my head if I didn't put it back on. It scared me, so I put my helmet on. I don't lace my skates in the same way or anything like that."

Activities before and after games: "If I'm feeling really tired I won't go to a pre-game skate; but I usually go and try to get back as soon as I can to get into bed again for a couple of hours. I usually cook spaghetti because it's fast, but if there are a couple of steaks in the freezer I'll have them; I'm indifferent to what I eat on a game day. I leave my place around 4.30, and usually play ping-pong before the game. After a game, if I'm really tired, I'll just come straight home and watch Saturday Night Live (if it's Saturday.) If I feel good, my girlfriend and I will go out for a drink at Jingles or Grapes."

Favourite books, films, TV, music: "I don't read at all; I've tried to read books but I just can't get past the first 20 pages. I love going to movies though; I'm a big Pink Panther fan – Peter Sellers can do dialogue so well. I really liked Prisoner of Zenda. I like to watch Saturday Night Live and movies on TV. Mork and Mindy is a good laugh and I love Star Trek. I love the Eagles, but I don't listen to country. We get a pass to the Gardens and I like to stand right in front of the stage; I saw Steve Martin, the Bee Gees, and Village People there."

Personal goals for the 1979-80 season and future in hockey: "I'd like to have a regular shift on the team – that's the main thing – and I'd like to score at least 30 goals. I think that's a reasonable figure right now. I want to say that I spent my whole career with one team, so I'd like to stay with the Leafs. I don't really see awards like the Hockey Hall of Fame as a goal; if that comes then it comes. I just like to be well-known."

Considering that he's only been a pro for two seasons, John Anderson has, at least objectively, done pretty well for himself. But not as well, and not as quickly, as the impatient young right winger with the lightning speed and the accurate shot had hoped for as the 1979-80 season began. In fact, as the 1978-79 hockey year drew to a close, he wearily told the Toronto Sun's John Iaboni: "It's been a long season. You think you're going well and then you run into some rough spots. I was starting to go well with seven goals in eight games at one point, then I sat on the bench for a while. It's tough not to get down sometimes."

Those seven goals represented just under half of his total for last year – 15, to be exact – as a part-time player in 71 Leaf games. But the fact that he stayed with the big team, under a system that encouraged defence and discouraged freewheeling and risk-taking says something about the regard in which he was held by Roger Neilson. Under the new and current regime, Anderson figures pretty heavily in the scheme of things. Floyd Smith, seeing him for the first time at training camp, was as impressed as most people are by the speed, and pleasantly surprised by Anderson's size. "It looks to me," Smith allowed, "that he's got all the tools to play in the NHL." For the Leafs? "For the Leafs."

Anderson, a local boy, was the team's first draft pick in 1977 after coming off three years with the Marlies in which he averaged just over 2.2 points per game and played on two Memorial Cup winners. In 1977 he joined the St. Catharines Junior All-Stars for the world junior hockey tournament in Czechoslovakia and scored 10 goals in seven games.

Anderson started the 1977-78 season for the Leafs, but he wasn't, in Neilson's opinion, ready for the NHL. In only 52 games with the Dallas Black Hawks he had 22 goals and 23 assists and then, in the playoffs, went on to set a Central Hockey League scoring record of 11 goals in Adams Cup play. He also added eight assists in those 13 games.

Unless a lot of people, including two very different coaches and two very different general managers, are wrong, there is some reason to believe that John Anderson is a "Leaf of the future" – unless, of course, this season is proving that for Anderson, the future has arrived.

(Robert Shaver)

Laurie Boschman

HEIGHT:	WEIGHT:	BIRTH:	HOME TOWN:	PETS:
6'0"	185 lbs	4 June 1960	Major, Sask.	Dutchess (German Shepherd)

MARITAL STATUS:
single

Why did you become a hockey player? "When I was young I got some equipment and just started playing hockey, so I don't really know what got me into it. It was just for the fun of it when I was a little kid. I got to become a little better at it so I just started to work at it. My dad brought some equipment home and I just started playing."

What would you have been if you did not turn pro? "I never really thought about doing anything else. Since I was 14 or 15 I started thinking that maybe I could play professional hockey. I wouldn't know what else I would do."

Sports celebrity pro and con: "All I'm thinking is that I'd like to be good at the game; I haven't really thought about the celebrity status. All I'm looking for now is to do well and make this team."

Lifestyle: "I like to do lots of things; I don't like to sit at home and just watch TV or whatever, I like to see everything. I'm more low-keyed than anything though. George Bigliardi's on Church Street is one of my favourite restaurants in Toronto, although I haven't been here that long."

Favourite people in hockey: "All the guys on the team have been just great with me. When I was coming up through hockey, I always watched Phil Esposito and Bobby Orr. Right now, I'd say the guys on this team are a great bunch. I respect them all."

Favourite and least favourite opponents: "It was a big thrill for me to play Montreal. Of course, Lafleur has done a lot in hockey and you just kind of keep your eye on him, watch what he does. Any least favourite players? Oh, not yet."

Are you superstitious as a hockey player? "I am superstitious but it's not so much the things I do at the rink or at home. If I'm having success with a certain thing, I'll try and keep doing it the same way."

Activities before and after games: "I just eat an early meal, 1.00 o'clock or so. I'll have steak or spaghetti but it just depends on what I feel like that day. After the practice, I go home and relax, watch TV for a while and get some rest before the game. I usually get up three hours before the game and walk around to wake myself up. I come down to the rink about 6.00 o'clock. Once there, I like to get the sticks ready, watch a little TV, play some ping-pong and just relax. After, I want to unwind. It takes a little while to get to sleep."

Favourite books, films, TV, music: "I like to go to movies once in a while. I watch a bit of television – mostly sporting events though. Rock, disco . . . I like it all. I've got a stereo so I enjoy my music. I don't read books but I do like magazines, *Sports Illustrated* and such."

Personal goals for the 1979-80 season and future in hockey: "I do have goals but I'd like to keep them to myself. I'd like to play well. I think I'll have a better indication of what I want to accomplish after a little more time."

When a great centre like Darryl Sittler can favourably compare a 19-year-old rookie centre with another great centre named Bryan Trottier, that says a great deal about the kid's future (or even present) in the NHL.

Perhaps the most exciting thing to happen to the Leafs this year – excepting perhaps, the return of Punch Imlach – was the signing of 19-year-old Laurie Boschman to a four-year contract, estimated to be worth between $350,000 and $375,000. "He has the makings of a superstar," enthused Imlach, after the Leafs managed to get the player they most wanted in the first round of the entry draft. "We feel very fortunate to get him. We didn't think he'd be around when we picked [ninth], we thought he'd go higher than that. He was the best centreman in the draft and we feel he can make the club this season."

Last year Boschman was on the highest-scoring line in junior hockey. He had 66 goals and 83 assists for the Brandon Wheat Kings, while his left winger, Brian Propp, had 94 goals and 100 assists and his right winger, Ray Allison, scored 60 times and added 93 assists. They were also first draft choices, of the Philadelphia Flyers and the Hartford Whalers respectively.

Boschman was as happy to be a Leaf as the Leafs were to have him. "Toronto has always been my favourite team, and I especially admire Darryl Sittler . . . It's just a sensational thrill."

With a year of junior eligibility left, and with the possibility of playing for the Canadian National Team, with which he'd trained three weeks before coming to the Leaf camp, Boschman retained a number of options. The Leafs wanted him so badly that they took the chance of drafting him under-age, meaning they couldn't send him to the minors without first offering him back to Brandon; but Boschman, obviously, was well worth that chance.

It's probably worth noting that Boschman also came with a reputation for getting penalties. His 149 points might have been considerably increased were it not for the 215 minutes he spent in the penalty box. "I've had a few fights," he allowed. "This is an aggressive league." And: "I like to play aggressively. I don't back down, but I don't like shooting my mouth off, either."

(Robert Shaver)

Pat Boutette

HEIGHT:	WEIGHT:	BIRTH:	HOME TOWN:	PETS:
5'8"	180 lbs	1 March 1952	Windsor, Ont.	none

MARITAL STATUS:
single

Why did you become a hockey player? "I've played hockey since I was five years old; it's probably everyone's ambition to be a player when they're young. You watch Hockey Night in Canada and you see the stars that you want to be like. I was just lucky enough to get a few breaks down the line."

What would you have been if you did not turn pro? "I went to university for three years but I didn't have anything else in mind."

Sports celebrity pro and con: "Toronto's a great city to play in, and I like the travelling and the company of the guys. I just enjoy playing hockey, it's a great living. I try to give as much attention to the kids as I can – sign autographs and that because I know I was young once. The worst thing you can do is be snobby. But at times it's kind of a pain, because people don't leave you alone. You can't go anywhere to relax and be yourself. People are always asking for autographs in restaurants, which is part of the game, I guess, but it's nice to have some peace."

Lifestyle: "I try to live like everybody else. I don't try to overdo it; I'm not a real high-liver. I enjoy certain things in life but I don't go overboard. Being active all the time is what I enjoy."

Favourite people in hockey: "We've got the type of team where everybody respects each other; it's a good team atmosphere. When I was younger, Bobby Hull was my idol. I also liked the whole Maple Leaf team."

Favourite and least favourite opponents: "It doesn't really matter who you play against; you've got to do the same job. Some players are a little better than others. You enjoy playing Montreal because they're the better team. But it doesn't really matter who you play because you end up playing each game the same way."

Are you superstitious as a hockey player? "If you do something the day of the game and have a good night, maybe the next game you'll go through the same routines – the time you eat, what you eat, when you get down to the rink. In hockey, you get into a certain pattern of doing things. Staying to that pattern is a way to keep your mind off of the game."

Activities before and after games: "I usually get up around 8.30 and have a skate down at the Gardens and fix my sticks. I'll go out and eat around 12.30 or 1.00, usually fish or spaghetti, stuff with lots of carbos. I'll then go home and lie down for an hour and after either read or watch TV, then come down to the rink around 5.30. Sometimes I'll play ping-pong in the dressing room or watch TV and read my mail, just relax. After a game, we'll go out somewhere, four or five guys. Depending on how tough the game was, it's usually hard to get to sleep."

Favourite books, films, TV, music: "I'm not much of a TV or movie man. I'll watch TV maybe an hour a day or three hours a week, usually to see sports like golf. I read quite a few books on the road because we travel so much. You have to have something to do on the planes and at the airports so I read quite a few novels. But I'll read anything. I'm not too much into music; I don't have any favourite singers so I won't go out and buy a certain album. I guess most of my recreation consists of sports."

Personal goals for the 1979-80 season and future in hockey: "I'd like to get 20 goals and play a little more offence, and to have the team scoring a little more. Last year we were strictly a defensive-type line. The big thing you hope for is to win the Stanley Cup: that's our major goal for the whole team. Yeah, the ultimate goal is the Stanley Cup."

Frank Orr of the *Toronto Star* once wrote of little Pat Boutette that his approach to hockey "creates the impression that he's really six-foot-three and weighs 210 pounds." Orr's partner in hockey coverage, Jim Kernaghan, expanded on that, writing: "There are two approaches open to the small man in hockey. One is to be quick and skilled, like Marcel Dionne or Dave Keon. The other is to play tough, aggressive hockey and never, never back down. That is Boutette's style . . . He doesn't tip-toe into the corners, he arrives more like a bowling ball."

At 175 pounds and five-feet, eight-inches, Boutette is the smallest Leaf overall, but it is interesting to note that only three other Leafs, Maloney, Williams, and Hutchison – all known to be among the ten toughest players in the NHL – had more penalty minutes last season. Boutette had 136 to go with his 14 goals and 19 assists. He is, in fact, terribly consistent as a scorer and penalty-getter, averaging 35 points and 124 minutes over four full Leaf seasons.

Boutette's evaluation of size in hockey is worth repeating. "It's simple," he says. "Back down once when you're fighting for space and you'll be backing down forever. That has nothing to do with size. If a player – five-feet-six or six-feet-five – doesn't challenge for a piece of the ice, word gets around that he has the brakes on." And, he adds: "Size doesn't mean much if you're afraid of the corners. I've always played an aggressive game, and I think I'm respected for it. It's necessary that opponents know that if they go into corners, you'll show up."

Boutette, despite his obvious tendency toward scrappiness, is no dead-end kid. He is, rather, one of the still-small new breed who went to university: after a year of junior in London, Ontario, he went on scholarship to the University of Minnesota, completed three years of studies (he plans to finish one day) and made All-America (second team) in his final season. He was the Leafs' ninth draft choice in 1972, and he had two fine years in Oklahoma City of the Central Hockey League before coming up to stay.

Some people have compared him with Dick Duff and, with all deference to the new Leaf assistant coach, the comparison seems far from inappropriate.

(Robert Shaver)

Dave Burrows

HEIGHT: 6'1½" **WEIGHT:** 190 lbs **BIRTH:** 11 Jan. 1949 **HOMETOWN:** Toronto, Ont. **PETS:** Bernie (a "great mutt")

MARITAL STATUS: married **WIFE AND CHILDREN:** Carol; sons Bret and Wade

Why did you become a hockey player? "I just really enjoyed hockey as a kid. It came fairly easy for me and when you're good at something, you really get into it. After that, it was just one team after another."

What would you have been if you did not turn pro? "I really don't know what other line of work I'd like to do but it would have to have something to do with the outdoors since I enjoy outdoor activities. But other than hockey, I don't really know what I'd like to do."

Sports celebrity pro and con: "Fame isn't a big thing with me; I can see how it would be with Sittler or Mac or the guys who are the stars. I enjoy the winning part of the game, how you feel after you win or when you've done a good job. That to me is the whole idea of sport – when you really feel like you've accomplished something. Naturally, when things aren't going good, especially in Toronto where hockey is the thing, you're going to hear a lot [from the fans]. But that's part of the game."

Lifestyle: "I have a home that's out in the country. I really enjoy being by myself, keeping my family life private. I like the open-air atmosphere so I don't enjoy being in cities. You're running around all winter catching planes and buses here and there and it's kind of hectic."

Favourite people in hockey: "I admire a lot of guys on this team for different things. You have to admire Dan Maloney's determination, Sittler's leadership abilities, Mackey's [McDonald's] shot, Borje's skating ability, Palmy's acrobatics, and so on. Danny Maloney and I went on a couple of fishing trips together so we enjoy doing the same type of things. I always admired Timmy Horton as a player when I was a kid and I really cherished the fact that the first year that I played, it was on the same team with him."

Favourite and least favourite opponents: "If you're talking about their skill, you don't really look forward to playing against them [opponents] because sometimes they can make you look pretty foolish. You've got to admire Guy Lafleur, or the way Perreault handles the puck – again, different guys for different reasons."

Are you superstitious as a hockey player? "Yeah, I'm superstitious. I put on my left shin pad before the right but it's more of a habit than superstition; you just seem to always do it a certain way. In Pittsburgh, I used to always be the third last guy out of the dressing room."

Activities before and after games: "I don't sleep in like a lot of guys do. I'll get up early, have a good breakfast and come down to the rink for a light skate. I'll eat at 1.30 or 2.00 and lay down for a couple of hours. I used to always have steak for lunch but now I'll eat almost anything, whatever I feel like. I'm one of the first guys in the dressing room. I feel more comfortable once I get my suit off so I can sit down before the game and relax, read the paper and get my sticks ready. I don't like to be rushed. After, I'll go out for a bite to eat and a couple of drinks. Le Baron and Jingles are my favourite spots. I've got a long drive home so I don't stay too late."

Favourite books, films, TV, music: "I'm starting to read more now than I ever have before. I really like hunting and fishing so I'll mainly read about that because I don't get the chance to hunt in the fall. I don't go to very many movies but I watch quite a bit of TV: Mork and Mindy for a laugh, and the outdoor shows like fishing. I also like the football games. I've got a wide variety of records. I was once really into rock but now I'm listening to more country like Waylon Jennings and Willie Nelson."

Personal goals for the 1979-80 season and future in hockey: "I've never really set any personal goals; my game is defensive, so it's hard to set goals. If you get into the playoffs and say to yourself that you've tried your hardest and things work out pretty good for you, then it's satisfying. I'd sure like to get a Stanley Cup ring; that's what we're all in here for."

In the six years that Dave Burrows spent with the Pittsburgh Penguins, before coming over to the Leafs for George Ferguson and Randy Carlyle at the start of the 1978-79 season, he developed into something of a living legend. Ken Carson, the former Penguin trainer who switched to baseball and the Toronto Blue Jays, told the *Star*'s Jim Proudfoot about it: nobody ever got around Dave Burrows.

"I remember one incident in a Montreal game," Carson said, "when Yvan Cournoyer got past him. It was a major event, something that hardly ever happened. The guys on the bench were looking at each other like they'd seen a flying saucer."

Burrows, as self-effacing as he is good, told Proudfoot about the incident too: "He just squished loose when I thought I had him. He didn't score, but I was still embarrassed. But there was more than one occasion when the guy got away when it was just me against him. That story's exaggerated, I'm afraid."

A native of Thistletown, which has been swallowed by Etobicoke, Burrows played his junior hockey with St. Catharines, did a minor pro stint from 1969 through 1971 and then became a Penguin mainstay. He brought impeccable credentials to Toronto, including that of clean player. Despite his size and position, the most penalty minutes Burrows ever had in one season was 51. "I enjoy the body contact," he once explained, "but I don't get my stick or my elbows up. There aren't too many times when I'll clobber a person. I have to get really whacked to get mad, and I need to get punched out a couple of times before I go after someone."

Burrows was happy to get back to his home town – he complained that neither the fans nor the writers understood hockey in Pittsburgh – and his home town team was happy to have him. Darryl Sittler, for one, made it known how much nicer it was playing with Burrows than against him: "I've played against him since junior hockey," Sittler said when Burrows arrived in town, "and he's frustrating because he's so efficient. You just don't see him getting beat very often."

Shades of Tim Horton and Carl Brewer? Not surprisingly, they were Burrows' childhood heroes. But heroes are no longer part of his life. "I found," he once said, "that the more I got involved with big names as players, the less they were idols."

(Robert Shaver)

Jerry Butler

HEIGHT:	WEIGHT:	BIRTH:	HOME TOWN:	PETS:
6'0"	180 lbs	27 Feb. 1951	Sarnia, Ont.	none

MARITAL STATUS:	WIFE AND CHILDREN:
married	Lynn; son Robbie

Why did you become a hockey player? "I always wanted to be a hockey player. It takes a lot of breaks and everything along the line to become one. It was just a matter of timing for me that I was drafted from that one year of junior; otherwise I'd have played one year and, if I hadn't made it, then gone back to college."

What would you have been if you did not turn pro? "I probably would have gone through for a physical education teacher."

Sports celebrity pro and con: "I enjoy doing what I do. The recognition isn't a prerequisite or anything; I've played in towns where I'm recognized and in towns where I'm not. I'm not the type of player who's going to demand a lot of public attention. It's not a big deal in my life. I don't get it too much as compared to say, Darryl, and Lanny. But it is a little hectic at times when you go to the rink every morning and the same people are there for autographs."

Lifestyle: "I'm pretty much a homebody. We don't go out that much in the off-season. We use hockey as a means to set up our life for when I'm finished. We're not extravagant but we do enjoy what we have."

Favourite people in hockey: "Playing on these different teams, I've met a lot of great people along the way. I haven't met too many that I could say anything bad about. I don't have any real close friends on Toronto as I had on some of the other teams I've played with. I'm very friendly with Bobby MacMillan who played in Atlanta and Larry Patey in St. Louis. Tiger (Williams) lives just two doors away so I drive in with him all the time."

Favourite and least favourite opponents: "Playing against guys I know, former team mates, makes the game a little more interesting."

Are you superstitious as a hockey player? "Everybody always has their little quirks but I don't put too much into that. I wouldn't wear the same stuff and I don't think there's anything I would do all the time."

Activities before and after games: "I'm usually up around 8.30 a.m. or so. I have coffee or juice and drive down to the rink for a pre-game skate and get the sticks ready. I'm usually home again by 12.00-12.30. I'll have a meal of spaghetti or even sometimes french fries with bread and some Coke but I haven't eaten too much steak in the last couple of years. I'll usually have a two-hour afternoon sleep and go down to the rink about 5.00 p.m. One of the ways I'll get up for the game is by talking to everybody in the dressing room. After, we'll go down to the Strip (Yonge Street) and have a couple of beers with something to eat until 1.00 or so."

Favourite books, films, TV, music: "I've been reading a lot. I've read most of Leon Uris's books and I like mystery novels. We don't really go to a lot of movies but I like the ones you can get a laugh out of. We watch quite a bit of TV in the wintertime. I'll watch the mysteries and the lawyer shows. I enjoy easy-listening music but I don't like to get into the heavy rock."

Personal goals for the 1979-80 season and future in hockey: "I'd love to score 20 goals. That's always been a goal but in the last couple of years it hasn't really been a realistic one at the start because of my being restricted to checking. With Roger [Neilson] gone it's going to be a whole new season. Probably everything's going to be different for me; we won't be checking as much as we have been, I think. I'd like to play as long as I'm able to contribute to the team. Everybody's goal is to win the Stanley Cup so it would be nice to stay in Toronto and win one here."

To know what Jerry Butler is made of, it helps to go back to the playoffs series between the New York Rangers and the Philadelphia Flyers in 1974. Butler, then a Ranger playing for Emile "The Cat" Francis, finished that series on the way to the hospital with a ruptured spleen, and Francis told Jim Coleman of the Southam Press about it:

Butler arrived for the last game of the series, on a Sunday night, in terrible pain; he was actually vomiting, but still insisting he could play. He took his first shift, but then Francis took him off. He went, on his own demand to play, back out in the second. This time Francis benched him for good, but Butler refused to undress; he stayed on to watch his team lose. By Monday night he was under the knife. "He must have been in great pain from Thursday night [the injury came in the second period], but he didn't say a damn word in the dressing room," Francis told Coleman. "He went out and played like a wild man in the third period [Thursday] and he set up our insurance goal with a pass to Ted Irvine. He must have been in great pain, but he kept his own secret. He wanted to play on Sunday, but he just couldn't hack it."

Butler went from the Rangers to St. Louis in 1975, and then on to Toronto early in the 1977-78 season for Inge Hammarstrom, a deal then-coach Roger Neilson described simply as "a checker for a scorer." (Hockey trivia fans take note: Butler played nine games for St. Louis and 73 for the Leafs that year, for a total of 82 – an NHL single-season record.)

Like Dan Maloney, Butler is a defensive hockey player, known for it and proud of it. He is quite candid in admitting that he lacks the scoring touch (he had a couple of 17-goal seasons with the Rangers and they were his best offensive years) but is not too concerned about it.

"I'm satisfied with my role as a checker," he says. "You just do what you're best at. The guys realize what we've done. When we can go out and check a big line and not allow any goals, we have a better chance of winning the game, and that's more where my ability lies. You don't score many goals from the boards."

(Toronto Sun)

Ron Ellis

HEIGHT: 5'9" **WEIGHT:** 184 lbs **BIRTH:** 8 Jan. 1945 **HOME TOWN:** Lindsay, Ont.

MARITAL STATUS: married **WIFE AND CHILDREN:** Jan; daughter, Kitty and son, Ronald Jr.

PETS: Tammy (German shepherd), Twilight, Blondie (horses)

Why did you become a hockey player? "At 19 I had a chance to accept a scholarship or turn pro and Punch Imlach felt I could become a pro. I always wanted to be a pro hockey player when I was young because it looked like a good career, a way that you could become successful quickly; and that was important to me."

What would you have been if you did not turn pro? "I was very interested in Phys. Ed. at school so I think, possibly, I would have done something along that line."

Sports celebrity pro and con: "I'm a very private person. I just like doing my job and I don't expect applause or rewards or notoriety; I don't demand that. The Toronto fans have been great to me and I certainly have no complaints, but there are times when you're out with your family and you do like some privacy; there are places where that's part of the game, like banquets. But let's be honest, it's a very lucrative career too."

Lifestyle: "My lifestyle is very reserved. I spend a lot of time with my family and enjoy going to the ranch for a horseback ride with them as much as going downtown for a meal. We enjoy the outdoors: riding, water-skiing and so on. I've played a lot of years when the salaries were not what they are today, so I have developed a lifestyle that's within my means."

Favourite people in hockey: "I've got a high regard for all the boys on the team, particularly Sittler whom you have to respect for his talent on and off the ice; he'll probably go down as the best captain of all time. McDonald, whom I feel I helped a bit, has turned into one of the top right wingers. Salming has to be respected for his talent."

Favourite and least favourite opponents: "I've played against Howe, Hull, Orr, and Lafleur – the four greatest players. In the old days it was a challenge for me to keep Hull off of the score sheet. Davie Burrows was a fellow I didn't like playing against – he's almost impossible to beat one-on-one so I'm glad he's with me now."

Are you superstitious as a hockey player? "No, I wouldn't consider myself superstitious but I do have systems. After you get yourself into condition, it comes down to a mental struggle. I may do the same things before a game only because they prepare my mind, but I don't do them because I'm superstitious."

Activities before and after games: "Last year, because of the distance I lived away, I wouldn't come in for the morning skate, but I wouldn't sleep in either. I have my game meal around 1.00 (I've gotten away from eating steak). I'm down at the Gardens by about 6.30 to prepare sticks and just relax or stretch; I'm pretty quiet before a game. After, my wife and I usually join the team mates and their wives and go to a little restaurant, usually to Bigliardi's, Gatsby's, or Harry's. I do like to have a substantial meal after a game."

Favourite books, films, TV, music: "I do like to read – real-life stories, biographies, and inspirational books. I'm trying to control watching TV so I'm becoming choosy with what I watch; I like documentaries more than anything. We used to go out and see a lot of movies when we were younger, but now we'll go to about two or three a year."

Personal goals for the 1979-80 season and future in hockey: "This is my fourteenth year with the Leafs and I have reached a lot of the goals which I set for myself. This year, I have a chance to play my 1,000th regular season game; that's a milestone for me. I'd also certainly like to play in another Stanley Cup game. I'm taking it a year at a time now so I have no long-range plans at all."

Leaving aside Ron Ellis, the hockey player, for the moment, let us consider Ron Ellis, the man. To put it succinctly, he is the kind of person anybody would be happy, proud, and even honoured to have for a next-door neighbour. Even those a little wary of born-again Christianity would have no trouble coming to terms with Ron Ellis because the only way he preaches his deep commitment is by living it.

As most people know, Ellis turned his back on a very successful 11-year career with the Leafs in 1975 and, in so doing, he took an era with him: he was the last Leaf to have played on a Stanley Cup winner. That retirement, which meant a considerable sacrifice financially, gave him the time he felt – or knew – he needed to come to terms with his life and the direction in which it was going.

After two years out of the professional game – he played Oldtimer hockey in a league run by his father, Randy Ellis, and with Team Canada in the 1977 world tournament in Vienna – Ellis returned to the Leafs, picking up where he left off. In 1977-78 he had his tenth consecutive 20-goal season (his 11th overall) and last year, while missing 17 games and playing others on a bad knee, he still managed 16 goals. As well he picked up his 600th NHL point. His 318 goals prior to this season made him the top-scoring Leaf right-winger of all time.

But it is as a digger and a checker that Ellis shines, and nowhere was that more in evidence than in that greatest of all hockey contests, the Russia-Canada series of 1972. Henderson's exploits are now legend, but it was Ellis who made a lot of them happen.

Ellis, at 34 when the season began, is the Leafs' elder statesman on the ice, but his commitment to a sound body is as great as it is to a sound mind. He did a summer youth fitness course at York University, losing 15 pounds and adding physical strength in the process, and is currently collaborating on a book about summer training for hockey. Two years ago, when Ellis began his comeback, Jim Coleman, the venerable columnist, spoke for just about every hockey fan, Leaf or otherwise, when he wrote: "Ellis is one of the gentlemen of the professional sports . . . He is the type of man who deserves success in his comeback and, certainly, he has the good wishes of everyone who knows him."

(Robert Shaver)

(Robert Shaver)

(Globe and Mail)

Paul Gardner

HEIGHT: 5'11½" **WEIGHT:** 185 lbs **BIRTH:** 5 March 1956 **HOME TOWN:** Fort Erie, Ont. **PETS:** none

MARITAL STATUS: married **WIFE:** Christine

Why did you become a hockey player? "I guess because I always enjoyed hockey. My dad played and I suppose I followed my brother, seeing that he was enjoying it and doing quite well. I was around 16 or 17 when I saw him go into the pros and I thought maybe I'd like to do that. I love the game and I'm so glad I'm here now."

What would you have been if you did not turn pro? "I don't really know. I thought about it two years ago when I hurt my back. I had thought of being a teacher; I enjoy kids and like working at hockey schools. And I would certainly like to get into the broadcasting area."

Sports celebrity pro and con: "I just love the game. A lot of people don't get to do something they like every day but I love going to work. You meet a lot of great people. I haven't had the problem of people bothering me yet – I suppose I haven't been in Toronto long enough. So far, nothing's really bothered me about being a celebrity."

Lifestyle: "I'm pretty easy going. I enjoy being with people and having a good time. Although hockey has given me a lot more money, I don't think I've really changed my lifestyle. I enjoy clothes and I like cars. I drive a 1976 Thunderbird. I love to eat out with my wife: Chinese food at Lichee Gardens is our favourite."

Favourite people in hockey: "On the Toronto team, I've enjoyed everybody. Rocky Saganiuk and I have done a little together because we came up at the same time. Ron Wilson and I get along too and Ian Turnbull and I have a lot of fun together. Mike Kitchen of the Colorado Rockies might be my closest friend because we broke in together."

Favourite and least favourite opponents: "When I was in Colorado, I used to always enjoy playing opposite Mike Palmateer but I used to regret playing against Tiger Williams; he used to bother me now and then, but that was just his game. I haven't run into anybody I really dislike."

Are you superstitious as a hockey player? "Yeah, I'm very superstitious. If something goes well I'll try and remember which way I dressed and do it the same way next time. I always hit Dave Burrows on the leg before I go out on the ice. After periods I like to be last off, and between periods I always take my sweater off."

Activities before and after games: "I like to skate in the mornings of a game day and shoot a lot of pucks. I used to always eat something heavy like a steak and potatoes before a game and follow it up with a nap. I usually get to the rink early and fool around; I like a fun dressing room where the guys are making jokes. That relaxes me. Playing ping-pong gets my reflexes going and I do that in the dressing room. After games, usually my wife and I will go out with some friends to cool down. I don't eat too much after – although I'm hungry – to keep my weight down. I have a tough time sleeping though; it's usually 3.00 or 4.00 in the morning before I can wind down to sleep."

Favourite books, films, TV, music: "I don't read enough but any sports that come on TV I'll see; Monday Night Baseball I'll never miss. I'm a fanatic on Bill Cosby, I have all of his albums. Sometimes I'll be eating my pre-game meal and put on one of his albums to loosen up."

Personal goals for the 1979-80 season and future in hockey: "I'd like to be a Maple Leaf for a long time if I can. I've scored 30 goals in my first three years and I'd like to repeat that but I don't want to start putting pressure on myself that I'm going to score 40 or 50. If I can just contribute to the Maple Leafs in any way Floyd Smith asks, I'm going to try and do that. I'd like to play my whole career here in Toronto; the people have been tremendous. I'd like to play until I'm 30 or so and then maybe get into the broadcasting field."

Paul Gardner didn't go directly from junior hockey to the NHL but few people have come much closer. A first draft pick of the Kansas City Scouts (soon to become the Colorado Rockies) in 1976, the former Oshawa Generals star played only 14 minor pro games before being called up. That night he scored a second period goal as the lowly Scouts tied the mighty Canadiens in Montreal. Then he scored two more goals in Boston and by the time his trial period expired, he had five goals in five games and was with the NHL team to stay.

He scored 30 goals that season, and did precisely the same the following year in Colorado. In fact, he was leading the league in the early going of 1977-78, but a back injury kept him out of all but 46 games. Then, last season, something went bad in Denver. Despite the fact he was second in team scoring with 23 goals and 26 assists, Gardner was on the bench with not much prospect of getting off with any regularity. "I don't really know why, because nobody said anything to me about it," he said after the Leafs liberated him from his fate by trading defenceman Trevor Johansen and the "retired" Don Ashby for him. "I do know that it's a great break to join the Leafs." (One theory was that Gardner was not trying hard enough defensively for the Rockies, but since he was acquired by Roger Neilson, that theory has to be somewhat suspect.)

Gardner finished last season with the Leafs, playing 11 games and adding seven goals to make it an even 30 once again. "I always played well in Toronto," he says, "and I guess I was fired up about it being my home town."

In case anyone's forgotten, Paul Gardner is the son of Cal Gardner, who toiled 11 seasons in the NHL with New York, Toronto, Chicago, and Boston. He retired in 1957, the year after Paul was born. Paul's older brother, Dave, is still playing pro hockey in the American Hockey League. But, as Paul recalls, Cal wasn't a "stage father."

"There was always pressure on me as a kid because of Dad and Dave," he said, "but I think the pressure was an incentive rather than anything else. It made me work harder. Dad never pushed Dave or I. He said if we wanted to play, that was fine. But if we didn't, that was all right too . . . He never hollered at us, he didn't go talking to our coaches. The most he would do would be to discuss the game riding back home in the car."

(Robert Shaver)

Paul Harrison

HEIGHT: 6'2" **WEIGHT:** 190 lbs **BIRTH:** 11 Feb. 1955 **HOME TOWN:** Timmins, Ont. **PETS:** none

MARITAL STATUS: married **WIFE AND CHILDREN:** Penny Anne; daughter, Chauncui

Why did you become a hockey player? "In small-town northern Ontario the Toronto Maple Leafs and Montreal Canadiens, they were *it*. Everyone who grew up in the same era wanted to be a hockey player."

What would you have been if you did not turn pro? "I probably would have been a gold miner because that's all there is up in the North. From about 16 on, all I wanted to do was play hockey."

Sports celebrity pro and con: "I probably would have to say the challenge – I really enjoy getting out there and stopping someone, or the puck. The standard of living is a big factor too because I would never be able to make the kind of living I'm earning now doing anything else with my other capabilities. I don't have the problem of too many people recognizing me on the street, because I always wear my mask during the game. It's great to be recognized but I'm sure that it gets to the point where you'd like to be left alone. A Mike Palmateer or Darryl Sittler can't go anywhere. I don't have that problem."

Lifestyle: "I'm very low-keyed. I'm not flamboyant by any means. I usually head home to my wife and little girl; I get a great charge out of my daughter. We might take in a movie once a month. One of my favourite restaurants is Le Baron, and there are some good Italian ones in Etobicoke, where we live."

Favourite people in hockey: When I was a youngster, Terry Sawchuk had to be my idol. Now, watching Palmy is amazing. He's so fast, his anticipation is so good; he's just a pleasure to watch."

Favourite and least favourite opponents: "I really get a charge out of playing Montreal; they're the team everyone wants to beat. I like playing against Lafleur because he's probably the ultimate on a one-on-one situation; if you've beat him you think you've really done something. I couldn't stand playing against Lemaire, though. He had my number last year; he always scored the big goals."

Are you superstitious as a hockey player? "There are definite little patterns that I follow. I always put my equipment on from right to left; but my routine before the game is not really superstitious, it's just a way to get myself mentally prepared."

Activities before and after games: "I'm up by 8.00 o'clock and I like to come down early to have my sticks taped and to check my equipment; I'll skate around for 15 or 20 minutes and work up a little bit of a sweat. I like to eat as early as I can – usually before noon – some pasta or spaghetti, anything with high carbohydrates. After sleeping for two or three hours, I get up around 4.00 to have a shower, walk around, and drink a cup of coffee. Once at the rink, I work on getting mentally prepared. I do my thinking at the rink, not at home during the afternoon; the more relaxed I am, the better I play. After, my wife and I will go out for something to eat, but with the schedule we have it's too hard to keep late hours."

Favourite books, films, TV, music: "I don't really read a lot but I've kind of gotten into this Holocaust thing lately. I also like mysteries and pocketbooks. I carry *Sports Psyching* around with me all the time – it's a general book on preparing for any kind of a game. Goaltending is 90 per cent mental, so you've got to be in control of what you're doing. I'm big on folk music and I play a little guitar; that's one of my ways of relaxing. I enjoy the Canadian artists like Valdy and Neil Young. I watch a lot of television, with M.A.S.H. being my favourite show."

Personal goals for the 1979-80 season and future in hockey: "I've yet to prove myself as a good NHL goaltender. It's pretty hard with a guy like Mike [Palmateer]; he's the best goalie in the league. I would like to play 40 games or at least 35. But goaltending is a team-oriented thing, you've got to work together. I'd like to stay in Toronto for as long as I can."

When he was a kid playing midget hockey in his home town of Timmins, Ontario, Paul Harrison made do one year with tube skates, a wire mask over his glasses, and shin-pads under regular goalie pads that were far too short. In order to get proper equipment he took a summer job in the gold mines, and while he was able to make the necessary purchases, he was also able to reach a certain conclusion: if he couldn't be a pro hockey player, he sure as heck didn't want to be a miner.

When he went down to the Oshawa Generals as an undistinguished 23rd draft selection, "I didn't even know what junior hockey was . . . I suppose the thought of playing pro entered my mind now and then, but not seriously until I started playing junior. By that time a lot of my friends were working in the gold mines. I knew that was not for me."

Hockey stardom never came easily for Harrison, even in junior, but class eventually told and he became the Generals' top goalie, playing in every playoff match in the two years he was in Oshawa. His credentials were good enough to make him the second draft selection of the Minnesota North Stars in 1975, but he rarely got to play. He bounced up and down between Minnesota and the AHL and it was only in 1977-78 that he got in enough games – 27 – to show what he could do, turning in a respectable (for that team, that year) 3.82 goals-against average.

He came to the Leafs at the beginning of last season as either a free agent (his theory) or in a trade for a fourth round draft choice (what former manager Jim Gregory insisted), but whatever the case, Harrison was "just glad to be here."

Last season, spelling off the stellar Mike Palmateer for 25 games, Harrison dropped his goals-against average to 3.51. He credits marriage and fatherhood with having a positive effect on his career: "It means more. I've got someone to work for, I'm not just being a hockey player for myself."

Harrison is one of those players who is constantly pushing himself to improve. He has, for example, changed his style from Tony Esposito (flopping) to Ken Dryden (stand-up) figuring that, "I'd better learn the style that would keep me here." And after games, he might analyze his mistakes all night. "I'm not a bad loser, but I'm conscientious . . . once you learn from your mistakes, you're not going to forget."

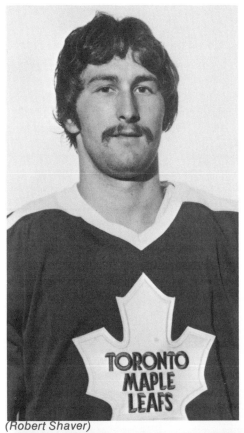

(Robert Shaver)

(Robert Shaver)

(Toronto Sun)

Greg Hotham

HEIGHT: 5'11" **WEIGHT:** 183 lbs **BIRTH:** 7 March 1956 **HOME TOWN:** London, Ont.

MARITAL STATUS: single

PETS: Puck (Newfoundland dog)

Why did you become a hockey player? "When I was four years old I started watching hockey, and after my parents bought me my first pair of skates, I though I'd want to be like those guys on TV. It's only a dream until you become bantam or midget, and then you realize that maybe you're good enough to play."

What would you have been if you did not turn pro? "I've never had anything else I wanted to do; I always concentrated on hockey."

Sports celebrity and pro and con: "I've never really been in the spotlight like I am now. Darryl is always in the spotlight and he knows how to handle it. I don't, but I guess it will come with experience. It gets tiring after a while. It's always nice to be recognized for what you do, but if you have a bad game or something, you don't want anybody to say anything to you – but I guess that goes along the job."

Lifestyle: "I think I'm a fairly shy and quiet person. I like to go out with my friends. Summer is the time that I can go out more, but that's also the time that I don't feel like going to dressed-up places. I like to be by myself and with my friends in the summer and it works out like that most of the time."

Favourite people in hockey: "I don't know too many people in hockey right now, especially in the NHL. Right now it's hard, when you're a rookie, for you to get to know the veterans; it takes time for that. I'll usually go out with a couple of the guys I played with last year, like Mark Kirton and Rocky Saganiuk."

Favourite and least favourite opponents: "I'd like to play against Montreal: you always look forward to the best. Playerwise, it's always something to play against guys like Guy Lafleur and Robinson."

Are you superstitious as a hockey player? "Oh, yeah. I'm superstitious. But I'm not going to say what I do because they're only lucky when nobody knows."

Activities before and after games: "We usually practise at 10:30 a.m. so I give myself an hour and a half to get down to the rink; I never have breakfast. For lunch at home I'll eat anything with carbohydrates like noodles, spaghetti or macaroni, and I don't eat steak very much at all. Then I'll sit around and watch TV for an hour and sleep for two hours or so. I like to get down to the rink early, check my sticks out and think a little bit about the game. I play ping-pong for a while because it's good for hand-eye co-ordination. After, depending on how I played (if badly, I'll go right home), I like to go out and have a couple of beers; it all depends on the schedule."

Favourite books, films, TV, music: "I love reading any mysteries like Agatha Christie, and I like watching a lot of movies – basically any kind of a film except musicals or love stories. In the wintertime I'll watch a fair bit of television, but very little in the summer; I'll see mostly comedies. But any show that has a mystery to figure out, like Columbo, I like. I listen to pretty well all kinds of music like rock, or disco, if I go out."

Personal goals for the 1979-80 season and future in hockey: "My main goal is making the team; I don't have any personal goals. I just want to play as well as I can and let things work out for themselves. Everybody wants to win the Stanley Cup; that's the ultimate in hockey. And I'd like to play as long as possible, and stay healthy too."

A couple of seasons ago the Leafs played an exhibition game with a touring Czech team and decided, since the game meant nothing to the NHL standings, to rest a few of the workhorses, like Borje Salming. A kid named Greg Hotham was called up from Saginaw (Michigan) Gears to fill in on the back line, and even though he acquitted himself well, the Leafs lost the game. Some of the fans grumbled that if Salming had been there, instead of young what's-his-name, the result would have been different. Nevertheless, there were those in the Leaf hierarchy who liked what they saw and kept Greg Hotham in mind.

Promoted to the New Brunswick Hawks last season, the fifth-round 1977 draft choice from the Kingston junior team contributed nine goals and 27 assists and played a strong defensive role with the American Hockey League team. Then came this year's training camp, with one defence position – the sixth – more or less up for grabs. Hotham grabbed and as the season began, he held. (A pre-season serious injury to Ron Wilson, an incumbent, undoubtedly helped, if only to let Hotham display more of his considerable wares.) In a pre-season game in Ottawa against the Bruins, Hotham scored two first-period goals and added an assist in a winning cause, and coach Floyd Smith began enthusing out loud about this third member –Rocky Saganiuk and Mark Kirton are the others – of his "Moncton Mafia."

"Some people can only go so high," Smith observed. "But it looks like he'll go higher."

And some other fairly astute observers were heard to remark that Hotham also seemed to have done wonders for Dave Burrows, his regular defence partner in pre-season. Burrows, they said, was looking more like he did as a great player in Pittsburgh than the way he did last season in Toronto. Hotham, not atypically for a Leaf rookie, is a young man with a pretty mature outlook. "I've been patient with my time in the minors," he said in pre-season. "The Leafs is what I've been working towards. I want to give it as good an effort as I can." And, as for Hotham the scorer: "I don't have the type of shot that can beat someone from the point, and I can't shoot for any particular spot. I just shoot for the net. Maybe I'll get a deflection."

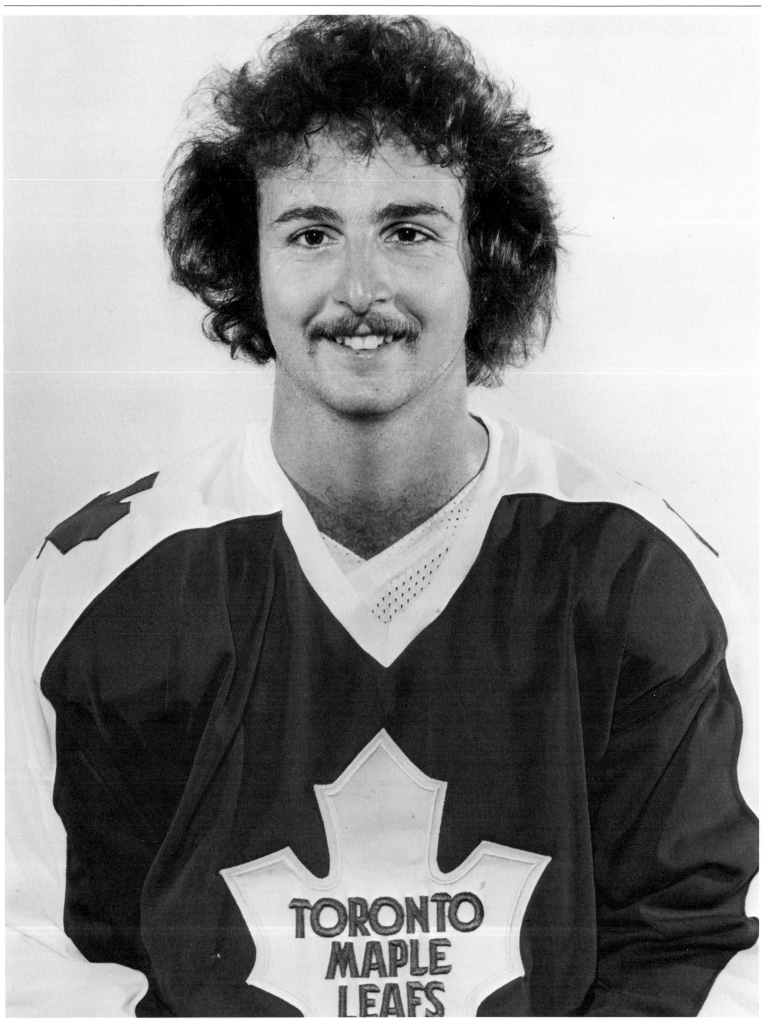

(Robert Shaver)

Dave Hutchison

HEIGHT: 6'2" **WEIGHT:** 205 lbs **BIRTH:** 2 May 1952 **HOME TOWN:** London, Ont. **PETS:** Buster (dog)

MARITAL STATUS: married **WIFE:** Alanna

Why did you become a hockey player? "Ever since I was a young kid in school, it was my goal in life to be a pro hockey player in the NHL. I was a fairly gifted athlete, but hockey was my favourite sport."

What would you have been if you did not turn pro? "I wouldn't know what I would be doing now, if not hockey; probably nothing too spectacular, maybe working at a factory job. Most of the guys I hung around with are doing the basic nine-to-five job now."

Sports celebrity pro and con: "Everybody likes the benefits and it's nice to have your friends and family appreciate you. I get recognized quite a bit because I've never worn a helmet so people get to see me more. But I like my privacy like everybody else. It's a drag when you're out with somebody and you're trying to play it low-key and people come over. I usually enjoy it but when the timing isn't too good, it's not fun."

Lifestyle: "I like to lead a slow-paced life. Although I'm an active person, I like to play it low-key; sleep in and take it easy. I used to buy expensive clothes when I was single but now I hang around in my jeans until the season starts. I go out with my wife for dinner often; we like La Castile, in Mississauga. Sometimes we'll get dressed up and go to a fancy restaurant and spend a hundred dollars and, on another night, we'll go to a small burger place just to get out."

Favourite people in hockey: "Bobby Hull and Bobby Orr are kind of my idols; I got lucky enough to play against Bobby Hull who was my idol as a youngster. Bobby Orr is a class guy. There are too many guys that I'd like to name off. I have lots of friends in Los Angeles. Danny Maloney has always been a good friend and so has Turnbull, but I get along well with all the guys."

Favourite and least favourite opponents: "Favourite opponents? Not really, because I'm very competitive so I don't enjoy playing against anybody unless they're good friends. But, every person on the other team isn't a friend of mine once the game starts; I dislike everybody that I play against."

Are you superstitious as a hockey player? "I have a few, but I'm not really superstitious. Every athlete in professional sports has his own tucked away, but I can't tell because they wouldn't work for me anymore."

Activities before and after games: "I like to get up in the morning and go down for a light skate and shoot some pucks. I'll come home about noon, have a bite to eat, and lie down for a couple of hours. When I get up I'll have a cup of tea and a cookie or something and listen to music. I like to be at the rink by at least 6.00. There I putter around with some sticks and try to get myself psyched up for the game time. I don't like to eat steaks on game days, that's for sure; I eat the light stuff. After, I like to unwind by going out with my wife or with a few guys on the team. I'll have something to eat, then go home."

Favourite books, films, TV, music: "I like a lot of music; I've got probably 200 albums, mostly rock. I enjoy the Eagles and Jackson Browne and, in fact, we're personal friends with the Eagles group. I like reading spooks and mysteries, like *The Shining*. I enjoy watching Clint Eastwood movies and spooky ones, but I'm not big on love stories. I've got a '58 Corvette so I'm big on cars; I've always been into cars and bikes. I watch Saturday Night Live and see Carson almost every night; that, plus sports shows, is all I ever watch."

Personal goals for the 1979-80 season and future in hockey: "I don't have any personal goals. My goals are all team goals: to win the Cup. When I ended up with the high plus-minus last year, that was kind of a thrill for me, but I'm not one to say I want to score ten goals."

When Dave Hutchison arrived in Toronto for the start of the 1978-79 season, part of the baggage he brought with him was a reputation as something of a "goon," which is generally applied to people long on muscle and short on skill. He told the *Star*'s Frank Orr then, and proved it over the course of last season, that he was much more than that.

"Getting speared in the gut doesn't make me as mad as when somebody attaches that [goon] label to me. I don't mind being called a policeman – if that means I can offer some protection to my team mates if an opponent is taking advantage of them – but the word goon says that my only job in hockey is to beat people up."

When Hutchison, along with Lorne Stamler, came to the Leafs from Los Angeles at the expense of Brian Glennie, the late Scott Garland, Kurt Walker, and a high draft choice, nobody was more pleased to see him than captain Darryl Sittler, an old team mate from the London Knights. "Hutchison," Sittler said, "is the kind of defenceman we needed. He moves people out of our goal area well, he doesn't allow any opponent to take advantage of his mates, and he has good hockey skills too."

His arrival in Toronto, which he calls the big break of his career, had a few people around the Gardens holding their collective breath. You see, Hutchison had a blood feud going with Dave Williams and had served a five-game suspension for an earlier stick-swinging battle. He vowed at the time that, "this thing will never be settled." But being team mates tends to make happier bedfellows, and he was heard to say, when he arrived, that all was forgiven and forgotten.

Hutchison began his professional career in the WHA with Philadelphia and Vancouver before putting in four solid defensive seasons with Los Angeles. Counting the WHA statistics, he will be reaching a milestone of sorts this season – 1,000 minutes in penalties.

As noted, he believes he's a better hockey player, all-round, than he's been given credit for; and he also thinks he has a pretty good explanation for some of his tendency to go a little wild on the ice from time to time. "Sometimes when I play only a few shifts here and there, I find that I get more penalties, I've been sitting on the bench itching to get into the game and when I do get on the ice I'm trying too hard and I get too rambunctious."

PHOTO BY
ROBERT SHAVER

(Robert Shaver)

Jim Jones

HEIGHT: 5'11" **WEIGHT:** 180 lbs **BIRTH:** 2 Jan. 1953 **HOME TOWN:** Woodbridge, Ont. **PETS:** Reggie (a dog)

MARITAL STATUS: married **WIFE:** Carolyn

Why did you become a hockey player? "I was brought up in a hockey-oriented society and, watching the Toronto Maple Leafs every Saturday Night, I just thought playing hockey and playing for the Toronto Maple Leafs would be pretty great. Everybody played hockey and it got into my system."

What would you have been if you did not turn pro? "I went to university for one year but I hadn't really thought about what I'd do if I didn't turn pro. So no, I didn't have anything else in mind."

Sports celebrity pro and con: "I really enjoy playing hockey but I don't look at myself as being a celebrity. People recognizing me in the street doesn't turn me off or on."

Lifestyle: "I'm your basic, cautious, fairly conservative type of person. My wife and I go out like everybody else, but not a lot. I'm definitely not extravagant."

Favourite people in hockey: "I don't think I have any favourite people."

Favourite and least favourite opponents: "I don't have a favourite player to play against. I respect Bobby Clarke for the type of hockey player that he is, but I don't really look up to him. I respect him for his talent and the way he plays but I don't like playing against Bobby Clarke."

Are you superstitious as a hockey player? "Yeah, I think I am superstitious. When I go into a game, I like to have nothing on my conscience. Superstitions just cloud my mind. But, I like to do my skates up in a certain manner; I like them done up that way always so I don't have to worry and I can concentrate on playing. I like to have my shin pads taped on in a certain way each time."

Activities before and after games: "I eat about 1.00 in the afternoon for an 8:00 p.m. game and usually keep the afternoon clear for some rest. I go down to the rink about 6.00 o'clock. For some games I'm more nervous than for others. [Jones attends all of the optional pre-game skates.] After, maybe I'll grab something to eat and come home. I'm not a real partying type. After the game I have trouble getting to sleep because of all the action."

Favourite books, films, TV, music: Arthur Hailey is Jones' favourite author, although he admits that he doesn't read a great deal. He does see quite a few movies, "but I like all different types." Jones doesn't watch any television except for sporting events. His favourite music is rock n' roll, mostly metal rock and his choice group is the Rolling Stones.

Personal goals for the 1979-80 season and future in hockey: "My goal is to be a member of the Toronto Maple Leafs. I'd like to make the team and go from there.

"I really enjoy playing hockey and I get a lot of fun out of it. I'd like to play for as long as I can but, when I finally can't play, doesn't really worry me."

When Jimmy Jones made the Leafs at the beginning of the 1977-78 season, a great many people were surprised. Among the many was Jones himself, who admitted, candidly, that "I didn't think I had much of a chance."

There was some good reason for his doubts about ever getting a real NHL opportunity. He'd been kicking around the minors since 1973 on an odyssey that included Roanoke down in the Southern League. Originally a Boston Bruin property ("How was I going to break into *that* team?"), Jones went to the Rochester Americans of the American Hockey League as a free agent (Boston offered him no contract) in 1977, and scored 24 goals, along with 34 assists, in just 74 games. That performance helped, but probably what helped more was the fact that Roger Neilson, who had coached him in his junior days at Peterborough, was an admirer; and Neilson, as everybody knows, was just taking over the Leafs at that time. Neilson wasn't looking for scoring, he was looking for somebody to kill penalties, and Jim Jones proved to be as good at that as just about anybody. Jones also turned out to be one hell of a defensive forward as well, as demonstrated beyond doubt the night in the 1977-78 playoffs when he held the great Marcel Dionne of the Los Angeles Kings to one uninspired shot on goal and even kept him from getting off a decent pass. Jones, on the other hand, also managed to assist on goals by Dave Williams and Jerry Butler in the 7-3 Leaf win.

While his play for Neilson resulted in a new contract at the beginning of last season, calling for a salary considerably in excess of the $37,000 he received as the lowest-paid Leaf of the year before, it remains to be seen how much use the Leaf regime will have for his specialties. Jones, who admitted that he had no bargaining position when his first Leaf contract was thrust upon him the night before the 1977 season opened, is not lacking in self-appraisal when it comes to his game, either.

"I know it has been said many times that I'm in the NHL because of my penalty-killing ability," he told the *Star*'s Jim Kernaghan last year. "It *is* the strongest part of my game and I do get a lot of satisfaction from it. Keeping the other team off the board when you're a man short is an achievement. It's not as good a feeling, I'm sure, as being on the power play, and scoring, but I do enjoy it."

(Robert Shaver)

Mark Kirton

HEIGHT:	WEIGHT:	BIRTH:	HOME TOWN:	PETS:
5'10"	170 lbs	3 Feb. 1958	Toronto, Ont.	Peppy (dog)

MARITAL STATUS:
single

Why did you become a hockey player? "I've played since I was four years old. You watch it on TV, you go out and play ball hockey and you say: 'I want to be like the pros.' Then you try to work at it as hard as you can. It finally turns into a business around junior, when there's more pressure."

What would you have been if you did not turn pro? "I always wanted to be a professional hockey player. Through high school I played every sport, but it just seemed that I ranked hockey number one."

Sports celebrity pro and con: "Sure, the fame is there when you're a rookie coming in, but I can see after two or three years that you could get tired of that. A guy like Darryl Sittler, his privacy is pretty well gone; he can't go anywhere without being recognized. Sure you feel great that everybody's watching you, but I can see where it could really hinder your lifestyle. I guess you have to get used to it."

Lifestyle: "I probably live along the same lifestyle as a lot of players, but it's a little different for me because I'm from Toronto. It's easier for me than for a guy from out west who comes to a new city: they have to adjust, where I don't have to make any adjustment. I just go about my daily life as I have for all the years that I've been here. I made it a point not to change my lifestyle since playing pro, because the worst thing you could do is get a big head."

Favourite people in hockey: "I always looked at Darryl Sittler in awe, and I liked Bobby Clarke for how hard he worked, and Doug Jarvis on faceoffs. You pick a little part of each guy's game and you try to put it in your own. But Darryl Sittler – the way he acts on and off the ice and how he leads – I find really interesting."

Favourite and least favourite opponents: "I like to play guys that have been around for a long time, and that I've watched, like Phil Esposito and Bobby Clarke."

Are you superstitious as a hockey player: "I wouldn't say I'm as superstitious as a lot of players, but maybe I will be someday. At this point I don't feel I've got that many. For example, I always go right to left when I put on my skates or pads. But I don't have any superstitions such that, when I score two goals I'll wear the same suit."

Activities before and after games: "I get up early and go for the morning skate, making sure I have breakfast before. For lunch I'll either have steak or spaghetti, nothing else. I like to sleep for a couple of hours in the afternoon but I have to get up around 5.00 to give me about an hour to walk around and wake up. What's great about the ping-pong table in the dressing room is that it wakes you up and gets your eyes going. I like to dress late because I don't like sitting around and waiting: I'll put my sweater on with a minute to go. After, I like to go out with some friends for a beer and something to eat."

Favourite books, films, TV, music: "I don't read that much, although sometimes I have this feeling I need to read and I'll go crazy for a couple of weeks then lay off for a few months. I'll see any type of movie: Silent Partner was a good one, and Close Encounters was super. I like sitting down at night and relaxing in front of the TV – All In The Family and Mork and Mindy are shows that I watch. I don't really have a favourite music group – except maybe Supertramp – and I have a variety of records."

Personal goals for the 1979-80 season and future in hockey: "I find that when I set personal goals, I put pressure on myself. So last year I said I'm not going to set any goals, just go out and play the game as hard as I can and see what happens. Of course, everyone wants to win the Cup. And I'd like to play as long as I can."

As National Hockey League teams go, the Leafs went into this season fairly well-to-do in terms of centres. Along with the inimitable Darryl Sittler they had steady Walt McKechnie, 30-goal man Paul Gardner, defensive ace Jim Jones, plus Bruce Boudreau, who's been sharing his seasons between Toronto and the New Brunswick Hawks. As a result, nobody was paying all that much attention to 21-year-old Mark Kirton, who arrived at the camp with only journeyman scoring credentials – 20 goals and 30 assists last season – with the Hawks in the American Hockey League.

But as the training camp progressed it started to become obvious that Kirton had a little more going for him than the bulk of the other candidates for the big team. John McLellan, former Leaf coach and present assistant general manager, said, simply: "I like the way he plays." And Floyd Smith concurred: "I thought Kirton was the best player in the rookie camp. He has great speed and he's a good checker." In Smith's scheme of things, speed was and is a major consideration; to play the kind of hockey he and Punch Imlach were aiming for, it was an imperative. So Kirton arrived at the right time. Along with Greg Hotham, another training camp surprise, Kirton survived the early cuts. In a pre-season game against Boston he scored a goal and added an assist. In fact, he played well offensively in all of his outings. But it was on defence that he really shone: paired with Jerry Butler up front on the penalty killing squad, the slim, light Kirton simply stood out – especially in that game against the Canadiens when he and Butler effectively killed one of the great power plays in hockey, and helped – immeasurably – the Leafs beat Montreal for the first time in three years.

Red Storey, the former referee who is now the "colourman" on the CKO-FM Leaf broadcasts, has never been all that short on enthusiasm, but in describing the play that night against the Habs, he almost outdid himself. "Finally the Leafs are killing penalties with a little bit of effort," he shouted into the microphone. "That young Kirton is not falling back too soon. He's going in there and forechecking and making defensive play interesting. This is the best I've seen the Leafs kill a penalty in years!"

(Robert Shaver)

Dan Maloney

HEIGHT:	WEIGHT:	BIRTH:	HOME TOWN:	PETS:
6'2"	185 lbs	24 Sept. 1950	Barrie, Ont.	Blewe (terrier)

MARITAL STATUS:	WIFE AND CHILDREN:
married	Susanne; daughter, Shelley and son, Thomas

Why did you become a hockey player? "I started off playing hockey like all the other kids and I was drafted by the Toronto Marlboros when I was 16. That's when the sincere interest started. In my last year of Junior A I was drafted in the first round by Chicago and I had to make my mind up to either play hockey as a professional or go to school. As it turned out things went pretty well."

What would you have been if you did not turn pro? "I would have liked to get into a veterinary line or work with wildlife."

Sports celebrity pro and con: "Hockey is something I always wanted to do and so I put all my efforts into it. I feel very fortunate because I know there are a lot of other people who would like to make a career of it and don't have the opportunity. Sometimes I don't really like all the attention we get but I don't think there are any negative aspects; autographs are no bother at all."

Lifestyle: "That's a tough question to answer. I spend as much time as I possibly can with my family because during the season my time is limited to be with them."

Favourite people in hockey: "I don't want to answer that question."

Favourite and least favourite opponents: "I don't want to answer that one either."

Are you superstitious as a hockey player? "Maybe I'm superstitious in some instances. Say, if I had a good night when both the team and I do well, probably in the next game I'll wear the same set of clothes or whatever. I don't think superstitions just pertain to hockey; everybody just has different hang-ups or superstitions."

Activities before and after games: "I usually get up fairly early and go down to skate on the morning of the game, get the sticks ready and kind of think about who I'm going to play against. I take a few shots and get a little bit of sweat on, concentrate on what I'm going to have to do that night. I'll have a large meal around 1.30 or 2.00 and then probably read for a few minutes and then lie down for a couple of hours. By 5.30 or 6.00 I'm at the rink. I then put in time by getting my equipment ready and talking to the guys and even playing some ping-pong to sharpen up. After the game, I run through my head what went on during the game and see if there are things that I can do to improve a little. Then I try to forget about the game. I'll usually go out with my wife for a bite but I don't eat right after because I'm too wound up. I don't fall asleep until 2.30 or 3.00."

Favourite books, films, TV, music: "My wife and I frequent a few movies but we don't have any special tastes for drama or westerns or anything like that. We manage to get out a couple of nights during the month. I always try to catch all the National Geographic television shows; I find those very interesting. I'll also watch the Wide World of Sports on the Saturday afternoon of a game. I read all of the sporting magazines and if I read books, they're history. I enjoy country and western music."

Personal goals for the 1979-80 season and future in hockey: "I don't always set up personal goals for myself but I like to improve from year to year, to personally do better than last year and for the team to do better. I've always felt that you're in the game for only one reason and that's to win the Stanley Cup. We haven't come very close to it yet. As a player's career goes on he becomes more aware that you only get so many chances in so many years to attain the Stanley Cup. It's always a very big goal in my mind."

Dan Maloney's first few games as a Toronto Maple Leaf were not exactly the happiest of his nine-year professional career. The fans were on him and on him hard for a couple of reasons: first, he'd come from Detroit at the expense of the popular and high-scoring Errol Thompson; and second, he had previously done a job on the equally popular Brian Glennie which resulted in criminal charges being laid (Maloney was acquitted). And, as *Star* columnist Milt Dunnell pointed out, "he arrived at a time when the Leafs played as if they all had their shoes on the wrong feet."

Maloney, who, by coaches' consensus, is the best fighter in the NHL, was always one of those guys who made up in guts what he lacked in skill. When he was with the Markham Waxers, a Junior B team, in 1967, coach Frank Bonello remembers, "He didn't have a lot of natural ability, but boy, did he ever work! It was easy to see he'd amount to something." Maloney played alongside Darryl Sittler in London, and in 1970 he was the Chicago Black Hawks' first draft choice.

In 1973, the Leafs went after him for the first time, and tried to trade Norm Ullman for him but Ullman wouldn't go. So Maloney went to Los Angeles for Ralph Backstrom. He was traded to the Wings in 1975.

Although Maloney isn't paid to score goals, he doesn't do all that badly. He's had three 25-goal NHL seasons and last year, working with various lines, he managed 17, along with 36 assists. But it is his tenacity and toughness that make him such a valuable property. (When criticism of the Thompson trade reached owner Harold Ballard, he said simply: "If you're going to buy gold you've got to pay the price.") So Maloney is pretty philosophical about his place in the scheme of hockey things. "Hockey boils down to style," he once observed, "and a freewheeling style will always attract people. But there's no way I can play that way. My style is to check, grind it out, and work hard."

And, as far as fighting is concerned (he picked up 157 minutes in penalties last year) he is also pretty philosophical: "There are times when fighting has to be done and, sure, toughness enters into that. But where toughness really enters the picture is when the other team knows we're going to put the body on them, that we're going to battle them hard for the puck in the corners and along the boards."

(Robert Shaver)

(Robert Shaver)

Lanny McDonald

HEIGHT: 6'0"   **WEIGHT:** 190 lbs   **BIRTH:** 16 Feb. 1953   **HOME TOWN:** Hanna, Alberta   **PETS:** none

MARITAL STATUS: married   **WIFE AND CHILDREN:** Ardell; daughter, Andra

Why did you become a hockey player? "My father played hockey when I was young. I enjoyed it and I liked listening to the games on the radio. I guess it was something that was a boyhood dream and I just wanted to follow it up, to see if I could make it."

What would you have been if you did not turn pro? "I'd hate to think what I would be if not a player because I enjoy this so much. I suppose I'd probably be in physical education; I enjoy working with kids."

Sports celebrity pro and con: "It's nice being able to know you're doing something that you love. Kids look up to you and that sort of thing, and, hopefully, you're setting a good example for them. A lot of other things, people bothering you, go with the territory. You learn to accept them; it's going to happen so you make the most of it."

Lifestyle: "I'd like to think I'm a family man: I like to spend a lot of time with my wife and little girl. I stay close to home and just enjoy life; I don't need to be on the go all the time. We enjoy getting out once in a while but most of the time is spent at home."

Favourite people in hockey: "Probably the person I've looked up to most since I've been in Toronto – a player who has always been my favourite when I was a youngster and still is – is Ronny Ellis. I've been very fortunate to have the chance to play with him, to have him teach me a lot of things. Secondly, it would be Darryl. After playing for three years, we know each other pretty well. Both of our families get along, so consequently we spend a lot of time together."

Favourite and least favourite opponents: "I don't have any favourite opponents because they're out there to beat you and you're out there to beat them. Sure, you have friends on other teams but those friendships have to wait until after the game. You have to treat them as opponents whether they're good guys or bad guys."

Are you superstitious as a hockey player? "Yeah, I'd say I'm superstitious. Probably 99 per cent of the players are. If things are going good I do the same thing, dress the same way, and use the same stick."

Activities before and after games: "On game days, I'm up around 8.30 for the practice. I'll have breakfast with the family and get to the rink by 10.00. Then I get my sticks together and make sure all my equipment is in ready shape. After, I head back home and have a bite to eat and maybe lie down for an hour or two. I eat either spaghetti or macaroni – they're high in carbohydrates I play some ping-pong before the game in the dressing room; it's very relaxing. You sit back and let your mind get away from you for a while so you don't have to worry about the game. Then, when it's around 7.00 o'clock you really key on it and make sure you're ready for the 8.00 o'clock start. After, a few of us will get together and take our wives out for supper."

Favourite books, films, TV, music: "I read the newspapers all the time, but as far as books are concerned, I only read on the road – whatever is the bestseller at the time, Harold Robbins and those kind. We try and get out to a movie every two weeks for a little break. I guess we're both romantic types, so we like a love story every once in a while. I enjoy nice, easy-listening music, something along the lines of the Bee Gees. After Andra goes to bed, we'll watch televison together."

Personal goals for the 1979-80 season and future in hockey: "I never set personal goals for myself; the only goal is the Stanley Cup. When you start setting personal goals you're putting pressure on yourself and that kind of pressure you don't need. When I get my first goal I'll go for number two and so on. You take whatever comes. Winning the Stanley Cup and playing international hockey; that's the ultimate, to play for your country. I've already done one [the latter] and, hopefully, before the end of my career, I'll accomplish the other."

Once, when he was still a kid, Lanny McDonald stood for an hour outside the hockey arena in Calgary waiting for one particular autograph. When Frank Mahovlich finally appeared, McDonald got what he was after, and he still has it. Soon, possibly this season, McDonald will have something else of Mahovlich's too: his all-time one-season record for goals. In the past three years, McDonald has scored 46, 47, and 43 goals respectively, and Big Frank's record of 48 is only a break or two away for the young right-winger.

Lanny McDonald is the *compleat* hockey player. When Scotty Bowman, somewhat of an authority on these matters, had McDonald on Team Canada, he was moved to say: "He plays flat out all the time. He does everything a coach asks. He's a superb team player and his enthusiasm rubs off on anyone close to him." But gaining that kind of recognition, and becoming one of the Leaf untouchables, did not come easy for McDonald. His first two seasons, which produced a total of only 31 goals, were not exactly what the team had in mind when it drafted him first in 1973; he was becoming trade bait.

As it turned out, fortunately for all concerned, the problem lay not in McDonald himself, but in his skates. The reason he was falling down all the time, and not getting off that big shot, was the rockering of the blades. Torchy Schell, the Leaf scout, spotted the trouble and it was corrected. He hasn't gone below 37 goals-per-season since. His three 40-goals-plus seasons are an all-time Leaf record.

Probably the biggest of his big nights, however, produced only one goal. But it was in overtime of game seven of the Stanley Cup quarter-finals against the New York Islanders in 1978. McDonald split the defence and Ian Turnbull flipped the puck to him; it dropped at his feet, he was in the clear, and all of a sudden the series was over.

McDonald, as noted, does everything well. In 1977-78 his plus-minus average was the best in the league, and it never occurs to him that just scoring is good enough. "I get excited about everything during a game," he says. "Blocking a shot is exciting to me. I like throwing a good check. I like backchecking. I like scoring. It is the game in its entirety that excites, not just one aspect of it."

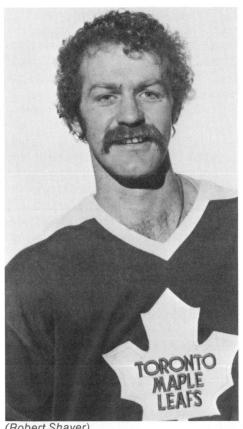

(Robert Shaver)

(Robert Shaver)

(Robert Shaver)

Walt McKechnie

HEIGHT:	WEIGHT:	BIRTH:	HOME TOWN:	PETS:
6'2½"	202 lbs	19 June 1947	London, Ont.	Sheba, (Siberian Husky)

MARITAL STATUS:
married

Why did you become a hockey player? "When I was young I was involved in most sports but my real love was hockey. I worked hard at it and was fortunate to make it. I think the greatest thing about being any kind of professional athlete – it's just like anything else in life – is you've got to love it to be a success at it. That's why I've done well in hockey, because I love it."

What would you have been if you did not turn pro? "Ever since I can remember, it's been nothing but hockey. I more or less sacrificed my education to dedicate myself to hockey."

Sports celebrity pro and con: "I've played 13 years pro and I don't feel I've worked a day in my life. No, the celebrity thing doesn't bother me at all. When I was a kid, I used to ask for autographs. Now when I see the kids, I think back that 'that is me.' "

Lifestyle: "I like to really relax during the season. My idea of going and doing things is going out and having a nice dinner or cooking something at home. I also like to stay at home in my apartment and listen to some music. Jingles, a restaurant up the street from the Gardens, is one I really enjoy. There are so many good restaurants in Toronto; I try to get around to as many as I can. But I don't go overboard in anything."

Favourite people in hockey: "One of my best friends is Brian Watson, who just retired this year. You'd never know that we were best friends when we played because he treats everybody the same way: he hit me as hard as anyone else. Dan Maloney and I have been good friends since the years in Detroit. I never had any guys that I worshipped when I was young, but my favourite team was Toronto."

Favourite and least favourite opponents: "I really enjoy playing against Phil Esposito; it's a great challenge to play him. They're all tough; there are no easy games in hockey. I haven't played an easy game yet."

Are you superstitious as a hockey player? "I wouldn't say I'm really superstitious. I don't wear the same things three days in a row or anything like that."

Activities before and after games: "I'm an early riser normally, and the day of the game I might get up even a little earlier. I enjoy going to a restaurant, getting a newspaper and relaxing. Then I like to work up a little sweat during the morning practice and eat early. I usually have some chicken or spaghetti around noon. Steak is too hard to digest. I'll get a couple hours of sleep in the afternoon, then get up around 4.00 or so and watch a little bit of TV. The older I get, the earlier I seem to be going down to the rink. I enjoy relaxing there and fixing sticks up. We get stats sheets before the game so I'm always interested to see how the other guys in the league are doing. After, I enjoy going out and that's when I usually have a good meal with a few beers."

Favourite books, films, TV, music: "I go to any movies that are getting a lot of good ratings. I like a little disco music although I can't take a lot. I do go to the odd club; I enjoy watching people there but I'm not one for dancing. I like groups like the Eagles, not heavy rock. I wish I read more but when I do, I enjoy history, the wars. I'll read the newspaper every day, almost from front page to back, to see how lucky I really am with all the problems in the world. I'll read anything from *People* magazine, to hockey magazines, to *Playboy*. Some nights I like to stay home and relax by watching the TV."

Personal goals for the 1979-80 season and future in hockey: "I never set personal goals. If the team's doing well, that's the main thing. Of course, I'd love to play on a Stanley Cup team; we have the makings of a darn good team in Toronto. That's definitely my goal."

There was a time when Walt McKechnie would have been known, as likely as not, as "Suitcase." Today any description of him would, of necessity, include "much-travelled." The tall centre has played on eight pro teams – including Minnesota, California, Boston, Detroit, and finally Toronto of the NHL – in his 12-year career prior to this season. Ironically, he has come full circle: a Leaf number one draft choice in the mid-sixties, McKechnie never wore the blue-and-white until last season, when he survived the training camp and went on to become the fifth-leading scorer on the team and one of its most valuable and popular players.

He contributed four goals and three assists to the team's short-lived playoff performance, including both goals in the 2-1 game that extinguished the Atlanta Flames. The first, a short-handed effort, was, by McKechnie's reckoning, the result of "the best shot I ever made in hockey." It was also, incidentally, his first playoff goal in the NHL: for the first time in his major league career he was on a team that actually made the playoffs.

As befits a man of his age – only Ron Ellis is older on this team – McKechnie plays the kind of hockey that pleases the more venerable fans: he is, for example, an accomplished stickhandler and a good, if not mercurial, skater. Superfan Peter Gzowski, in fact, has publicly named McKechnie his favourite Leaf.

For part of last season he centred a checking line of veterans, with Dan Maloney on his left and Ellis on his right, and one night in Los Angeles McKechnie scored the second – only the second – hat-trick of his long career. "Everything went in tonight," he enthused. "One even went in with what Maloney and I described as the Grand River Roll when we were in Detroit together. It curved into the net about five feet."

The Leaf rediscovery of Walt McKechnie came at a time when he was on the edge of leaving the game entirely, and his 25-goal, 36-assist performance last season pretty well shows that he has plenty left to contribute. "Playing with the Leafs has given me my heart back for the game," he says. "I look forward to practice the way I used to. I feel like a kid again."

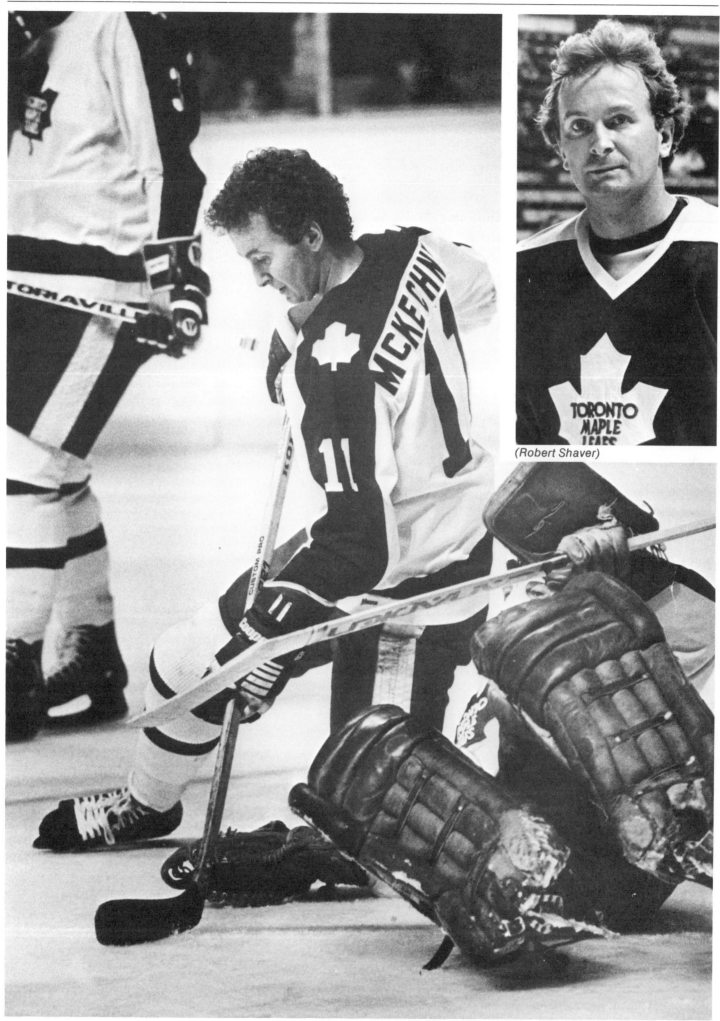

(Robert Shaver)

Mike Palmateer

HEIGHT: 5'9" **WEIGHT:** 170 lbs **BIRTH:** 13 Jan. 1954 **HOME TOWN:** Toronto, Ont. **PETS:** none

MARITAL STATUS: single

Why did you become a hockey player? "It was just a goal I had when I was young. My parents got me started young and they just kept on taking me."

What would you have been if you did not turn pro? "To be honest, I don't really know. When you make up your mind for hockey, you're usually late in your teens and I had hockey on my mind at that time. Nothing else mattered."

Sports celebrity pro and con: "It's a dream to become a star. I would say the best things about it are my summers and the money. The lack of privacy is not great though. I never mind signing autographs for the kids but when you're sitting in a restaurant having dinner and someone comes up as you're sticking a salad in your mouth and asks for an autograph, that gets a little hectic."

Lifestyle: "I have a busy life; I don't have much of a chance to sit around. I'm always on the go. Whenever I have a free afternoon I end up playing golf or tennis. I'd rather go out and spend $75 on a dinner than buy a $20 pair of jeans. I usually go down to George's Spaghetti House or Le Baron or Grapes – that's about it."

Favourite people in hockey: "I consider everybody on my team a friend. I had heroes when I was growing up – Roger Crozier, Frank Mahovlich, those guys."

Favourite and least favourite opponents: "I don't really have favourite opponents. What I look forward to is playing the top teams. If I could play 60 out of 80 games, I'd like to play them all with the top ten teams."

Are you superstitious as a hockey player? "No, not really. I might have a few little quirks but I don't hold anything by them like the tee shirt I wear or the way I tape my stick. They don't really mean anything; they're more or less habits. Boy, if you have superstitions you're in trouble."

Activities before and after games: "The night before a game, I always try to get a good sleep – I need a lot of rest before I play. Usually I go down to skate in the morning, depending on how tired I am. For lunch I'll have a steak or something at 1.00 – in fact, I could eat a steak at 7.30 and still play the game. I don't get queasy stomachs. I'll sit around, read a magazine or something, then sleep in the afternoon. I'm down an hour or so before the game. I have a kind of ritual though – I like to have time to drink a coffee and read the stats, but I don't think about the game until I start it. But I might look over the other players to see who I'm playing against. After, I usually go out and have a couple of beers, getting back in time to catch the late show. It takes me a long time to unwind; a good movie will get my mind off of the game."

Favourite books, films, TV, music: "I enjoy TV a lot but I don't see too many of the shows – mainly I watch the movies when they come on: if there's a good movie I might hold something up that I was going to do to see it. I enjoy sports but when I watch them on TV I get this incredible urge to play them. I always watch the football and baseball playoffs but other than that, I don't have time to sit around. I really enjoy going to the movies – comedies or adventures like Woody Allen and James Bond. I don't read a great deal, mostly fishing and hunting books or magazines, although at night I'll pick up a James Bond book; I've got them all."

Personal goals for the 1979-80 season and future in hockey: "I always want to keep my average under three. I'd certainly like to finish as high up as I can in the Vezina race. I wouldn't mind taking a shot at the all-star team one of these years. I want to make the all-star team and I want to play the Russians. It's just a matter of time before I play them."

As incredible as it sounds, Mike Palmateer, the baby-faced and eccentric incumbent in the Leafs' nets, is the first great goaltender developed solely within the Leaf system. Lorne Chabot, Turk Broda, Johnny Bower, Terry Sawchuk, and Jacques Plante all came from other organizations.

But the fact that he came up through that system, the Junior B Markham Waxers and Junior A Marlboros, did not, apparently, mean all that much. In the 1974 draft, he was the Leafs' fifth pick, and the league's 85th choice overall. Either what is so patently there today was not there then, or perhaps nobody recognized it. But after two years in the minors he arrived at the Gardens to inform then-general manager Jim Gregory in his inimitable way that, "Your hunt for a goaltender is over." And the rest, as they say, is history. Palmateer bumped Wayne Thomas quickly and for good in that 1976-77 season, played 50 games and recorded an astounding 2.67 goals-against average. The next year he was even better. And so on. This past season he was awarded the J.P. Bickell Memorial Cup, a memorial to the first president of the Gardens, as the outstanding Leaf player of the year. There is a greater significance: that particular trophy had not been awarded since 1972. *Toronto Star* sports writer Jim Kernaghan went so far as to suggest that Palmateer was the most valuable player in the whole league, and should have won the Hart Trophy as well.

Palmateer is so good that it allows him to be, even at his ripe young age, a "character." Never mind his rambling-and-scrambling, flopping-and-dropping style in the nets: that's simply what works best for him. But how many other goalies talk out loud to themselves – and opposition players – in the middle of the game, and how many can be heard singing songs while the action progresses at the other end of the rink?

With Ken Dryden gone, Palmateer is, arguably, the best goalie in the game, as good as he believes he is, and as good as he's proven to be in matches like the one on November 17, 1976. He stopped 40 shots against the Canadiens that night, shutting them out 1-0. It was the first time the Habs had been held scoreless in 192 games, including playoffs. Of course nobody can do that game-in, game-out, but Palmateer has made it clear that nobody – but nobody! – gets something for nothing from him.

Dennis Miles

Joel Quenneville

HEIGHT:	WEIGHT:	BIRTH:	HOME TOWN:	PETS:
6'1"	192 lbs	15 Sept. 1958	Windsor, Ont.	none

MARITAL STATUS:
single

Why did you become a hockey player? "I got into hockey when I was younger. I really liked it a lot and stuck with the game most of the way. Finally, I got a chance to play junior and improved. Things only got better for me, and making the NHL was my biggest thrill."

What would you have been if you did not turn pro? "I was very good in school. I would have gone on to pursue a higher education; in fact, I went for two years of university biology. I was hoping for something in the science area."

Sports celebrity pro and con: "People look up to you a lot. The kids think it's a big thrill to get your autograph and I don't mind doing it because it means so much to them. Back home, people idolize me; being from Windsor they really wish me well. I feel like I've accomplished something. I don't have anything that I detest about the fame, yet."

Lifestyle: "I'm a single guy. I like going out on the town, enjoy the night life. I'm not much of a cook so I'm always going out for dinner. When you've got a little more money to spend you can live it up a little more."

Favourite people in hockey: "I think Palmy's [Mike Palmateer] quite a character; I chummed around with him this year. All the guys have been great; they really make me feel welcome. It's like a whole big family and I enjoy that."

Favourite and least favourite opponents: "Last year Mark Napier walked around me twice in one game and that haunted me all year. Very rarely does anybody go around me, and he beat me out of my jock strap twice. I wouldn't want him coming down my wing too often.

"Trottier – he amazes me out there, the way he handles the puck and sets up his wingers."

Are you superstitious as a hockey player? "Oh yeah, I'm superstitious as hell! I always put on my equipment in the exact same order as before, unless things are going bad; then I've got to change it. I'll do everything exactly the way I did before, when I had a good game, and I'll follow that whole routine for the following games. I'll always take my teeth out as soon as I get into the dressing room, but I don't hang anything up in the stall."

Activities before and after games: "Almost every game day I'll get up at 9.00 or 10.00 a.m. and go down for a skate, then eat around 12.30 and relax. I'll usually watch some TV and fall asleep. I'll get up again around 5.00 and get down to the game a half-hour later. Then I'll sit around to get psyched up and play some ping-pong. Listening to music at home really psychs me up because it seems that when I'm on the ice I can hear it. After, I usually go out for a drink or get something to eat. I can never get to sleep after a game; it's usually 2.00 or 3.00 before I do."

Favourite books, films, TV, music: Joel read the *Amityville Horror* and *Penthouse* is a favourite. As for movies, he enjoys comedies. Except for sport shows (football), Quenneville watches little TV. "I like going down to the Gardens once in a while when they have concerts." He enjoys rock music by groups like The Who and the Rolling Stones.

Personal goals for the 1979-80 season and future in hockey: "I'd like to become really settled, get more time than I did last year, and pick up my game in offence. I know I can play offence. I would like to be an all-star in the long-term; it might take a long time, who knows? But the number one goal would be to win the Stanley Cup."

Joel Quenneville is a very bright young man, an honours student in high school, strong in maths and sciences, who had (and still has, to some degree) plans to enter medicine one day. But there was one thing he turned out to be dead wrong about: when he was playing his first Junior A season with his hometown Windsor Spitfires, he just didn't think he had the potential to make it to the pros. By the second season he had, subjectively and objectively, "vastly improved." And by the third season . . . well, all he did was score 27 goals and assist on 78 others to become only the second defenceman in the history of the Ontario Major Junior League to top 100 points in a season. The first man to do so, incidentally, was the Norris Trophy winning Denis Potvin of the Islanders.

Quenneville, on the strength of that performance, was the Leafs' first draft choice in 1978 (and 21st overall). He did some time in Moncton last season, but was up with the big team for 61 games – although on a team wih Salming, Turnbull, Burrows, and Hutchison, and a team that was stressing defence, he didn't get all that much chance to show his scoring stuff, adding only two goals and nine assists to the team's cause.

On the Imlach-Smith Leafs, however, he should get a pretty good shot at displaying his offensive wares. "Actually," he told the *Toronto Star*, "the defensive side of the game is the easiest part, because if you can do just a few things well, you can get the job. There are so many more things that can go wrong when you carry the puck up the ice."

One advantage that Quenneville has over most of the other Leafs is his ability to speak French, which, it was figured by the brass, meant that in games against the Canadiens, he would know what the Habs were shouting to one another on the ice and respond accordingly. The only trouble was, Quenneville said, most of what the Canadiens were shouting at one another was unfit to print.

Quenneville is also the owner of a nice sense of humour, as evidenced by his response to his first-ever NHL goal, a shot that somehow dribbled its way between and under the pads of Philadelphia's Rick St. Croix last season, and turned out to be a game-winner. Pretty it wasn't, a truth not lost on the young defenceman, but, "When I tell my grandchildren about it some day, I'll have deked five guys to get it."

(Robert Shaver)

Rocky Saganiuk

HEIGHT: 5'8" **WEIGHT:** 190 lbs **BIRTH:** 15 Dec. 1957 **HOME TOWN:** Edmonton, Alta. **PETS:** Charlie (Cocker-Terrier)

MARITAL STATUS: married **WIFE:** Bonnie

Why did you become a hockey player? "I went into it when I was just a little guy, nine years old or so. My dad's really athletic, so it got into the family. When you're young and you're good at something, you just keep at it. Things kept on going well for me."

What would you have been if you did not turn pro? "I probably would have gone into construction work because of my father's building business."

Sports celebrity pro and con: "I like pleasing people with the job that I do. If I do my job well I like the reaction that I get out of the crowd. I like kids and help them out as much as I can. Just this week, in Moncton, I must have signed a thousand autographs . . . There's nothing that I mind. I have no regrets about being what I am right now."

Lifestyle: "During the hockey season I'm very dedicated to my sport and to the team. I spend a lot of time with guys on the team. Come summer, I just sit down and relax with the family. I'm not a miser but I'm not extravagant with my money. Our only trips are usually to the mountains."

Favourite people in hockey: "Right now, the guy that I really admire is Eddie Johnston, the fellow who coached me in Moncton. Joel Quenneville and John Anderson and I get along really well. I really like Dan Maloney on the ice. Ronny Ellis and all the older fellows . . . I look up to them a lot."

Favourite and least favourite opponents: "I like to play against Montreal; they're fast skating. I always admired Bobby Clarke because he gave 110 per cent. I don't like playing against Detroit because they have Errol Thompson. He's so fast that it's hard to stay with the guy. A couple of times he made me look foolish. He's not a goon, it's just he's so fast."

Are you superstitious as a hockey player? "I come in between periods and I have to go to the washroom. I don't know why I do it, I just got into the habit. Darryl Sittler gave me a little rabbit's foot that I've got above my stall."

Activities before and after games: "I go to all the morning skates. After that, I'll have my dinner around 12.00 or 1.00 o'clock. I usually get around three hours sleep before the game. I'll just sit by myself and think about what I'm going to do; try and psych myself up. Once I get to the arena I do a lot of talking in the dressing room and try to get my adrenalin flowing. Once I'm on the ice I always take one good, quick skate. Last year I'd go out with the guys for a bite to eat and a drink. I just love seeing my friends after a game. But this year it will be a little different with my wife. I don't usually have trouble going to sleep."

Favourite books, films, TV, music: "I just got into reading this year – mysteries, kooky stuff like *Amityville Horror*. I like comics too. I'm 23 years old and I read comics like a 12-year old. I like all kinds of music and I tape my own cassettes. I watch a lot of TV; it can be anything. I especially like the sports movies and my favourite show would be Quincy."

Personal goals for the 1979-80 season and future in hockey: "Every rookie wants to win the 'Rookie of the Year' and that's going to be my goal this year. I think I've got a good chance of winning. The main thing is to win the Stanley Cup and try to help the team to do that. I'm such a team man that I like to help the guys in any way I can; I love to win. I'd like to play another 12 years after this one. I just hope my heart stays in the same shape, that I've still got the heart to play."

As debuts go, it's hard to think of one more auspicious than that enjoyed by Rocky Ray Saganiuk when he joined the Leafs from Moncton farm club last spring. In the first period of that game, against Pittsburgh, he took a pass from Walt McKechnie and scored his first NHL goal. Later he assisted on goals by Dan Maloney and Borje Salming. The Leafs won the game, Saganiuk won the first star and, more important, he won the hearts of the Leaf fans, some of whom were muttering "where has this guy been all year?"

He'd been with the New Brunswick Hawks, and if he'd stayed down there, instead of coming up to Toronto for the last 16 games of the schedule, he'd have blown away the 30-year old AHL goal-scoring record of 53. As it was, he finished with 47 goals down there, made the first all-star team at right wing, and was named the league's most valuable player.

Saganiuk is, in the parlance, a "little guy" and when he was struggling through the pre-junior ranks he remembers being told every step of the way that his size was against him. "Everyone told me I didn't have a chance," he once recalled. "The trend at that time was to go after the bigger types, like [Colorado's] Barry Beck." But he made the Flyers' Bobby Clarke his model and he hung tough and determined. And his size, he accurately observed, gives him an edge with the fans. "When a player is small like me and things work out for him, the fans usually are with him."

What's more, he doesn't back down. In his second Leaf training camp, after being drafted second by the team in 1977 on the strength of 60 goals and 49 assists for the Lethbridge Broncos, he found himself into it with none other than Dave Williams. "I looked at him and he looked at me," Saganiuk told the *Globe*'s Allen Abel, "and I knew I couldn't walk away. I had to fight him. [Fortunately for somebody, big Dave Hutchison intervened.] Five minutes later he (Williams) skated up to me and said: 'Way to go, kid. That's the way you gotta be to make it in this league.'"

But even a kid named for Rocky Marciano and Sugar Ray Robinson is not necessarily invulnerable. During the 1977-78 season, when the Hawks were still in Dallas, an illegal cross-check broke two vertebrae in his neck. He was paralysed for a few minutes, and it was only after ten days in hospital that he learned yes, he would be able to play hockey again.

(Robert Shaver)

Borje Salming

HEIGHT: 6'1" **WEIGHT:** 195 lbs **BIRTH:** 17 April 1951 **HOME TOWN:** Kiruna, Sweden

MARITAL STATUS: married **WIFE AND CHILDREN:** Margitta; son, Anders and daughter, Theresa

Why did you become a hockey player? "I never had it in mind to become a professional hockey player. I started when I was seven years old, when my brother took me down to the ice. I was 17 when I moved down to the big league in Sweden and played three years there, but even then I never thought about being a professional player. Everything just came."

What would you have been if you did not turn pro? "I tried to go to school but I played on my own team plus the national team. I was in university for two years but it was really hard because I was away from school so much. Hockey was just a hobby but I didn't really know what else I wanted to be. I was at school studying to be an engineer."

Sports celebrity pro and con: "It's really a drag sometimes but I guess when it's (fame) not there I'll find it lonely. It's nice when people recognize you because you're famous, but for me it doesn't matter. Sometimes you get tired of it – all the sports writers talking with you – but it's part of the game."

Lifestyle: "I like to relax a lot of the time. I don't take up too much of my time with lots of stuff; I want to be home most of the time. I'd like to live outside of town on a lot of land, like a farm; that's my ideal lifestyle."

Favourite people in hockey: "I get along with most of the guys on the team; we've got really good guys. If you're a winning team you feel good together but if you start to lose, everything gets tied up – then it's a little bit tough."

Favourite and least favourite opponents: "I don't really have any favourite opponents. But Montreal is the best team to play against."

Are you superstitious as a hockey player? "I'm not superstitious. I don't put my left skate on before my right or anything like that and I don't care about eating the same meal; it makes no difference to me."

Activities before and after games: "I go to the team meeting at 10.30 and get home by 1.00 in the afternoon. I eat with my family so I have whatever they do; it's nothing special; I don't care what my pre-game meal is. Usually, I'll sleep in the afternoon and get down to the rink about 6.30. I usually get there in the last minute because I don't like to sit around too much. After, I'll go out for a steak – you've got to eat something after a game – either that or I'll go home because it's usually so late. When we come in from an out-of-town game at 1.00 in the morning, I find it hard to sleep."

Favourite books, films, TV, music: "Now, I'm sort of relaxing more and reading lots of books, mostly Swedish ones although I read English ones too. Right now I'm reading *Holocaust.* I also like war books – reality and not too much fiction. I go to movies every so often; I read in the papers to see what's best at the time. I like to watch sports on TV in the afternoons of Saturdays and Sundays. I also like cartoons. This year, we have some Swedish music with us."

Personal goals for the 1979-80 season and future in hockey: "I've been here six years now, and we've been in the quarter-finals for five years and the semi-finals one year, so I wouldn't mind being in the finals. Certainly to win the Stanley Cup wouldn't be too bad – I'm starting to get old. The Stanley Cup would be my goal."

If Borje Salming isn't the best defenceman in all of hockey, there aren't many people who would try to slip a bookmark between him and the guy above him. Like Bobby Orr before him, Salming continues to do things on the ice that nobody has ever seen before, much less thought possible; to go with all of his considerable physical skills and intelligence, he has something that can best be defined as "creativity." He simply invents new moves, new ways of doing things.

Salming's prowess since he joined the Leafs from the Swedish National Team in 1973 has not been lost on anybody. He is a perennial all-star, making the first or second team in five of his six NHL seasons. And the Molson Cup, which goes to the Leaf who's named in the most three-star selections over the season, is just about his to keep; in years that he hasn't won it, he's been runner-up or third in line.

Not counting Stan Mikita, who was born in Czechoslovakia but learned his hockey in Canada, Salming is the first great European player to become a star in the NHL. In fact if "superstar" had not become such a debased term, there would be no hesitation in hanging it on him.

The purity of his play, plus the (rightly) perceived decency of the man, have made him a particular favourite of Toronto fans, who have always deeply appreciated those qualities. When a serious eye injury knocked him out of the playoffs in 1978, he received literally thousands of telegrams and letters at his Wellesley Hospital room, the greatest response in that hospital's long history of hockey celebrity patients.

Although Salming is a pretty big guy, his almost ascetic look and his elegance on the ice tend to give the impression that he's fragile. But he can take a beating, as he did one playoff night against the Flyers in 1976, and continue to come up with the big plays, offensively and defensively: despite the pounding, which included an eight-stitch cut, he scored the winning goal. And playing 40-to-50 minutes of important games is much more the rule for him than the exception.

Salming is the all-time season leader for the Leafs in assists by a defenceman, with 66 in 1976-77, and while that alone doesn't make him the greatest Leaf rearguard ever, the statement can be made without too much fear of contradiction.

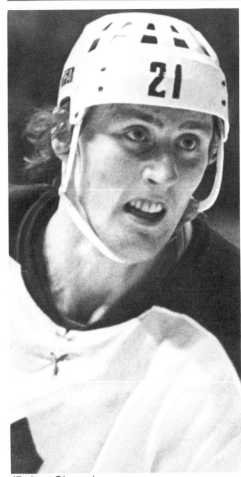

Darryl Sittler

HEIGHT:	WEIGHT:	BIRTH:	HOME TOWN:
6'½"	195 lbs	18 Sept. 1950	St. Jacobs, Ont.

MARITAL STATUS: married

WIFE AND CHILDREN: Wendy: son, Ryan and daughter, Meaghan

Why did you become a hockey player? "I've enjoyed playing hockey as long as I can remember. Making it to the NHL has always been my goal."

What would you have been if you did not turn pro? "I probably would have become a crane operator or a draftsman. I took drafting in high school. My father was a crane operator; I worked with him during the summers when I was going to school and enjoyed that type of work."

Sports celebrity pro and con: "It's all part of being successful. I am at peace with myself when I am with my family, friends, or alone. It's nice to be recognized for things you accomplish. I realize that many young boys and girls look up to NHL stars. I feel it is only proper to set a good example for them. All I have to do is remember my thoughts when I was young, how I idolized NHL players, and how much their autographs meant to me."

Lifestyle: "I am basically a family oriented person. I do get many requests to do public relations for companies, charities, and commercials. In the summer, I try to spend as much time with my family at our cottage as I can. I also enjoy hunting and fishing."

Favourite people in hockey: "Jean Beliveau has always been my hero and still is."

Favourite and least favourite opponents: "I've always enjoyed playing in international competitions, like the Challenge Cup. In the NHL I have no favourite opponents."

Are you superstitious as a hockey player? "Generally no. I'm not superstitious with any consistency."

Activities before and after games: "I usually get up around 8.30 and have a small breakfast at home. Around 9.30, I leave for the rink. At 10.30, I'm on the ice for about half an hour. I am usually back home by 12.30 and have a pre-game meal, one high in carbohydrates, like spaghetti or macaroni. I sleep in the afternoons from 2.00 to 5.00. I leave for the rink then. When I arrive, I do some stretching exercises and prepare my sticks for the game. After the game, if we are not going out of town, I go out for dinner with my wife and other members of the team."

Favourite books, films, TV, music: "I very seldom watch television. When I do, it is generally sports; baseball, football, and so on. I sometimes watch Johnny Carson before I go to bed. I read very few books, though if I do, it is on airplanes or on the road. I read the newspapers and different magazines. I'm not much of a music buff, but occasionally I listen to soft music."

Personal goals for the 1979-80 season and future in hockey: "Everybody's goal is to win the Stanley Cup, and that's mine. I try to play each game with as much intensity and consistency as possible, so that I have peace of mind with myself."

If someone set out to build a Toronto Maple Leaf hockey player from scratch, using all the finest parts and ingredients, chances are he'd eventually end up with Darryl Sittler.

After two relatively unproductive seasons in his rookie and sophomore years, Sittler matured into the team leader, with or without the puck, on and off the ice; his captaincy – an honour not bestowed lightly by the Leafs – was and is a simple confirmation of the obvious. And it is not just the team and its loyal fans who recognize Sittler's value as both hockey star and human being: hardly a week passes that does not see 40 or 50 requests for speeches and appearances, and these have included, among others, dinner invitations from a prime minister and the Queen.

Sittler came to the Leafs in 1970, a first-round draft choice from the London Knights. Born and raised in the small Mennonite farming community of St. Jacobs, Ontario, he came into the game of hockey with qualities that didn't need to be taught. "I'm a strong person when I set out to do something I want to do," he says. "Even when I was 17, I didn't drink or miss curfews. I was born with will power." And a mind of his own: when Leafs owner Harold Ballard tried to stop him from participating in Hockey Showdown this past pre-season, Sittler won his case in court and did so anyway.

On a team with 53 years and countless great players under its belt, Sittler holds most of the all-time offensive records, from most points in a season, 117, through most assists in a season, 72, through most 30-goal seasons, six. He also produced, on February 7, 1976, the most awesome display of one-game offensive hockey in the NHL's history: he scored six goals and added four assists as the Leafs crushed the Bruins. There was a nice irony to that night, an irony not lost on Sittler: at the time some of the sportswriters (and other students of the game) were grumbling that what the team needed to be a contender was a high-scoring centre. "I wonder," Sittler asked rhetorically after the game, "if they'll still be looking for a centre?"

That night to remember will endure as long as there are hockey fans left to remember it, and pass it on, but that will not be Darryl Sittler's only legacy. Like Syl Apps and Teeder Kennedy, he is already the stuff Leaf legends are made of.

(Robert Shaver)

(Toronto Star)

Ian Turnbull

HEIGHT:	WEIGHT:	BIRTH:	HOME TOWN:	PETS:
6'0"	205 lbs	22 Dec. 1953	Montreal, Que.	Davie (a dog)

MARITAL STATUS: married

WIFE AND CHILDREN: Inge; son, William and daughter, Thea

Why did you become a hockey player? "I'm in hockey, probably because of the fact that I had a certain amount of talent in that field; it was something that I liked to do, that plus the money."

What would you have been if you did not turn pro? "I probably would have stayed in school and gotten a degree in business administration."

Sports celebrity pro and con: "It's a nice lifestyle, there's no question about it. I basically treat it as a job. People asking for my autograph doesn't bother me, but all the hours and travelling gets to me after a while."

Lifestyle: "I'm pretty low-key. More and more. I think that staying home with the family is quite nice, although I do enjoy going out with my wife for an evening. I don't buy a lot of things and I'm pretty interested in business and how it works."

Favourite people in hockey: "I get along well with just about everybody. Growing up, I looked up to the usual players – Bobby Hull, Gordie Howe, and other people."

Favourite and least favourite opponents: No preferences.

Are you superstitious as a hockey player? "I think most players are superstitious to a certain degree. We all have our idiosyncracies. I always put my left shin pad on the left leg and all that; I never cross over. Sometimes I'll eat the same meal if I had a good game or drive to the rink the same way. I had a lucky horseshoe at one time that a kid sent me, but I don't know where the hell it is now."

Activities before and after games: "I go down to the rink for a pre-game skate and come back home to grab a bite to eat, watch a little television and lie down for a couple of hours. I'll eat a sandwich, or bacon and eggs, or spaghetti. I used to have a steak all the time but I don't eat that as often before a game anymore. I like to get down to the rink around 6.30 and listen to the stereo. After, I'll go out for supper because usually I'm pretty hungry by that time."

Favourite books, films, TV, music: "I read a fair amount, usually a lot of periodicals and magazines. I'll read business books and get into some pocket books on the road, the best-sellers. We don't go out to movies as often as we used to; with a couple of kids it becomes tougher since good baby-sitters are hard to find. But I do enjoy going out to see films. We go to the theatre, the Royal Alex, where we have tickets. I watch a fair amount of television, like good documentaries and NFL football, Monday night and all weekend long. I like all types of music and I have quite a cross-section of records. I listen to Steely Dan and enjoy the new Rickie Lee Jones album, but I like everything: bluegrass, country, rock, and so on."

Personal goals for the 1979-80 season and future in hockey: "I don't really look at any personal goals. I hope everything goes well for me this year but I look at it more in terms of team goals. I'm hoping that the team will at least make it to the finals. I've been around seven years, so I figure the big goal now would be to play on a Stanley Cup championship team. That's what I'm looking forward to."

The past few seasons have not been memorable for Ian Turnbull – at least not for the right reasons. His free-spirited style of play and his interest in scoring goals as well as attempting to prevent them had little place in coach Roger Neilson's scheme of things. In fact, according to owner Harold Ballard (see Interview) it was only his personal intercession that prevented Turnbull from being traded away last year.

The young defenceman, now in his sixth season with the Leafs, was drafted in 1973 from the Ottawa 67s, more than just partly on the basis of his 82 scoring points in junior hockey that year. With Bobby Orr and Brad Park having changed the nature of the game for defencemen, making it quite all right for them to carry the puck up the ice and shoot it, Turnbull was a man with a future. Now, perhaps, he'll get the chance to realize that future: the Imlach-Smith regime wants him to carry the puck and, when possible, tuck it behind opposing netminders. Which is something he knows how to do, as proven by that February 2 night in 1977 when he popped in five as the Leafs beat the Red Wings 9-1. Not even The Great Orr had ever scored that many goals in a single night. He was also Leaf playoff scoring leader last year and the year before.

What's more, it seems a little unfair to peg Turnbull as just an offensive defenceman: in two of his five seasons he led the team in the significant plus-minus statistics, which reflect Leaf goals versus opposition goals scored while a player is on the ice.

If by any chance the team finds itself wealthy enough in rearguards to afford the switch, it is not unthinkable that Turnbull, who has already done some front-line duty, could end up playing there a little (or a lot) more. "Maybe," Imlach was musing in pre-season, "we can make a centre out of him, just like I did with Red Kelly." Kelly, most will recall, simply became one of the great centres in Leaf history, inspiring the team to four Stanley Cups during the sixties.

For Turnbull, the Rolls-Royce-driving wine bar owner, any place on the ice this year promises to be an improvement in his professional life. "I hope I get a chance to play my game," is really all he asks. And he was up for this season: "We've all matured," he observed. "We know what to do and I think we can come along to a great year."

(Robert Shaver)

(Robert Shaver)

David Williams

HEIGHT: 5'8" **WEIGHT:** 188 lbs **BIRTH:** 3 Feb. 1954 **HOME TOWN:** Weyburn, Sask. **PETS:** none

MARITAL STATUS: married **WIFE AND CHILDREN:** Brenda; sons Ben and Clancy

Why did you become a hockey player? "I liked the money and the life and it was something I always wanted to do."

What would you have been if you did not turn pro? "I never think of the negative side. At the time, I just set out to be a hockey player and I was going to do it."

Sports celebrity pro and con: "I just like the game. Of course, in this city being a celebrity is all part of the game. But I've never really thought about what I like most. Sometimes a lot of aggravation comes with being in the public's eye. There are so many times that you have to turn your back and walk away where a normal guy could stand and tell someone what he thinks: you get stung by the diplomatic situation that you're in. I don't like being diplomatic."

Lifestyle: "I just like being busy; it doesn't matter whether I'm shovelling grain or water-skiing. I do go out quite a bit with my wife: we like some of the restaurants in the country; there are some good Mennonite ones around Kitchener. I'm very, very conservative."

Favourite people in hockey: "King Clancy – I just like him; he's a great guy [named one son after him] and Conn Smythe."

Favourite and least favourite opponents: "Other than our team, I hate them all." Who are your least favourite opponents? "Mr. Ballard. Yeah, I'm serious." [Other than that, he has no favourite players and he will meet any team; it doesn't matter.]

Are you superstitious as a hockey player? "I'm superstitious about talking about superstitions. But I'm deep into that stuff. My superstitions are my own thinking and even my wife doesn't know why I do stuff. I once borrowed a rabbit's foot from Darryl but it didn't do me any good. I guess it started when I was about 14 year's old playing top-level midget hockey. It's gotten worse though."

Activities before and after games: "I usually get up no later than 9.30 and come down for the skate. I'll have my meal around 1.30 or so – either a pasta dish or fish; it's either fish or an Italian dish every time. I never eat steak, except in the summers. I never used to sleep in the afternoon but I believe in it now. Before 5.00 I'm down at the rink again, and I make sure that all my sticks and equipment are ready to go. The first thing I do after the game is have something to eat. Where I eat varies; either we stay downtown, eat in the west end, or go home. But I never go out [for beers etc.]. I'm too tired."

Favourite books, films, TV, music: "I've hardly been to any movies in Toronto although I enjoy seeing them. I'm really into Canadian music: Murray McLachlan, Anne Murray, Gordon Lightfoot, those type of singers. I don't read a lot of anything but if I do read, it's only true stories. My favourite author is Peter Newman – *The Canadian Establishment, The Bronfman Dynasty,* that sort of stuff. The only part of the paper I ever read now is the business section because I'm interested in the way the country's being run. The National News is my favourite TV show; I try to get it every night to see how the other half are living but I don't watch that much TV. [He also enjoys W-5 and 60 Minutes.]

Personal goals for the 1979-80 season and future in hockey: "My goal is just to play well, to have things go well. You can have all the personal goals that you want but if the team doesn't win you're still a jerk. You can score a thousand goals and say that you did your part, but if you don't win you haven't contributed anything. I'd like to see us get 100 points this year, that's what I'm aiming for. Before I leave hockey I'd like to feel that I've performed every duty in the game well – backhand, forehand, passing and so on. I'd also like to get the ring, for the Stanley Cup."

For four full seasons and the better part of a fifth, the name of Dave "Tiger" Williams has been synonymous with a punch in the mouth. He is the stuff that hockey purists' nightmares are made of, rendering the word "aggressive" almost obsolete. What can you say, after all, about a guy who averages well over five hours a season in the penalty box, who hunts bear with a bow and arrow (a rug in Harold Ballard's Gardens' office attests to his skills in that area), and signs his Christmas cards Tiger instead of Dave?

Only what Hermann Goering once said about his German people, that they have hard hands, but soft hearts.

Despite his attempts to correct the problem by attending a three-week-long skating school a summer or so ago, Williams will probably never be confused with, say, John Anderson out there on the ice. But in fairness, he is an honest workman, strong on positional play, going fearlessly into the corners with anybody who cares to challenge him for the territory, and reminding the opposition that his team mates are off limits to elbows, sticks, and fists. At the same time, he makes a scoring contribution, averaging 19 goals and about the same number of assists over the past four years. And as far as penalties are concerned, he managed last season to break – downward – the 300-minute barrier for the first time as a full-time Leaf (is he getting soft?) with a mere 298 minutes. That may sound like a lot, but consider that in 1977-78 he had 351 minutes, topping the Leaf record he set the year before (338 minutes), which had topped the Leaf record of 306 minutes he set in the 1975-76 season.

When the Leafs drafted Williams second in 1974 they had a pretty fair idea of what they were getting. As a member of the Junior A Swift Current Broncos for two seasons he accumulated 576 penalty minutes. As well, he had two somewhat productive seasons as a scorer: 44 goals and 58 assists, then 52 goals and 58 assists. And, unlike a number of young pros today, there was never any doubt in Dave Williams' mind as to what he wanted to do with his life. When he was still in high school in his home town of Weyburn, Saskatchewan, he was asked to fill out a form which included a question about career designation. Williams wrote, simply, "NHL."

(Robert Shaver)

Ron Wilson

HEIGHT: 5'11" **WEIGHT:** 180 lbs **BIRTH:** 28 May 1955 **HOME TOWN:** Windsor, Ont. **PETS:** "Just a few fish"

MARITAL STATUS: married **WIFE AND CHILDREN:** Maureen; daughter Kristen

Why did you become a hockey player? "My family has been involved in hockey. I was born and bred and raised on hockey. So it was natural for me to go into it."

What would you have been if you did not turn pro? "I really don't have any idea. I always had it in my mind to be a hockey player."

Sports celebrity pro and con: "Celebrity? I kind of like it all. But there's a lot of pressure put on you by the public to win. Of course you want to, but people do put a lot of pressure on you, especially in Toronto because it's such a hockey city. Otherwise, I enjoy the attention because I realize that I'm only going to get it for a few years. When I was growing up, Dave Keon was my hero, then Bobby Orr. Now I wear 14, which was Keon's number, so that's a really big thrill for me."

Lifestyle: "I'm fairly easy going but I don't like to lose whether I'm playing hockey, golf or even pool. Otherwise, I'm more or less a homebody and I like to spend a lot of my time with my family. We've got a nice house but, that's about as far as I'll go spending my money. I'm kind of a quiet guy off the ice."

Favourite people in hockey: "Besides myself? [Laugh] I guess I look up to a Lanny McDonald. Or Darryl Sittler: he's well respected, an all-star, and a good team leader. Lanny is such a super guy off the ice. I really like Jim Gregory and Roger Nielson but they're not around any more."

Favourite and least favourite opponents: "I'm kind of in awe playing Guy Lafleur. I look up to any of the all-stars in the league. I don't have anybody in the league mad at me yet so I can't say there's somebody I don't like to play against."

Are you superstitious as a hockey player? "Yeah, I am a little superstitious. Before each game and period I always whack the goalie three times on the pads. I'll eat the same meals if I had a good game before, but I'm not like guys who wear the same clothes. Last year I had a four-leaf clover stuffed in my glove for a while, but I lost it."

Activities before and after games: "Usually I go down to the rink and skate to loosen up and get the feel of the sticks I'll use. Then I come home and watch a bit of TV. I usually eat around 2.30 or 3.00 and always take a nap for two or three hours. Last year I used to take the GO Train into the games. When I get in, I like to get dressed in a hurry. After, we'll always go out for something to eat but I'm not a lively person. I don't like to party and I don't like to stay out late, so we'll usually get in by 12.30 or 1.00."

Favourite books, films, TV, music: Mystery novels are Wilson's favourites. Since he was an economics major at college, and hopes to work on an MBA in the next couple of years, he brushes up on that subject by reading texts. "I go to every movie that comes out, especially on the road. I saw The Deer Hunter twice. I'll go see anything, as long as it's entertaining." Quincy is his favourite television show and Ron watches all sporting events. He listens to Doobie Brothers and Beach Boys records and catches the occasional repertory theatre in Providence, Rhode Island.

Personal goals for the 1979-80 season and future in hockey: "I'd like to be able to play a regular shift. I wouldn't set any goal-scoring or point-scoring goals for myself; I just want to play a lot to give myself a chance to score 15 or 20 goals. As far as the team's concerned, getting up to first place is a goal. I'll just play until I stop enjoying it. If I don't play a lot this year or next year I may hang up the game because it's no fun sitting on the bench. I like to get in on the action."

Even more so than team mate Paul Gardner, whose father, Cal, retired the year after he was born, Ron Wilson grew up with hockey. His father, Larry Wilson, played and coached in the NHL until his death this past summer; the Detroit Red Wing coach had a heart attack while jogging. Ron's uncle, Johnny Wilson, remains in the game as coach of the Pittsburgh Penguins. But while hockey was his father's life, and continues to be his uncle's, it is not Ron's – at least not exclusively. "That's why I went to college in the first place," he told Allen Abel of the *Globe and Mail.* "My dad moved around too much playing hockey."

Wilson, a "thinking-man's hockey player," graduated from Providence College where, as a defenceman, he not only led his team in scoring for four straight years, but also made the Dean's List as an honour student in economics. He intends to live in the Rhode Island city, which is his off-season place of residence now, and do post-graduate work.

All that having been said, it should be noted that Ron Wilson is a pretty fair country hockey player. He not only has the genes, but a fine mind that allows him to quickly dissect and assess what's happening on the ice and adjust accordingly. As Floyd Smith has pointed out, however, Wilson's size tends to work against him as a defenceman, albeit one of the rushing variety. As well, the Leafs are defenceman-rich. But Wilson's versatility should be in his favour: in his first pro year, 1977-78, in Dallas, he led the team with 31 goals and 38 assists as, predominantly, a right winger. (He played 15 of his 67 Dallas games on defence before being switched; he had begun the season with the Leafs, but played little in the first 13 games, managing only two goals and one assist.) He has also played some centre, a position he prefers to the wings, but still a second choice to defence.

Last year in Moncton he averaged a point-a-game (31 for 31) and in Toronto, doing spot duty, he had five goals and 12 assists in 46 games.

Among Wilson's fans are his former coach, Roger Neilson, and his present one, Floyd Smith. "He's a very intelligent hockey player, " Smith says, "and he moves the puck exceptionally well for a defenceman and he shoots well. If there is a drawback, it's his size. He has all the natural skills and ability.

(Robert Shaver)

(Robert Shaver)

(Ice Photo Studio)

Scott Garland

Scott Garland didn't wear the Toronto Maple Leaf uniform for long, but, as with the 400 or so other young men who have pulled it on over the past 53 seasons, he wore it proudly. He wasn't exactly a star, but he was an effective journeyman who might have had a rewarding career somewhere in the NHL had it not been for that terrible fluke accident on a Montreal expressway last June. A tire blew, his car went out of control, and when help arrived Garland was already dead; strangely, the only mark on his body was a bruise on the back of his head.

Garland, only 27 when he died, came up to Toronto from Oklahoma City at the end of the 1975-76 season after nearly four solid, if unspectacular, seasons in the Central Hockey League, and emerged as one of the better Leafs in the playoffs that year against the Philadelphia Flyers. The following year he cracked the Toronto line-up and managed nine goals and 20 assists in 69 games of mostly spot duty. By 1977-78, after returning to the Leafs from 20 games and six goals in Tulsa, injuries kept him either on the bench or out of the line-up entirely. At the end of that season he was sent to Los Angeles, along with Brian Glennie and Kurt Walker, for Dave Hutchison and Lorne Stamler. Last season he played for Springfield in the American Hockey League.

Born in Regina, Garland lived in Montreal at the time of his death. He is the third Leaf in recent memory to die in a car crash; George Hainsworth, the great war-time goalie, and the legendary Tim Horton are the others.

Toronto Maple Leafs
NHL Totals

	Regular Schedule					Playoffs				
	GP	G	A	PTS	PIM	GP	G	A	PTS	PIM
Anderson	88	16	13	29	12	8	0	2	2	0
Boschman	0	0	0	0	0	0	0	0	0	0
Boutette	317	59	78	137	496	38	6	13	19	95
Burrows	585	26	117	143	301	25	1	4	5	23
Butler	417	70	86	156	376	41	2	3	5	77
Ellis	948	318	296	612	199	67	18	8	26	20
Gardner	181	90	79	169	86	6	0	1	1	2
Hutchison	311	10	52	62	840	26	1	10	11	91
Jones	147	13	18	31	68	19	1	5	6	11
McDonald	442	204	225	429	462	45	20	17	37	22
McKechnie	693	160	263	423	368	15	7	5	12	2
Maloney	557	147	215	362	1133	37	4	7	11	31
Quenneville	61	2	9	11	60	6	0	1	1	4
Saganiuk	16	3	5	8	9	3	1	0	1	5
Salming	448	78	282	360	382	42	8	18	26	39
Sittler	923	288	397	685	600	58	24	38	62	108
Turnbull	413	82	225	307	449	49	12	29	41	88
Williams	352	87	114	201	1480	44	5	11	16	240
Wilson	59	7	13	20	4	3	0	1	1	0
Hotham	0	0	0	0	0	0	0	0	0	0
Kirton	0	0	0	0	0	0	0	0	0	0

Toronto Maple Leafs
NHL Totals

	Regular Schedule					Playoffs				
Goaltenders	GPI	MINS	GA	SO	AVE	GPI	MINS	GA	SO	AVE
Harrison	60	3385	220	2	3.90	2	90	7	0	4.67
Palmateer	171	10033	493	13	2.95	24	1453	65	2	2.72
Crha	0	0	0	0	0	0	0	0	0	0

A Night to Remember

Wayne Lilley

Brian McFarlane, Dave Hodge, and Bill Hewitt, who prove regularly that nostalgia isn't everything *(Hockey Night In Canada)*

Until a few years ago, the ascent to the radio broadcast booth in Maple Leaf Gardens was not for the timorous. Known as the gondola because it resembled the cabins beneath the blimps so popular when the Gardens was built in 1931, the narrow, 50-foot-long booth was reachable only after a trip involving six doors, 89 steps, a short ladder, and a precarious tiptoe over a catwalk to its door 74 feet above the ice.

But it was not so much vertigo that had Peter Maher's stomach churning as he made his way to the broadcast booth prior to the Maple Leafs' first home game in the fall of 1978. For one thing, the radio broadcast location had changed; it was now on the same side of the Gardens as the press box, no more difficult to reach than the Greys. Rather, it was the awesome responsibility he faced that had Maher's digestive tract doing gymnastics that night: he was conscious of the fact that he would begin doing a job that previously had been held by a legend, Foster Hewitt. "Foster was my idol almost all my life," says Maher. "It was an eery feeling following him as the radio broadcaster of the Leafs."

Maher carefully avoids the word "replace" with reference to his new position and its old occupant. "Nobody can *replace* Foster," he says. In fact, he suggests he would not even pretend to do so except for the circumstances that gave him the opportunity. Earlier in the summer, radio station CKFH, which Foster Hewitt began in 1951 and still owned, lost its bid to broadcast Leaf hockey games on radio. A new FM station, CKO of Toronto, connected to an all-news radio network across Canada, had won the rights by offering the Leafs more money. From a number of broadcasters who auditioned for the job of play-by-play announcer with CKO, Maher had emerged on top.

The first night on the job, of course, would be worrisome enough for Maher. Although he'd had experience calling hockey games in his native New Brunswick, he'd never done a Leaf game, or any other National Hockey League game, for that matter. As well, for fledgling CKO, the job Maher did would have much to do with the station's survival. But the biggest worry of Maher was what Foster would think. "I was hoping he wouldn't think I was someone who took his job away," he says.

Had Maher known Foster Hewitt better (the two had never met by the end of the first season) he would have realized that Foster Hewitt bore him no bitterness but viewed his successor with a mixture of respect and disappointment. On the one hand, as a businessman he regretted losing the broadcast rights. But even that regret seemed coloured as much by sentiment and respect for Toronto fans as it was by financial loss. The move of the broadcast to FM from AM, he'd argued, would mean fewer listeners would be able to get the games since fewer had FM receivers. Coming from Foster, who's spent a lifetime making sure fans got their money's worth, there was nothing hollow about the argument.

On the other hand, Foster Hewitt is one of the most modest and gracious men ever to speak into a microphone and would be quick to encourage Maher even if he was competing with CKFH. "It's been a lot of fun over the years," says the veteran, now 75. "But you have to know when to stop and I just sort of faded out of the picture."

As any hockey fan knows, he did no such thing – and couldn't if he wanted to. But he was witnessing one more change among the many that had gone on in broadcasting since he first called the opening game in Maple Leaf Gardens in 1931. And while the man who never missed an opener in the Gardens for the next 43 years would finally do so, he left a legacy unlikely to be duplicated ever in Canada or anywhere else.

Apart from signifying the end of an era, though, Maher's first radio broadcast from Maple Leaf Gardens was noteworthy for another, subtler reason. When the governing body of broadcasting in Canada, the Canadian Radio-Television and Telecommunications Commission (CRTC), granted CKO its broadcasting licence a few years ago, it did so with the proviso that the station follow a mandate of "all-news radio." To be sure, there had been a definite trend on the part of television's Hockey Night in Canada program towards electronic journalism instead of pure entertainment. But in bidding for and winning the contract to broadcast the Leaf games, CKO was suggesting that hockey games were a legitimate part of its all-news format.

It remained for the CRTC to settle, for the moment at least, an awkward question that had dogged writers and broadcasters for years: if the Commis-

sion allowed CKO to broadcast, it would be tantamount to considering sports as news. But if sports coverage indeed does constitute news, why must radio and television stations pay a handsome dollar for the right to broadcast? Futhermore, is it right that team owners and league officials should have the right to manipulate "news" by placing certain clauses in contracts before granting broadcast rights?

The argument pointed up once again the curious netherland that sports occupies: owners like to think of hockey as entertainment, yet when reporters point to sloppy play or players as a drama or movie critic might lambaste a bad film or play, teams complain. But for the moment, none of that rhetoric seemed to matter. What mattered was that the high-pitched voice that had come to so many of us via the glowing tubes of a wooden-cased radio from Eaton's would no longer be present. An era had ended.

Foster Hewitt's reign as the most popular voice on the air in Canada had begun almost as suddenly as it ended. Upon graduation from the University of Toronto, he'd gone to work for the *Toronto Daily Star* where his father was sports editor. When the *Star* bought radio station CFCA, he began splitting his duties between writing and announcing on radio. Somewhat reluctantly, the 19-year-old agreed to attempt to broadcast the first hockey game on radio in March 1923 between Toronto Parkdale and Kitchener.

"I suggested they get someone from the radio station's sports department," he recalls now. "But they said there was no one experienced enough." He also admits to some attraction to the idea of being the first in Canada to broadcast a hockey game. But even so, he might have felt some misgivings when he arrived at the aging Mutual Street Arena. In those days, ice-making was not as perfect an art as it has become since, and to assist the freezing, the building deliberately was kept cool. The presence of a single match, though, could have heated the three-foot-square broadcast booth from which he found he would be operating. And the presence of his own body was more than enough to heat it well above the temperature outside. And did. By the mid-point of the game, it was a struggle to keep the glass clear of condensation so he could see the ice. Adding to the problem was the unsophistication of the broadcast techniques of the time; Foster had to speak into a telephone that relayed his words back to the station for broadcast, and frequent interruptions in telephone conversations in 1923 were hardly unusual.

Notwithstanding such difficulties, the broadcast proved a success, especially when the game went into 30 minutes of overtime, heightening the drama. Furthermore, with no one to compare his performance to, Foster struck his own style, and that too seemed to meet listeners' approval. There was no question the timbre of his voice was different from the rounded tones of most radio announcers' voices – but despite that, or maybe it was because of it, the broadcasts became a hit. From the outset, Foster Hewitt showed a rare ability to describe the play so vividly that imaginations could "see" the game emanating from their balky receivers. In short order, Foster became a fixture at Mutual Street Arena, broadcasting minor league games and eventually graduating to the NHL games of the Toronto St. Pats.

Make no mistake: it was a labour of love for the man who'd grown up with sports in Toronto and who, as a university boxer, had won the Canadian Intercollegiate flyweight championship a little more than a year before he made his initial hockey broadcast. And it was a love that was reciprocated both by fans, and by 40-years worth of street hockey-playing urchins and shinny-playing river skaters adopting the shrill Hewitt voice to call their own games as they played, inevitably adding, from time to time, Foster's patented phrase, "He shoots! He scores!"

But while Foster saw his workload grow as he began broadcasting the NHL games in Mutual Street Arena, not even he could have predicted the career ahead of him. It began in earnest when the inimitable Conn Smythe talked the St. Pats owners into cutting their asking price for the team so the Toronto-based group Smythe had put together could buy the NHL franchise. Thus, when the season opened in 1926, Foster was on hand to broadcast the first game ever played by the renamed St. Pats, the Toronto Maple Leafs, which occurred on February 14, 1927.

While Smythe was building the Leafs into one of sports' legends, Foster was aiding and abetting; nonetheless he did so independently, with the integrity

he always projected. (Throughout his career, he refused to openly tout a sponsor's product, for instance; the product Foster sold was hockey and he was the best salesman in the world.)

As the Leafs began to impinge on the consciousness of an increasing number of fans, however, there remained one irksome factor to overcome so far as Smythe was concerned. Mutual Street Arena, still the home of the Leafs, had improved little if at all from the time Smythe bought the team. And the conditions in which Foster Hewitt broadcast games hadn't become noticeably better either. The former fact, of course, resulted in Smythe's building of Maple Leaf Gardens, the finest emporium of hockey in the world. But the latter fact was not forgotten. When Maple Leaf Gardens opened its doors in 1931, one of its features was the broadcast "gondola" which Foster Hewitt would make as famous as the building itself. For two generations, fathers took pride in pointing out to their youngsters, on first trips to the Gardens, the structure atop the intricate web of ladders and landings. For all the elaborate opening night ceremonies for the benefit of fans and dignitaries in the Gardens, it was Foster Hewitt's familiar opening, "Hello Canada and hockey fans in Newfoundland and the United States . . ." that would carry the event to millions, eventually making the Toronto Maple Leafs the best-known team in the world.

In fact, Foster had played a role in the building of the Gardens itself. Although he remained aloof from commercial announcements, he'd casually let it be known during a broadcast a few years earlier from Mutual Street Arena that Frank Selke had prepared a book on the Leafs as part of the Gardens' fund-raising drive. The mention resulted in 90,000 orders flooding the Leaf office, helping fill Smythe's war chest. The result was not lost on canny advertising men of the time who reasoned that if Foster could do that then sponsors of the broadcast might expect similar rewards in product sales. General Motors agreed to sponsor Hockey Night in Canada. The relationship lasted until 1936 when Smythe talked Imperial Oil into taking over sponsorship of the broadcasts.

The year 1936 was significant for another reason as well. One of the longest standing traditions of the Leafs has

been Young Canada Night (usually the Saturday night of the game closest to Christmas), to which the Gardens encouraged parents to bring their youngsters. In those days, tickets to Leaf games could still be bought at the box office fairly readily and, in fact, broadcasts of the games didn't begin until 9.00 o'clock lest they discourage attendance. To participate in his own way, Foster decided to introduce his son Bill on the air to do a small portion of the play-by-play.

Even at eight years of age, Bill displayed some of his father's professionalism. Prior to doing his stint on the air, he would arrive at the Gardens before the game started and sit earnestly before the microphone, practising. By the time he got on the air, he became the envy of every kid in Canada.

Indeed, by the time Bill Hewitt began doing his Young Canada Night guest spots in 1936, Hockey Night in Canada had truly become a national phenomenon. In 1933, Foster's popularity had grown to the point that the CBC had picked up his broadcast to send to stations across its network. Despite a starting time that varied across five different time zones in Canada, hockey became the most popular radio show in the nation. According to writer Jack Batten, a 1942 survey showed that 74 per cent of those questioned listened to Leaf games at some time or other during the season.

The year of the inaugural network broadcast was doubly memorable for Foster Hewitt because it included one of the most unusual games he would ever broadcast. The semi-final match between the Boston Bruins and the Leafs on April 3 was to decide which team would advance to the Stanley Cup playoff finals against New York a night later. But if that didn't provide enough tension to make the game exciting, throughout its course no less than three goals were called back by referees. At the end of regulation time, the score remained tied and fans settled in for the climactic overtime period that would decide the outcome. None anticipated waiting the equivalent of another full game and a half before the tie-breaker would come, however. Yet not before 1.45 a.m. would Leafs' Ken Doraty finally beat the Boston netminder after 164 minutes and 47 seconds of play.

The situation that arose around the game was as interesting as the score. When the game ran beyond sportswriters' deadlines, they filed stories without being able to offer a final score; so long was the game, though, that they were able to return to watch its finish even as fans in the stands could saunter out onto Carlton Street between overtime periods and pick up an early edition of the Toronto papers which referred to "the game played in Toronto last night," the game they were still watching. Some Toronto listeners to Foster's broadcast became so intrigued at this history-in-the-making that they trundled down to the Gardens to watch the last part live. Weeks after the game, Foster heard from one fan who thanked him for entertainment throughout a 240-mile drive to Windsor, Ontario. By twiddling his car-radio knobs as one station faded out, he'd been able to find another along the network and heard the same game throughout the more than five-hour journey.

For the players, Foster recalls in his book *Hockey Night in Canada*, the length of the game was bad enough. But for him, having to announce the play throughout without the benefit of a line change or a penalty, it was devastating. "It was the only time I can recall broadcasting in a daze," he says. "I couldn't even hear my own voice."

Remarkably, though, the voice never let him down during the game, surely one of broadcasting's more astounding feats. In fact, Foster's voice never let him or hockey fans down at all, although he once did find it soaring to unprecedented octaves during one "He shoots! He scores!" When he recovered, a little abashed, he apologized on air to fans by observing sheepishly that he "blew a fuse." For the next few weeks, sympathetic listeners sent Foster fuses of all manner and description from every corner of the country.

Such responses weren't unusual either. During World War II, the Royal Canadian Navy asked Hockey Night in Canada to appeal to Canadians to assist the war effort by supplying binoculars that were needed. The fans responded by sending over 1,000 pairs to the CBC studios. Foster's personal commitment went even further during the war. Following his broadcasts, he went immediately to the radio station studio where he would listen to tapes of the game, then produce a tape of the highlights for broadcast on short-wave radio around the world. The Leaf fans among Canadian troops sent let-

ters of thanks from China, India, Guadalcanal, New Guinea, and Australia. Foster even received a letter smuggled out of Tobruk, a city under siege at the time.

Almost as popular as the play-by-play of Foster was the between-periods banter that had come to make up The Hot Stove League. In the early years of radio broadcasting (early television would have the same problem), the two intermissions between periods of hockey proved awkward spots to fill. Producers tried music of various kinds but nothing seemed to fit – and in fact most efforts tended to detract from the game On a whim, it was decided to let a couple of knowledgeable hockey writers, Bobby Hewitson of the *Toronto Telegram* and Elmer Ferguson of the *Montreal Star*, engage on air in a kind of freewheeling bull session of the sort that went on in the press box during intermissions. The effect of the sportswriters' ability to convey the impression, like racetrack touts, that they had inside information proved the perfect touch; and when Harold "Baldy" Cotton joined the intermission show, his career as a Leaf and his job as a Boston Bruin scout (as well as his impish sense of humour) only enhanced the impression. The addition of moderator Wes McKnight, whose nightly sportscast on radio station CFRB bordered on gospel in Toronto, well-rounded the team. Even the name The Hot Stove League, was just right, conjuring up as it did images of coteries of the Leaf faithful around the stove, amidst cracker barrels, feet up on crates, in corner stores in hamlets acoss Canada, listening to the game with a reverence matched only by the solemnity of CFRB's Jack Dennett as he introduced the sponsor, Imperial Oil.

No less profound than Dennett's voice, though, was the effect The Hot Stove League regulars had on Leaf broadcasts and on hockey itself. We waited while Elmer Ferguson hemmed and hawed before announcing the three stars of the game because the announcement (originally a promotion for Imperial Oil's now-forgotten Three Star brand gasoline) had become an institution – and remains so now, even spreading to other NHL cities. But if Fergie's three stars were sometimes disputable – Fergie himself on occasion appeared to forget why he chose them – there was no disputing what Foster said. Such was his credibility and hawk-like eyesight that he had be-

come more than a national institution: he was, in truth, our ultimate arbiter of what had gone on down on the ice during the game. In disputes that resulted in players being called before league president Clarence Campbell, Foster's versions of the incidents in question were accepted by everyone as being as reliable as videotape.

In all, Hockey Night in Canada during the golden years of radio had become quintessential Canadiana. But by the 1950s, it seemed only a matter of time before hockey would turn up on television as new antennas sprouted on rooftops in cities close to the US border, where American stations could be picked up. Inevitably, the CBC too began a television network to serve the nation, and inevitably Hockey Night in Canada from Maple Leaf Gardens – still starting about halfway through the game – became the top show on the new medium despite initial worries that the bulky cameras would be unable to follow the puck in the world's fastest game.

Of course, they could and did. And there was even a logical succession of second generation broadcasters ready to make the transition to television a smooth one. Ever since his first time on the air at eight years of age, Bill Hewitt had been groomed to one day take over his father's job. In 1951, he handled the network radio broadcasts, inheriting, like a deserved peerage, the right to imitate the famous "He shoots! He scores!" But it was only natural that Foster, who had called the first game ever on radio from the Gardens 20 years earlier, should do the same on the first hockey telecast.

If television did nothing else, it confirmed for fans that Foster Hewitt was indeed the one man most able to accurately describe what was happening on the ice. The new visual medium also put faces to names that had so long entertained fans as part of The Hot Stove League. In fact, even Murray Westgate, a Toronto actor who was portrayed as an Esso service station operator on Hockey Night in Canada broadcasts, and the late George Feyer, the remarkably facile artist who actually created commercials on screen with his marker, became stars.

Still, television in the 1950s and even the early 1960s was relatively cumbersome technically. Indeed, it was as much a spectator of the game as fans in the Gardens. It did not, for instance, halt play for commercial breaks; instead, messages were run across the screen during the game in such a way that no one would miss the action.

Especially during the 1960s, Hockey Night in Canada rapidly became one of the finest productions of any kind, anywhere. Bill Hewitt had matriculated to the role of play-by-play man (while Foster "retired" to do the same for his radio station CKFH). Under the guidance of Ralph Mellanby, the Canadian Sports Network, which produced the program, added technical innovations such as replays of highlights, and a new breed of broadcasters, familiar with television, joined the production.

Ironically, Brian McFarlane, who joined Bill Hewitt as a colour man, always ready with a timely anecdote to fill a pause in the action, and who remains one of the longest standing members of the broadcast team, was passed over in his first attempt to work for Hockey Night in Canada. In 1961, he'd trekked to Toronto to audition for the hosting job but lost out to Ward Cornell, a broadcaster from London, Ontario, who had long experience in football but little in hockey. McFarlane, an excellent Junior A and college player, accepted a position with CFRB only to be offered the job of colour man with the American network, CBS, which was then doing the NHL Game of the Week. Two years later he was offered a similar position with Hockey Night in Canada and he's been there ever since.

Inevitably, the pressure of live television produced gaffes from time to time. On one occasion, Cornell managed to mix up Leaf president Stafford Smythe and Frank Selke Jr., son of one of the team's builders. But the fans who huddled around television sets each Saturday night never really seemed to mind. Not only did television not eliminate movie theatres as some had predicted, it did not diminish the popularity of the Toronto Maple Leafs, as some alarmists had thought it might.

Yet in a way, Hockey Night in Canada was maturing, as television fare, faster than hockey itself. Basically, the NHL had remained the same – the smallest major professional league in professional sport, still with the same six teams it had had for 25 years. But by the late 1960s, that too would change as the league expanded to 12 teams and shortly thereafter to 18. Expansion, though, bore its own crisis. The dilution of talent that resulted was

accompanied by a rare lull in fan interest that pushed the television people to even loftier heights of technical excellence. And that in turn led to other changes.

As hockey moved into the 1970s, surely the most litigious years in sports history, it seemed to do so on the crest of a wave of investigative journalism borne out of Watergate. Increasingly, ever since the appearance of player agents, sheafs of lawsuits had mounted in two countries. The sports pages, it seemed, had become something closer to a court record than traditional reporting.

Against that backdrop, Hockey Night in Canada faced a twin-edged quandary. Because Canadian Sports Network paid Maple Leaf Gardens for television rights, and agreed to a certain level of discretion in what it would and would

The young Bill Hewitt, then known as Billy and, sometimes 'Faster Foster,' about the time he was taking over the radio duties *(Hockey Night In Canada)*

not say about players, teams, officials, and management, the popular term "credibility gap" seemed to apply. Fans watching games on television often read coverage of the Leafs in newspapers that contained much harsher – often deservedly harsher – criticism than broadcasters gave. The other edge of the quandary was that coverage of the game under the aegis of Mellanby and producer Bob Gordon often produced replays that made the broadcasters' see-no-evil, speak-no-evil embargo a difficult one to maintain.

The most immediate concern of broadcasters, anxious to avoid on-air blunders and mix-ups, was identifying accurately all the new faces that expansion brought. The problem, notes Brian McFarlane, who does post-game interviews, was magnified at playoff time when teams often brought players in from the minor leagues to shore up rosters. "In 1975 when the Philadelphia Flyers won the Stanley Cup, I was doing interviews in the dressing room. For the series, they had brought up Jack McIlhargey whom I didn't know. But even if I had known him, I might not recognize him out of uniform as he stepped out of the shower. It's uncomfortable interviewing someone you don't know."

The rise of the World Hockey Association created a problem for the broadcasters as well. For a long time, the NHL refused to recognize the existence of the league on grounds that admitting it was there would legitimize the new professional league that had "stolen" so many NHLers. Broadcasters working for CSN, which in turn was contracted to the NHL, had to steer awkwardly around such questions as where Bobby Hull was playing, despite the fact that fans who read newspapers knew perfectly well where he was playing.

Little by little, however, objectivity began creeping into the broadcasts, at least when the occasion obviously demanded it. Camera coverage had become so good that viewers at home could see clearly, via four separate and excellent angles on videotape, that, say, a referee missed a flagrant foul. To ignore the fact was to insult viewer intelligence, and crews began to comment even on the officiating where it seemed warranted.

Still, Brian McFarlane, who is hardly outspoken on the air, could be excused for being a bit gunshy, having

experienced – as he has – the wrath of the fans. During a 1969 game in which the Leafs were trounced by Boston, Toronto's Forbes Kennedy was on his way to setting a playoff single-game record. "He bounced off about 18 Boston players and then appeared to knock down a linesman with a punch. I mentioned that he could be subject to a fine when Clarence Campbell looked at the videotape. And sure enough, he was suspended and fined $1,000. But he never played another game in the league and some people descended on me, claiming Forbes never touched the official and that I was responsible for ending his career."

On another occasion, McFarlane had Gordie Howe as a guest during a playoff broadcast of a game between Boston and New York Rangers. Phil Esposito of Boston crossed the blue line, stumbled, and fell but the referee gave a penalty to a Ranger who was nearby. Naturally, Howe, never a sympathizer of referees, agreed with McFarlane that the error (which later showed up clearly on videotape) should be pointed out. "The referee wasn't happy and neither was the league," says McFarlane. "But we had to call what we saw with our own eyes."

If McFarlane didn't point out such things by the mid-1970s, it would have been almost dead certain that either Howie Meeker or Bob Goldham – whoever happened to be the guest analyst that night – would have. In fact, their knack for dissecting plays on videotape, albeit in different ways, has not only added immeasurably to fans' knowledge, but developed into wonderful entertainment. The perky Meeker, almost gleeful as he picks apart a play with surgical skill, is a show in himself; Goldham's professorial drollery brings a wry sense of humour to his analysis which enhances, rather than detracts from, its incisiveness. Understandably, neither Meeker nor Goldham is particularly popular with the players and officials whose shortcomings are scrutinized before a national audience.

All the electronic wizardry that has kept Hockey Night in Canada in the forefront of television programs in Canada has not been without its cost, both in money and sentiment. Sadly, one of the traditions that has slid by the wayside has been The Hot Stove League. Although it's resurrected to fill an intermission from time to time

throughout the season, somehow it has never been quite the same without Fergie, Baldy, and the rest of the regulars. But then, maybe a meandering conflab among old sweats wearing cardigans would be out of place today.

Certainly Hockey Night in Canada loses nothing as entertainment from the crisp, journalistic style it has adopted in recent years, increasing the program's credibility. Dave Hodge, hired eight years ago as the Hockey Night in Canada host, arrived on the scene as the new wave began and remains as its foremost symbol. Although Hodge disclaims being responsible for the change, he concedes that as a broadcast journalist (recruited from the traditional breeding ground of Hockey Night in Canada talent, radio station CFRB), he is more comfortable allowing his instinct for the newsworthy in sports decide what questions he asks in interviews, or what he might say on camera.

In fact, Hodge says with some justification that, given the program's record, Hockey Night in Canada should no longer have to defend itself from charges of being the shill of either the NHL or the teams. "I don't know how things were done before," says Hodge, one of the most credible and capable sportscasters in Canada. "But I just do the job the best way I know how. And people who watch the show should know by now that there is nobody watching over me or writing scripts for me."

But Hodge was presiding when Hockey Night in Canada lost its innocence – at least in the view of many observers. And paradoxically, the incident that prompted it was one of modern hockey's more lamentable occasions, which began as the 1976 Stanley Cup series between the Philadelphia Flyers and the Leafs.

Although the Leafs had a few scrappers on the team, they had an equal number of pacific stars such as Borje Salming, Inge Hammarstrom, and Errol Thompson, to whom fighting was somewhat foreign. Moreover, coach Red Kelly, a former Lady Byng trophy winner, was hardly the sort to goad his players into violence.

Not so the Flyers, an expansion team with a nucleus of talent revolving around Bobby Clarke and goalie Bernie Parent, but far better known for a roster of players significant for their size and aggressiveness: having been nicknamed the Broad Street Bullies, truculent skaters such as Dave Shultz, Don Saleski, and Ed Van Impe seemed bent on living up to the name.

Given the feverish pitch of playoff hockey, it was inevitable that the Flyers would use the same intimidation tactics that had brought the team Stanley Cups in each of the two preceding years. But when mayhem did result, instead of being relegated to hockey history as just another brawl, the Leafs-Flyers series took a different turn. Following one game a couple of players who'd been involved in fights – including some with timing officials and even one who reportedly made contact with a Toronto policeman – were charged by Ontario attorney-general Roy McMurtry with assault with a deadly weapon.

The charges understandably caused some consternation throughout the NHL. Previously, the league had been left to discipline itself. Legal authorities in jurisdictions where games were played in the US and Canada had overlooked the fact that much of what went on would be an indictable offence had it occurred on the street, instead of the ice. To McMurtry, and to many Canadians, however, the increasing trend to violence in professional ranks of hockey was threatening the game itself by setting a poor example for youngsters. If the league couldn't or wouldn't clean up its own act, he decided, he would do so in Toronto.

McMurtry had a strong case for doing what he did. If stick-swinging was legal just because those who owned teams and governed the league sanctioned it – or appeared to, inasmuch as they refused to take sufficient measures to eliminate it completely – then by extension, wouldn't it be legal for anyone to stage as entertainment, say, a gunfighting duel? Put another way, suppose a player deliberately killed another during a game. Would that too be overlooked by legal authorities and merely result in a fine and suspension from the league? Of course, it would not, but McMurtry's point was made. But let's return to the role of Hockey Night in Canada: the issue presented a real problem for the broadcasters. For one thing, they had brought the whole disgraceful affair into living rooms across the country and therefore felt some responsibility; they rose to the occasion. Brian McFarlane, a more than passingly good player in his youth, expressed dismay at what the cameras showed during the game. For

good measure, host Hodge signed off the evening of the game by apologizing to viewers for the display on the ice.

If that wasn't enough to assure fans that Hockey Night in Canada had matured into more than an apology for the league and team owners to which it was contracted, the broadcasters seized upon the news value of the legal charges and in the next telecast from Toronto invited Roy McMurtry onto a between-periods intermission session with the NHL's referee-in-chief Scotty Morrison to debate the affair. "People said Ballard [Leaf owner Harold] wouldn't allow us to do it," says Hodge. "And I'm not sure he even knew McMurtry was in the building. But we never asked anyway. We felt it had to be done and in the end, nobody said anything; and I think we made a contribution to the game and to broadcasting."

Hodge's pride in being a journalist had already done much to do away with the characteristic "Hi mom" type of interview with players, according to Brian McFarlane. "You just can't say too much about Dave and the way he

Of all the changes that Hockey Night In Canada has undergone, one of the most positive had to be the arrival of Dave Hodge, who brought a sense of journalism into the job *(Hockey Night In Canada)*

handles his job," says McFarlane. Hodge, though, would prefer not to appear a crusader and if he sometimes appears so, he notes, it's often merely a function of doing live television rather than a seizing of every opportunity to inject a personal distaste for violence.

Last season's playoff series between the Leafs and Atlanta supports his contention. In a game in Toronto, the penalty total quickly mounted to something on the order of the 1976 debacle between Leafs and Flyers, the only difference in 1979 being the fact that Leafs had become more aggressive. In any case, when fighting halted play with a few minutes to go at the end of a period and carried on for about 15 minutes, the broadcasters were having difficulty filling the resulting air time without sounding like war correspondents. Finally the officials decided to break for the intermission and tack the remainder of the period on the next one, further elongating the intermission period.

"A lot of our plans for the intermission were upset by what happened," says Hodge. "One of the Atlanta players was tossed out of the game and his coach wouldn't let him do the interview we had planned. Then we had technical problems with some taped material and we couldn't go with that. So there we were live with 35 minutes to fill and I was on camera with the producers saying, 'Talk.' What else could I do but talk about what we'd just seen?

"I was criticized for going on and on with the anti-violence thing," he adds, "but I don't back down from a thing I said. Yet I might not have said it if we'd been in a different position. As it was, it wasn't an opportunity but a necessity of live television."

Live television is no less pressurized an environment for the play-by-play and colour commentators, says Bill Hewitt. "For the last four or five years we've worn headsets and that means while we're talking, someone might be talking to us, giving a commercial cue or announcing what replay is coming up and things like that. And sometimes we have guests in the booth too, so it takes a lot of concentration. The whole program is a team effort now and not an individual thing as it once was."

Although the NHL has expanded once again, the integration of the new teams could prove smoother this time, but still not without its problems for tra-

ditional Leaf and Vancouver fans on the Prairies, or Montreal Canadiens fans in Quebec. The addition of Quebec City, Winnipeg, and Edmonton, though happily bringing more Canadian cities into the fold, is bound to divide loyalties. On the other hand, the fact that the newcomers have been operating as teams in the once unmentioned World Hockey Association should make them a stronger part of the NHL from their beginning than some previous expansion teams were.

Over the years, Hockey Night in Canada has not only wrought changes on hockey, but on Maple Leaf Gardens as well. No longer, in the days of virtual full-time sellouts, do television viewers have to wait until half-way through the game before the broadcasts begin. Earlier, one of the most publicized changes at the Gardens was the decision to use brighter lights on the ice to accommodate colour television cameras. So shocked were the players at first at the extra brightness that goalies complained of losing the puck in the glare and one Leaf, Kent Douglas, even went so far as to paint dark strips under his eyes in the fashion of football punt returners bothered by bright sun. Players have adjusted, however, and Brian McFarlane notes only half jokingly that were goalies today forced to play beneath the old lights used for black and white television, they would complain of having to field pucks in the gloom.

Broadcast facilities have also changed. From the beginning, telecasters had their own booth in the Gardens and an ice-level studio made possible player interviews during and after the game. But portable cameras have made virtually every corner of the Gardens into a TV studio, isolating nuances of the game – a player having a skate blade repaired, the expression on a coach's face – and have made hockey more intimate than ever before. Significantly, members of the sportswriting fraternity (in a brand new press box, by the way) swivel to watch television monitors carrying Hockey Night in Canada to review the plays they have just witnessed; television, which once seemed unable to match print media depth in covering the Leafs, now contributes to that depth. And it's still a pretty good way to check up on happenings on the ice, even if Globe and Mail columnist Scott Young's version of the game, as viewed through his omnipresent bino-

culars, and not the monitors, remains one of the best.

Nor is there any suggestion that Hockey Night in Canada will be anything less than journalism and superb entertainment in the future. Muffling Meeker, for instance, would be about as easy as duplicating Darryl Sittler's 10-point night (which television carried live to living rooms across the country both on the hockey telecast and later during national newscasts). Dave Hodge's instinct for the newsworthy is unlikely to be blunted either, and the technical crews are almost sure to get even better. Already, Hodge points out, the technical teams used on hockey telecasts and those shooting live sports of other kinds are among the most skilled in television, constantly in demand when such events as state funerals, royal visits and the like, call for live coverage. Even technologically there is a closer kinship between news and sports than many realize.

It is with justifiable pride and sense of tradition that 32-year-old Peter Maher enters the radio broadcast booth at the Gardens. Unfortunately, though, he'll never have the opportunity to announce a game from the most famous perch in Canada, because during renovations a few years ago, the famed gondola, home of Foster Hewitt and Hockey Night in Canada in the Gardens for more than a quarter-century, was dismantled in the name of progress; and without anybody who could have stopped the desecration, including Gardens' owner Harold Ballard, knowing about it, the gondola was burned.

By any standard, the destruction of the most illustrious structure in broadcast history in Canada was an oversight that has quite rightly been decried by Hewitt, Hockey Hall of Fame curator Lefty Reid, and former NHL president Clarence Campbell. That a lack of communication could result in such a fate for the very seat of hockey communication is indeed ironic.

Fortunately, however, Hockey Night in Canada has always been more than a physical structure. It has been a force stronger than steel girders and wood and thus endures in the tradition of Foster Hewitt as an ongoing tribute to the most popular game in Canada.

Statistics and Records

Stan Obodiac

(Toronto Sun)

Toronto Maple Leafs
Standings 1978–79

Player	End-of-Season GP	G	A	PTS	PIM	PP	SH	GW	GT	Playoffs GP	G	A	PTS	PIM	PP	GW
Sittler	70	36	51	87	69	12	0	4	0	6	5	4	9	19	2	0
McDonald	79	43	42	85	32	16	0	2	2	6	3	2	5	0	0	0
Salming	78	17	56	73	76	4	0	2	0	6	0	1	1	8	0	0
Turnbull	80	12	51	63	80	4	0	0	0	6	0	4	4	27	0	0
McKechnie	79	25	36	61	18	7	1	6	1	6	4	3	7	2	1	1
Gardner (Col.)	64	23	26	49	32	14	0	0	1							
(Tor.)	11	7	2	9	0	2	0	1	0							
(Total)	75	30	28	58	32	16	0	1	1	6	0	1	1	2	0	0
Maloney	77	17	36	53	157	0	0	5	1	6	3	3	6	2	1	1
Williams	77	19	20	39	298	6	0	4	1	6	0	0	0	48	0	0
Boutette	80	14	19	33	136	0	0	2	1	6	2	2	4	22	0	0
Ellis	63	16	12	28	10	4	0	1	0	6	1	1	2	2	0	0
Anderson	71	15	11	26	10	0	0	2	3	6	0	2	2	0	0	0
Hutchison	79	4	15	19	235	0	0	0	0	6	0	3	3	23	0	0
Jones	69	9	9	18	45	0	0	0	1	6	0	0	0	4	0	0
Wilson	46	5	12	17	4	4	0	0	1	3	0	1	1	0	0	0
Butler	77	8	7	15	52	0	2	2	0	6	0	0	0	4	0	0
Burrows	65	2	11	13	28	0	0	0	0	6	0	1	1	7	0	0
Monahan	62	4	7	11	25	0	2	0	0	0	0	0	0	0	0	0
Quenneville	61	2	9	11	60	0	0	1	0	6	0	1	1	4	0	0
Saganiuk	16	3	5	8	9	1	0	1	0	3	1	0	1	5	0	0
Boudreau	26	4	3	7	2	0	0	0	1	0	0	0	0	0	0	0
Stamler	45	4	3	7	2	0	0	1	1	0	0	0	0	0	0	0

Goaltenders	GPI	MINS	GA	EN	SO	AVE	W	L	T	GPI	MINS	GA	EN	SO	AVE	W	L
Palmateer	58	3396	167	3	4	2.95	26	21	10	5	298	17	0	0	3.42	2	2
Harrison	25	1403	82	0	1	3.51	8	12	3	2	90	7	0	0	4.67	0	2
Hamel	1	1	0	0	0	.00	0	0	0	0	0	0	0	0	.00	0	0
Total	80	4800	252	3	5	3.15	34	33	13	7	389	24	0	0	3.70	2	4

Individual Scoring Leaders for Art Ross Trophy

Players	Team	GP	G	A	PTS	PIM	PPG	SHG	GW	GT
Bryan Trottier	NY ISLANDERS	76	47	87	134	50	15	0	8	2
Marcel Dionne	LOS ANGELES	80	59	71	130	30	19	0	7	5
Guy Lafleur	MONTREAL	80	52	77	129	23	13	0	12	1
Mike Bossy	NY ISLANDERS	80	69	57	126	25	27	0	9	2
Bob MacMillan	ATLANTA	79	37	71	108	14	8	1	4	1
Guy Chouinard	ATLANTA	80	50	57	107	14	11	0	5	2

Individual Scoring Leaders for Art Ross Trophy (cont'd.)

Players	Team	GP	G	A	PTS	PIM	PPG	SHG	GW	GT
Dennis Potvin	NY ISLANDERS	73	31	70	101	58	12	3	2	1
Bernie Federko	ST LOUIS	74	31	64	95	14	7	0	1	3
Dave Taylor	LOS ANGELES	78	43	48	91	124	13	0	4	0
Clark Gillies	NY ISLANDERS	75	35	56	91	68	11	0	5	1
Dennis Maruk	MINN-WASH	78	31	59	90	71	6	2	3	3
Darryl Sittler	TORONTO	70	36	51	87	69	12	0	4	0
Butch Goring	LOS ANGELES	80	36	51	87	16	13	4	2	2
Rick Middleton	BOSTON	71	38	48	86	7	12	1	5	1
Lanny McDonald	TORONTO	79	43	42	85	32	16	0	2	2
Gil Perreault	BUFFALO	70	27	58	85	20	6	0	4	0
Eric Vail	ATLANTA	80	35	48	83	53	5	1	5	1
Brian Sutter	ST LOUIS	77	41	39	80	165	12	0	1	1
Peter McNab	BOSTON	76	35	45	80	10	4	0	4	3
Bill Barber	PHILADELPHIA	79	34	46	80	22	10	6	4	0
Anders Hedberg	NY RANGERS	80	33	46	79	33	6	0	5	2
Phil Esposito	NY RANGERS	80	42	36	78	31	14	0	7	2
Ivan Boldirev	CHI.-ATL.	79	35	43	78	31	14	0	4	2
Steve Shutt	MONTREAL	72	37	40	77	31	10	0	6	0
Terry O'Reilly	BOSTON	80	26	51	77	205	3	0	5	1

Top Plus Players

Following are the 20 leaders in the NHL plus-minus calculations, based on at least 40 games played during the 1978-79 regular season:

		GP	OFF PCT	DEF PCT	PCT DIFF
Brad Park	BOSTON	40	43.1	24.8	18.3
Dave Taylor	LOS ANGELES	78	42.5	26.5	16.0
Bryan Trottier	ISLANDERS	76	47.1	31.3	15.8
Pierre Mondou	MONTREAL	77	33.2	17.6	15.6
Dave Hutchison	TORONTO	79	40.6	25.3	15.3
Marcel Dionne	LOS ANGELES	80	47.2	34.2	13.0
Mike Bossy	ISLANDERS	80	37.5	26.1	11.4
Clark Gillies	ISLANDERS	75	35.0	23.6	11.4
Brian Sutter	ST. LOUIS	77	40.1	29.6	10.5
Blake Dunlop	PHILADELPHIA	66	26.3	15.9	10.4
Stan Smyl	VANCOUVER	62	33.0	22.6	10.4
Ron Stackhouse	PITTSBURGH	75	46.9	36.7	10.2
John Van Boxmeer	COLORADO	76	47.6	37.5	10.1
Borje Salming	TORONTO	78	51.2	41.1	10.1
Robert Picard	WASHINGTON	77	51.0	41.3	9.7
Ted Bulley	CHICAGO	75	36.1	26.5	9.6
Nick Libett	DETROIT	68	31.1	21.5	9.6
Denis Potvin	ISLANDERS	73	49.4	40.1	9.3
Doug Risebrough	MONTREAL	48	27.1	17.9	9.2
Tom Gorence	PHILADELPHIA	42	28.5	19.6	8.9

Individual Leaders

GOALS:	Mike Bossy	NEW YORK ISLANDERS, 69
ASSISTS:	Bryan Trottier	NEW YORK ISLANDERS, 87
POINTS:	Bryan Trottier	NEW YORK ISLANDERS, 134
PENALTY MINS.:	Dave Williams	TORONTO MAPLE LEAFS, 298
POWER-PLAY GOALS:	Mike Bossy	NEW YORK ISLANDERS, 27
SHORTHAND GOALS:	Bill Barber	PHILADELPHIA FLYERS, 6
GAME WINNING GOALS:	Guy Lafleur	MONTREAL CANADIENS, 12
GAME TYING GOALS:	Marcel Dionne	LOS ANGELES KINGS, 5
THREE-GOAL GAMES:	Mike Bossy	NEW YORK ISLANDERS, 5
SHUTOUTS:	Ken Dryden	MONTREAL CANADIENS, 5
GOALTENDER WINS:	Dan Bouchard	ATLANTA FLAMES, 32
BEST PERSONAL GOALS AGAINST AVERAGE:	Ken Dryden	MONTREAL CANADIENS, 2.30

Record of Goaltenders for 1978-79 Season

All goals against a team in any game are charged to the individual goaltender of that game for purposes of awarding the Vezina Trophy.

Code—GPI—Games played in. MINS—Minutes played. GA—Goals against. SO—Shutouts. AVE—60 minute average. EN—Empty net goals. (Not counted in personal averages but included in team totals.)

WON-LOST-TIED record based on which goaltender was playing when winning or tying goal was scored.

Goaltenders	Team	GPI	MINS	GA	EN	SO	AVE	W	L	T
Ken Dryden	MONTREAL	47	2814	108	2	5	2.30	30	10	7
Michel Larocque	MONTREAL	34	1986	94	0	3	2.84	22	7	4
MONTREAL	TOTAL	80	4800	204		8	2.55	52	17	11
Glenn Resch	NY ISLANDERS	43	2539	106	0	2	2.50	26	7	10
Bill Smith	NY ISLANDERS	40	2261	108	0	1	2.87	25	8	4
NY ISLANDERS	TOTAL	80	4800	214		3	2.68	51	15	14
Bobbie Moore	PHILADELPHIA	5	237	7	0	2	1.77	3	0	1
Bernie Parent	PHILADELPHIA	36	1979	89	2	4	2.70	16	12	7
Rich St. Croix	PHILADELPHIA	2	117	6	0	0	3.08	0	1	1
Wayne Stephenson	PHILADELPHIA	40	2187	122	4	2	3.35	20	10	5
Peter Peeters	PHILADELPHIA	5	280	16	2	0	3.43	1	2	1
PHILADELPHIA	TOTAL	80	4800	248		8	3.10	40	25	15
Pierre Hamel	TORONTO	1	1	0	0	0	.00	0	0	0
Mike Palmateer	TORONTO	58	3396	167	3	4	2.95	26	21	10
Paul Harrison	TORONTO	25	1403	82	0	1	3.51	8	12	3
TORONTO	TOTAL	80	4800	252		5	3.15	34	33	13
Don Edwards	BUFFALO	54	3160	159	1	2	3.02	26	18	9
Bob Sauve	BUFFALO	29	1610	100	0	0	3.73	10	10	7
Randy Ireland	BUFFALO	2	30	3	0	0	6.00	0	0	0
BUFFALO	TOTAL	80	4800	263		2	3.29	36	28	16
Gerry Cheevers	BOSTON	43	2509	132	1	1	3.16	23	9	10
Gilles Gilbert	BOSTON	23	1254	74	1	0	3.54	12	8	2
Jim Pettie	BOSTON	19	1037	62	0	1	3.59	8	6	2
BOSTON	TOTAL	80	4800	270		2	3.38	43	23	14

(cont'd.)

Goaltenders	Team	GPI	MINS	GA	EN	SO	AVE	W	L	T
Tony Esposito	CHICAGO	63	3780	206	9	4	3.27	24	28	11
Mike Veisor	CHICAGO	17	1020	60	2	0	3.53	5	8	4
CHICAGO	TOTAL	80	4800	277		4	3.46	29	36	15
Denis Herron	PITTSBURGH	56	3208	180	3	0	3.37	22	19	12
Greg Millen	PITTSBURGH	28	1532	86	2	2	3.37	14	11	1
Gord Laxton	PITTSBURGH	1	60	8	0	0	8.00	0	1	0
PITTSBURGH	TOTAL	80	4800	279		2	3.49	36	31	13
Rejean Lemelin	ATLANTA	18	994	54	2	0	3.26	8	8	1
Dan Bouchard	ATLANTA	64	3624	201	2	3	3.33	32	21	7
Yves Belanger	ATLANTA	5	182	21	0	0	6.92	1	2	0
ATLANTA	TOTAL	80	4800	280		3	3.50	41	31	8
Mario Lessard	LOS ANGELES	49	2860	148	2	4	3.10	23	15	10
Ron Grahame	LOS ANGELES	34	1940	136	0	0	4.21	11	19	2
LOS ANGELES	TOTAL	80	4800	286		4	3.53	34	34	12
Gilles Meloche	MINNESOTA	53	3118	173	4	2	3.33	20	25	7
Gary Edwards	MINNESOTA	25	1337	83	1	0	3.72	6	11	5
Pete Lopresti	MINNESOTA	7	345	28	0	0	4.87	2	4	0
MINNESOTA	TOTAL	80	4800	289		2	3.51	28	40	12
Glen Hanlon	VANCOUVER	31	1821	94	1	3	3.10	12	13	5
Gary Bromley	VANCOUVER	38	2144	136	1	2	3.81	11	19	6
Dunc Wilson	VANCOUVER	17	835	58	1	0	4.17	2	10	2
VANCOUVER	TOTAL	80	4800	291		5	3.64	25	42	13
John Davidson	NY RANGERS	39	2232	131	1	0	3.52	20	12	5
Wayne Thomas	NY RANGERS	31	1668	101	0	1	3.63	15	10	3
Doug Soetaert	NY RANGERS	17	900	57	2	0	3.80	5	7	3
NY RANGERS	TOTAL	80	4800	292		1	3.65	40	29	11
Jim Rutherford	DETROIT	32	1892	103	2	1	3.27	13	14	5
Rogie Vachon	DETROIT	50	2908	189	1	0	3.90	10	27	11
DETROIT	TOTAL	80	4800	295		1	3.69	23	41	16
Bill Oleschuk	COLORADO	40	2118	136	2	1	3.85	6	19	8
Michel Plasse	COLORADO	41	2302	152	6	0	3.95	9	29	2
Doug Favell	COLORADO	7	380	34	1	0	5.37	0	5	2
COLORADO	TOTAL	80	4800	331		1	4.14	15	53	12
Gary Inness	WASHINGTON	37	2107	130	2	0	3.70	14	14	8
Jim Bedard	WASHINGTON	30	1740	126	1	0	4.34	6	17	6
Bernie Wolfe	WASHINGTON	18	863	68	0	0	4.73	4	9	1
Rollie Boutin	WASHINGTON	2	90	10	1	0	6.67	0	1	0
WASHINGTON	TOTAL	80	4800	338		0	4.23	24	41	15
Ed Staniowski	ST LOUIS	39	2291	146	4	0	3.82	9	25	3
Phil Myre	ST LOUIS	39	2259	163	2	1	4.33	9	22	8
Dave Grant	ST LOUIS	4	190	23	1	0	7.25	0	2	1
Terry Richardson	ST LOUIS	1	60	9	0	0	9.00	0	1	0
ST LOUIS	TOTAL	80	4800	348		1	4.35	18	50	12

Final 1978-79 Statistics

Scoring and penalty statistics up to and including games of Sunday, April 8, 1979, compiled from records of official scorers.

PRINCE OF WALES CONFERENCE

Norris Division

	GP	W	L	T	GF	GA	PTS	PCTG
MONTREAL	80	52	17	11	337	204	115	.719
PITTSBURGH	80	36	31	13	281	279	85	.531
LOS ANGELES	80	34	34	12	292	286	80	.500
WASHINGTON	80	24	41	15	273	338	63	.394
DETROIT	80	23	41	16	252	295	62	.388

Adams Division

	GP	W	L	T	GF	GA	PTS	PCTG
BOSTON	80	43	23	14	316	270	100	.625
BUFFALO	80	36	28	16	280	263	88	.550
TORONTO	80	34	33	13	267	252	81	.506
MINNESOTA	80	28	40	12	257	289	68	.425

CLARENCE CAMPBELL CONFERENCE

Patrick Division

	GP	W	L	T	GF	GA	PTS	PCTG
NY ISLANDERS	80	51	15	14	358	214	116	.725
PHILADELPHIA	80	40	25	15	281	248	95	.594
NY RANGERS	80	40	29	11	316	292	91	.569
ATLANTA	80	41	31	8	327	280	90	.563

Smythe Division

	GP	W	L	T	GF	GA	PTS	PCTG
CHICAGO	80	29	36	15	244	277	73	.456
VANCOUVER	80	25	42	13	217	291	63	.394
ST. LOUIS	80	18	50	12	249	348	48	.300
COLORADO	80	15	53	12	210	331	42	.263

PCTG Arrived at by dividing possible points into actual points.

Teams Home-and-Away Record

At Home **Norris Division**	GP	W	L	T	GF	GA	PTS	**On the Road** GP	W	L	T	GF	GA	PTS
MTL.	40	29	6	5	186	96	63	40	23	11	6	151	108	52
PITT.	40	23	12	5	152	120	51	40	13	19	8	129	159	34
L.A.	40	20	13	7	163	120	47	40	14	21	5	129	166	33
WASH.	40	15	19	6	151	162	36	40	9	22	9	122	176	27
DET.	40	15	17	8	148	137	38	40	8	24	8	104	158	24
Total	200	102	67	31	800	635	235	200	67	97	36	635	767	170

| | **At Home**
Adams Division | | | | | | | | **On the Road** | | | | | | |
	GP	W	L	T	GF	GA	PTS		GP	W	L	T	GF	GA	PTS
BOS.	40	25	10	5	171	123	55		40	18	13	9	145	147	45
BUFF.	40	19	13	8	150	130	46		40	17	15	8	130	133	42
TOR.	40	20	12	8	148	118	48		40	14	21	5	119	134	33
MINN.	40	19	15	6	143	116	44		40	9	25	6	114	173	24
Total	160	83	50	27	612	487	193		160	58	74	28	508	587	144

Patrick Division

	GP	W	L	T	GF	GA	PTS		GP	W	L	T	GF	GA	PTS
NY. I.	40	31	3	6	201	89	68		40	20	12	8	157	125	48
PHIL.	40	26	10	4	158	113	56		40	14	15	11	123	135	39
NY. R.	40	19	13	8	161	140	46		40	21	16	3	155	152	45
ATL.	40	25	11	4	179	126	54		40	16	20	4	148	154	36
Total	160	101	37	22	699	468	224		160	71	63	26	583	566	168

Smythe Division

	GP	W	L	T	GF	GA	PTS		GP	W	L	T	GF	GA	PTS
CHI.	40	18	12	10	128	117	46		40	11	24	5	116	160	27
VAN.	40	15	18	7	113	126	37		40	10	24	6	104	165	26
ST. L.	40	14	20	6	146	156	34		40	4	30	6	103	192	14
COL.	40	8	24	8	111	159	24		40	7	29	4	99	172	18
Total	160	55	74	31	498	558	141		160	32	107	21	422	689	85

Over All

	GP	W	L	T	GF	GA	PTS		GP	W	L	T	GF	GA	PTS
Total	680	341	228	111	2609	2148	793		680	228	341	111	2148	2609	567

Toronto Maple Leafs All-Time Record

| | **At Toronto** | | | | | | | **On Road** | | | | | | | **Total** | | | | | | |
Against:	GP	W	L	T	GF	GA	PTS	GP	W	L	T	GF	GA	PTS	GP	W	L	T	GF	GA	PTS
ATLANTA	16	9	5	2	60	43	20	17	6	10	1	59	66	13	33	15	15	3	119	109	33
BOSTON	258	140	74	44	875	636	324	257	77	134	46	685	821	200	515	217	208	90	1560	1457	524
BUFFALO	27	13	11	3	88	86	29	28	10	16	2	73	100	22	55	23	27	5	161	186	51
CHICAGO	245	138	63	44	828	555	320	245	94	114	37	610	690	225	490	232	177	81	1438	1245	545
COLORADO	6	5	1	0	27	18	10	6	3	1	2	21	18	8	12	8	2	2	48	36	18
DETROIT	248	132	77	39	774	592	303	247	78	128	41	555	693	197	495	210	205	80	1329	1285	500
LOS ANGELES	31	20	5	6	134	82	46	31	11	17	3	75	95	25	62	31	22	9	209	177	71
MINNESOTA	31	19	3	9	124	81	47	31	14	13	4	100	103	32	62	33	16	13	224	184	79
MONTREAL	292	149	99	44	870	727	342	292	79	177	36	704	1022	194	584	228	276	80	1574	1749	536
NY ISLANDERS	17	9	5	3	59	51	21	16	6	8	2	45	56	14	33	15	13	5	104	107	35
NY RANGERS	245	143	65	37	845	600	323	246	94	101	51	701	718	239	491	237	166	88	1546	1318	562
PHILADELPHIA	30	11	11	8	98	85	30	29	5	18	6	58	109	16	59	16	29	14	156	194	46
PITTSBURGH	31	14	10	7	116	96	35	31	12	15	4	101	109	28	62	26	25	11	217	205	63
ST. LOUIS	29	21	4	4	114	72	46	29	12	11	6	74	63	30	58	33	15	10	188	135	76
VANCOUVER	22	10	8	4	82	65	24	22	7	11	4	71	74	18	44	17	19	8	153	139	42
WASHINGTON	12	8	1	3	61	30	19	12	7	4	1	47	36	15	24	15	5	4	108	66	34
DEFUNCT CLUBS	232	158	53	21	860	515	337	233	84	120	29	607	745	197	465	242	173	50	1467	1260	534
Totals	1772	999	495	278	6015	4334	2276	1772	599	898	275	4586	5518	1473	3544	1598	1393	553	10601	9852	3749

Final Statistics 1979 Stanley Cup Playoff Results

Preliminary Rounds

Series "A"

Apr.	10	VANCOUVER	3	at PHILADELPHIA	2
Apr.	12	PHILADELPHIA	6	at VANCOUVER	4
Apr.	14	VANCOUVER	2	at PHILADELPHIA	7

(PHILADELPHIA won series 2-1)

Series "B"

Apr.	10	LOS ANGELES	1	at NY RANGERS	7
Apr.	12	NY RANGERS	2	at LOS ANGELES	1*

*—Phil Esposito scored at 6:11 Overtime   NY RANGERS won series 2-0)

Series "C"

Apr.	10	TORONTO	2	at ATLANTA	1
Apr.	12	ATLANTA	4	at TORONTO	7

(TORONTO won series 2-0)

Series "D"

Apr.	10	PITTSBURGH	4	at BUFFALO	3
Apr.	12	BUFFALO	3	at PITTSBURGH	1
Apr.	14	PITTSBURGH	4	at BUFFALO	3*

*—George Ferguson scored at 0.47 Overtime   (PITTSBURGH won series 2-1)

Quarter-Final Rounds

Series "E"

Apr.	16	CHICAGO	2	at NY ISLANDERS	6
Apr.	18	CHICAGO	0	at NY ISLANDERS	1*
Apr.	20	NY ISLANDERS	4	at CHICAGO	0
Apr.	22	NY ISLANDERS	3	at CHICAGO	1

*—Mike Bossy scored at 2.31 Overtime   (NY ISLANDERS won series 4-0)

Series "F"

Apr.	16	TORONTO	2	at MONTREAL	5
Apr.	18	TORONTO	1	at MONTREAL	5
Apr.	21	MONTREAL	4	at TORONTO	3*
Apr.	22	MONTREAL	5	at TORONTO	4**

*—Cam Connor scored at 25.25 Overtime   (MONTREAL won series 4-0)
**—Larry Robinson scored at 4.14 Overtime

Series "G"

Apr.	16	PITTSBURGH	2	at BOSTON	6
Apr.	18	PITTSBURGH	3	at BOSTON	4
Apr.	21	BOSTON	2	at PITTSBURGH	1
Apr.	22	BOSTON	4	at PITTSBURGH	1

(BOSTON won series 4-0)

Series "H"

Apr.	16	NY RANGERS	2	at PHILADELPHIA	3*
Apr.	18	NY RANGERS	7	at PHILADELPHIA	1
Apr.	20	PHILADELPHIA	1	at NY RANGERS	5
Apr.	22	PHILADELPHIA	0	at NY RANGERS	6
Apr.	24	NY RANGERS	8	at PHILADELPHIA	3

*—Ken Linseman scored at 0.44 Overtime   (NY RANGERS won series 4-1)

Semi-Final Rounds

Series "I"

Apr.	26	NY RANGERS	4	at NY ISLANDERS	1
Apr.	28	NY RANGERS	3	at NY ISLANDERS	4*
May	1	NY ISLANDERS	1	at NY RANGERS	3
May	3	NY ISLANDERS	3	at NY RANGERS	2**
May	5	NY RANGERS	4	at NY ISLANDERS	3
May	8	NY ISLANDERS	1	at NY RANGERS	2

*—Denis Potvin scored at 8:02 Overtime   (NY RANGERS won series 4-2)
**—Bob Nystrom scored at 3:40 Overtime

Series "J"

Apr.	26	BOSTON	2	at MONTREAL	4
Apr.	28	BOSTON	2	at MONTREAL	5
May	1	MONTREAL	1	at BOSTON	2
May	3	MONTREAL	3	at BOSTON	4*
May	5	BOSTON	1	at MONTREAL	5
May	8	MONTREAL	2	at BOSTON	5
May	10	BOSTON	4	at MONTREAL	5**

*—Jean Ratelle scored at 3:46 Overtime   (MONTREAL won series 4-3)
**—Yvon Lambert scored at 9:33 Overtime

Final Round

Sun.	May 13	NY RANGERS	4	at MONTREAL	1
Tues.	May 15	NY RANGERS	2	at MONTREAL	6
Thurs.	May 17	MONTREAL	4	at NY RANGERS	1
Sat.	May 19	MONTREAL	4	at NY RANGERS	3*
Mon.	May 21	NY RANGERS	1	at MONTREAL	4

*—Serge Savard scored at 7.25 Overtime   (MONTREAL won series & Stanley Cup 4-1)

Player Statistics

Player	Team	GP	G	A	Pts	Pim
Jacques Lemaire	MONTREAL	16	11	12	23	6
Guy Lafleur	MONTREAL	16	10	13	23	0
Phil Esposito	NY RANGERS	18	8	12	20	20
Don Maloney	NY RANGERS	18	7	13	20	19
Bob Gainey	MONTREAL	16	6	10	16	10
Larry Robinson	MONTREAL	16	6	9	15	8
Jean Ratelle	BOSTON	11	7	6	13	2
Mike McEwen	NY RANGERS	18	2	11	13	8
Ron Greschner	NY RANGERS	18	7	5	12	16
Don Murdoch	NY RANGERS	18	7	5	12	12
Rick Middleton	BOSTON	11	4	8	12	0
Yvon Lambert	MONTREAL	16	5	6	11	16
Denis Potvin	NY ISLANDERS	10	4	7	11	8
Steve Shutt	MONTREAL	11	4	7	11	6
Walt Tkaczuk	NY RANGERS	18	4	7	11	10
Carol Vadnais	NY RANGERS	18	2	9	11	13

Goaltending Statistics

Goaltender	Team	GPI	MINS	GA	SO	ENGA	AVE	WON	LOST
Bill Smith	NYI	5	315	10	1	0	1.90	4	1
Glenn Resch	NYI	5	300	11	1	0	2.20	2	3
NY ISLANDER Totals		10	615	21	2		2.05	6	4
John Davidson	NYR	18	1106	42	1	0	2.28	11	7
Michel Larocque	MTL.	1	20	0	0	0	0.00	0	0
Ken Dryden	MTL.	16	990	41	0	0	2.48	12	4
MONTREAL Totals		16	1010	41	0		2.44	12	4
Gerry Cheevers	BOS.	6	360	15	0	1	2.50	4	2
Gilles Gilbert	BOS.	5	314	16	0	0	3.06	3	2
BOSTON Totals		11	674	32	0		2.85	7	4
Bob Sauvé	BUF.	3	181	9	0	0	2.98	1	2
Tony Esposito	CHI.	4	243	14	0	0	3.46	0	4
Denis Herron	PITT.	7	421	24	0	1	3.42	2	5
PITTSBURGH Totals		7	421	25	0		3.56	2	5
Mike Palmateer	TOR.	5	298	17	0	0	3.42	2	3
Paul Harrison	TOR.	2	91	7	0	0	4.62	0	1
TORONTO Totals		6	380	24	0		3.70	2	4
Mario Lessard	L.A.	2	126	9	0	0	4.29	0	2
Rejean Lemelin	ATL.	1	20	0	0	0	0.00	0	0
Dan Bouchard	ATL.	2	100	9	0	0	5.40	0	2
ATLANTA Totals		2	120	9	0		4.50	0	2
Robbie Moore	PHIL.	5	268	18	0	0	4.03	3	2
Wayne Stephenson	PHIL.	4	213	16	0	3	4.51	0	3
PHILADELPHIA Totals		8	481	37	0		4.62	3	5
Gary Bromley	VAN.	3	180	14	0	1	4.67	1	2
VANCOUVER Totals		3	180	15	0		5.00	1	2

(cont'd.)

Team Statistics

Team	GP	PIM	Bench MINS	AVE	ADV	PPG	TS	PPGA	SHG	SHGA
ATLANTA	2	129	0	64.5	13	3	10	1	0	1
TORONTO	6	192	0	32.0	19	3	30	9	1	0
LOS ANGELES	2	45	0	22.5	10	2	8	3	0	0
PHILADELPHIA	8	173	2	21.6	31	6	49	8	0	5
NY RANGERS	18	286	2	15.9	72	14	67	8	6	1
VANCOUVER	3	47	0	15.7	19	2	11	4	0	0
NY ISLANDERS	10	144	0	14.4	31	3	27	3	1	0
BUFFALO	3	41	0	13.7	8	1	13	0	0	0
PITTSBURGH	7	84	0	12.0	28	2	19	4	0	1
BOSTON	11	131	4	11.9	25	6	32	8	1	0
CHICAGO	4	45	0	11.3	9	0	11	2	0	0
MONTREAL	16	178	0	11.1	51	15	39	7	0	1
Total	45	1495	8	33.2	316	57	316	57	9	9

Leafs 1979-80 Schedule

HOME

October

Wed.	10—NY RANGERS
Sat.	13—COLORADO
Wed.	17—MINNESOTA
Sat.	20—VANCOUVER
Wed.	31—HARTFORD

November

Sat.	3—BUFFALO
Wed.	14—ST. LOUIS
Sat.	17—BOSTON
Wed.	21—EDMONTON
Sat.	24—CHICAGO

December

Sat.	1—PHILADELPHIA
Wed.	5—MONTREAL
Sat.	8—NY ISLANDERS
Wed.	12—COLORADO
Sat.	15—ATLANTA
Wed.	19—LOS ANGELES
Sat.	22—DETROIT
Wed.	26—WASHINGTON
Sat.	29—WINNIPEG

AWAY

October

Sun.	14—PHILADELPHIA
Fri.	19—WASHINGTON
Wed.	24—VANCOUVER
Fri.	26—COLORADO
Sat.	27—LOS ANGELES

November

Fri.	2—HARTFORD
Wed.	7—ST. LOUIS
Sat.	10—WINNIPEG
Sun.	11—EDMONTON (aft.)
Sun.	18—QUEBEC
Sun.	25—NY RANGERS
Tues.	27—ATLANTA
Wed.	28—WASHINGTON

December

Mon.	17—MINNESOTA
Thurs.	20—BOSTON
Sun.	23—MONTREAL
Thurs.	27—BUFFALO

Leaf Milestones, 1979-80

Goals	Needs	Milestone
Gardner	10	100
Williams	13	100
Turnbull	18	100
Sittler	12	300

Assists		
Gardner	21	100
Neely	20	100
Sittler	3	400
Salming	18	300
McDonald	25	250
Ellis	4	300
Butler	14	100
Boutette	22	100

Points		
Gardner	31	200
Sittler	15	700
Salming	40	400
Maloney	38	400

Games		
Gardner	19	200
Williams	48	400
Sittler	77	1000
Salming	52	500
Quenneville	39	100
Maloney	43	600
Ellis	52	1000
Burrows	15	600
Boudreau	19	100
Anderson	12	100
Palmateer	29	200

Leafs 1979-80 Schedule (cont'd.)

HOME		AWAY	
January			
Wed.	2—NY ISLANDERS	Wed.	16—PITTSBURGH
Sat.	5—QUEBEC	Thurs.	17—NY ISLANDERS
Mon.	7—PITTSBURGH	Sat.	19—MONTREAL
Wed.	9—MONTREAL	Tues.	22—ATLANTA
Sat.	12—VANCOUVER	Thurs.	24—LOS ANGELES
Wed.	30—DETROIT	Sat.	26—EDMONTON
		Sun.	27—VANCOUVER
February			
Sat.	2—CHICAGO	Sun.	3—CHICAGO
Sat.	9—LOS ANGELES	Thurs.	7—BOSTON
Wed.	13—PITTSBURGH	Sun.	10—DETROIT
Sat.	16—HARTFORD	Sun.	17—NY RANGERS
		Tues.	19—NY ISLANDERS
		Wed.	20—CHICAGO
		Sat.	23—WINNIPEG
		Tues.	26—ST. LOUIS
		Wed.	27—COLORADO
March			
Sat.	1—PHILADELPHIA	Sun.	2—DETROIT
Sat.	8—QUEBEC	Wed.	5—PITTSBURGH
Wed.	12—ST. LOUIS	Sun.	9—QUEBEC
Sat.	15—NY RANGERS	Thurs.	20—PHILADELPHIA
Mon.	17—ATLANTA	Tues.	25—MINNESOTA
Wed.	19—WINNIPEG		
Sat.	22—BUFFALO		
Mon.	24—WASHINGTON		
Sat.	29—EDMONTON		
April			
Wed.	2—BOSTON	Tues.	1—HARTFORD
Sat.	5—MINNESOTA	Sun.	6—BUFFALO

The Molson Cup

The Molson Cup Three Stars evolved from one of NHL hockey's oldest traditions – the selection at game's end of the three players judged most valuable in a particular contest. For many years, no special recognition was accorded the "stars" who caught the selectors' collective eye. Then came the Molson Cup, born to add substance to the star selections, to reward consistently high levels of performance, to recognize major contributions to the team's success over an entire season.

Members of the Toronto Maple Leafs are awarded five points each time they are selected a star of a regular season game. The player who has accumulated the greatest number of points during the season wins the Molson Cup.

Since its inception with the Leafs, the Molson Cup has been awarded to only two players, Darryl Sittler and Borje Salming. These two, more than any others, have greatly contributed to Leafs' success in recent years. Sittler has won the award three times and Salming, with his win last season, has now equalled Darryl's Molson Cup trophy collection.

Molson Cup 1978-79
Final Standings

Borje Salming	110	Paul Gardner	15
Mike Palmateer	95	Pat Boutette	15
Lanny McDonald	75	Ron Ellis	10
Walt McKechnie	55	Jerry Butler	10
Darryl Sittler	45	Dave Burrows	10
Dan Maloney	45	Bruce Boudreau	5
Ian Turnbull	35	Garry Monahan	5
Paul Harrison	25	Joel Quenneville	5
John Anderson	20	Jimmy Jones	5
Dave Williams	20	Lorne Stamler	5
Rocky Saganiuk	15	Ron Wilson	5

Autographs

(Jerry Hobbs)

Paul Harrison
Darryl Sittler
Lanny McDonald
Mike Palmateer
Ian Turnbull
Ron Ellis
Borje Salming
Dave Williams
Pat Boutette
Jim Jones
Jerry Butler
Paul Gardner

Rocky Saganiuk
Joel Quenneville
Jiri Crha
Dave Hutchison
Dan Maloney
John Anderson
Walt McKechnie
Ron Wilson
Dave Burrows
Laurie Boschman
Greg Hotham
Mark Kirton